Ritual in an Oscillating Universe

Ritual in an Oscillating Universe

WORSHIPING ŚIVA IN MEDIEVAL INDIA

Richard H. Davis

PRINCETON UNIVERSITY PRESS
PRINCETON, NEW JERSEY

Published by Princeton University Press, 41 William Street,
Princeton, New Jersey 08540
In the United Kingdom: Princeton University Press, Oxford

Library of Congress Cataloging-in-Publication Data

Davis, Richard H.
Ritual in an oscillating universe : worshiping Śiva in
medieval India / Richard H. Davis.
p. cm.
Includes bibliographical references and index.
ISBN 0-691-07386-4 (alk. paper)
1. Siva (Hindu deity—Cult—India—History.
2. India—Religious life and customs. I. Title.
BL1218.2D38 1992 294.5'38—dc20 91-3954 CIP

Publication of this book has been aided by
the Hilles Fund of Yale University

This book has been composed in Adobe Times Roman

Princeton University Press books are printed
on acid-free paper, and meet the guidelines
for permanence and durability of the Committee
on Production Guidelines for Book Longevity
of the Council on Library Resources

Printed in the United States of America

10 9 8 7 6 5 4 3 2 1

Contents

Illustrations vii

Preface ix

Acknowledgments xiii

Abbreviations xv

INTRODUCTION
Locating the Tradition 3

CHAPTER ONE
Ritual and Human Powers 22

CHAPTER TWO
Oscillation in the Ritual Universe 42

CHAPTER THREE
Becoming a Śiva 83

CHAPTER FOUR
Summoning the Lord 112

CHAPTER FIVE
Relations of Worship 137

CONCLUSION 163

Notes 165

Glossary 181

Selected Bibliography 189

Index 195

Illustrations

FIGURES

1.	Emission and reabsorption of the *tattvas*	45
2.	Imposition of mantras onto the hand	49
3.	Locations of domains	54
4.	Subtle anatomy and domains	56
5.	Diagrams for establishing pots	65
6.	Śiva's entourages	67
7.	Transfer of five *kalās* to the *pāśasūtra*	97
8.	Śiva's supports	122
9.	Divine throne and divine body	127
10.	Locations of the twelve *kalās*	130
11.	The meeting of worshiper and Śiva	135

PLATES
(*following page 74*)

1. Naṭarāja (Rajaraja Museum, Thanjavur)
2. Imposition of *brahmamantras* onto the hands
3. Imposition of *brahmamantras* onto the worshiper
4. Ejection of the attributes
5. Imposition of *brahmamantras* onto the liṅga
6. Ascending pronunciation and invocation

Preface

IN THIS ESSAY, I attempt to take seriously a simple postulate that seems to me fundamental to the study of ritual: that those who compose and perform the ritual are conscious and purposeful agents actively engaged in a world they themselves constitute, in large measure, through their practices of knowing and acting.

The "world" in which Śaiva ritual takes place is not the familiar world of Western science or "common sense" that modern Westerners often believe common to all people. Nor does it occur in some sociologically defined universe of a particular community or society, as social anthropology might portray. Rather, Śaiva liturgy is performed in a world that is ontologically organized and constituted by Śaiva siddhānta: a world that oscillates, that is permeated by the presence of Śiva, in which humans live in a condition of bondage, and where the highest aim of the human soul is to attain liberation from its fetters. Within that world, the Śaiva worshiper acts with and upon forces, objects, and categories that are defined for him by Śaiva ontology, and his goals in practicing ritual are based on the possibilities and purposes of human attainment depicted in Śaiva soteriology.

My aim in this study is to explicate, insofar as I am able, both the world envisioned in Śaiva siddhānta and the way in which daily worship reflects and acts within that world. This world is assuredly not the one we think we live in, but nevertheless it is a world we can enter, partially and temporarily, through a mental "reenactment," as R. G. Collingwood put it. The Śaivas themselves would call it *bhāvanā*, "imaginative re-creation." For the Śaivas, as for Collingwood, this reconstructive praxis is primarily intellectual and rational, rather than simply a matter of empathy. By rethinking ourselves the convictions and intentions a well-versed Śaiva ritualist of the twelfth century would have brought to his daily practice, we can mentally place ourselves in his temple and reenact his worship of Śiva.

To enter that world, it will be necessary to attend to two different modes of discourse in Śaiva literature: the propositional discourse of philosophical knowledge (*jñāna*) and the practical discourse of ritual action (*kriyā*). These are, in the Śaiva view, integral and necessary to one another. According to the Śaiva siddhānta tradition, a Śaiva *āgama* should have four sections or "feet" (*pādas*) to be a complete, self-standing treatise. One section, the *jñānapāda*, describes how the world is; it sets forth, in metaphysical and theological terms, the fundamental order of the universe as envisioned by Śaiva siddhānta. A second section, the *kriyāpāda*, prescribes how one should conduct oneself in that world, utilizing the most powerful and efficacious forms of action. (The other two sections, dealing with yogic disciplinary practices [*yogapāda*] and proper day-to-day conduct [*caryāpāda*], are also necessary but clearly subordinate in importance to the first two.) And just as *jñānapāda* and *kriyāpāda* are equally necessary to a complete *āgama*, Śaiva authors insist that an aspirant who wishes to advance within the world of Śiva must exert himself both to know that world and to act properly and effectively within it.

Unfortunately, the applicability of this principle to my own study was not always so apparent to me. When I first began to study the Śaiva *āgamas*, I was like a commentator whom Rāmakaṇṭha criticizes. In his own commentary on the *Mataṅgapārameśvarāgama*, Rāmakaṇṭha contrasts himself with this other, unnamed commentator of the same text who ended his explication after the *jñānapāda*.

> A certain commentator who knew only philosophy completed an extensive examination of the knowledge section (*jñānapāda*), and altogether disregarded the three practical sections concerning ritual action, yoga, and proper conduct. Whereas I, honoring the Lord Śiva, will here compose a lucid exposition of those sections as well, because the types of action prescribed here conform (*anuga*) completely with the meanings of the philosophical discourse.

He was engaged only by philosophy; I was concerned solely with ritual. As a historian interested in temple ritual and its relation to medieval Indian political formations, I wished to read only those practical portions of the *āgamas* dealing with *kriyā*, and not waste time with what I considered speculative metaphysics. I believed I would be able to discern the significance of medieval Śaiva ritual texts directly by locating them in the context of the social and political structures of medieval South India. I was certainly mistaken in this presumption.

To be fair to myself, the commentator that Rāmakaṇṭha criticized and I are not the only ones ever to have pursued such shaky, one-legged inquiries. In fact, the large majority of scholarly studies dealing with Indian rituals make no recourse to the philosophical foundations on which the rituals are based. They characteristically present Indian rituals as instances of highly elaborate routinized behavior either divorced from any formative consciousness or based on severely flawed apprehensions of the world. On the other side, it is only the rare study of an Indian philosophical school that makes any extended reference to such practical corollaries as modes of proper conduct or ritual activity. Scholars most often portray Hindu theology as the exercise of great intellectual ingenuity with little or no concern for practical consequence. So in focusing my attention on only one limb of the body of thought and action I wished to study, I was simply following the habitude of my scholarly field.

As I commenced reading the account of daily worship in *Kāmikāgama*, however, I soon realized that I was missing something. At first I saw it as a problem of terminology or technical language. What were the five *kalās*, or the twelve *kalās*, or the thirty-eight *kalās*, to which the text kept referring? Who were the Vidyeśvaras, the Maṇḍaleśvaras, and numerous other superhuman characters who periodically showed up in the ritual terrain? What did it mean for the worshiper to "make his hand into Śiva" (*śivīkaraṇa*)? Why should a *bubhukṣu* and a *mumukṣu* do things in reverse order? My Sanskrit dictionaries were of little or no avail in tracking down the significance of these, and many other, mystifying terms. With timely help from more experienced scholars in South India, however, I learned that many of the terms I could not comprehend in the *kriyāpāda* were discussed in the *jñānapāda*, and so I began reading philosophical digests and commentaries in addition to my ritual texts. Soon I was able to ferret out the meanings of most of the bothersome terms and to gain a preliminary idea of what was going on in the ritual.

Yet clearing up perplexing terminology was only a first step. It slowly dawned on me that the shared terminology of the two sections was not fortuitous. As the Śaivas would put it, the fetter that was causing my ignorance gradually "ripened," and its grip upon me loosened, enabling me finally to see the principle of "conformity" (*anuga*) or connectedness of *jñāna* and *kriyā* to which Rāmakaṇṭha so clearly refers. The two sections were *meant* to be mutually explanatory; with good reason were they called two feet of the same entity. Belatedly I started to follow a more conscious two-footed approach in my own reading and research, stepping back and forth between ritual texts and philosophical texts, and found that each helped clarify and explicate the other. The rituals served to illuminate and objectify Śaiva philosophical categories and topics, while philosophy helped me to understand the purposes and strategies of Śaiva ritual.

More than that, I began to see that the Śaiva texts envision a world—*the* world, they would say—in which the capacities of humans to know about that world and to act within it are two interrelated modalities of a unitary power of consciousness. According to Śaiva siddhānta, every animate being, beginning with Śiva, has a soul, whose principal characteristic is "consciousness" (*cit*). Consciousness, in turn, manifests itself through two primary powers: the power to know (*jñānaśakti*) and the power to act (*kriyāśakti*). Yet these two powers are not fundamentally distinct. Śiva's power, Aghoraśiva tells us, is in essence a single power. However, because of an "apparent" distinction (*upādhi*) between the spheres of knowing and practical activity, this power seems to take on forms suitable to its tasks in each domain (*TPV* 3). Similarly, what we humans experience as two separate capacities, to know and to act, is, in the highest sense, the integral power of consciousness as it directs itself toward the seemingly distinct domains of the knowable and the doable. From the highest point of view, the powers of consciousness are one and the domains in which the powers act are one; from our more limited human perspective, the unitary power appears divided and the single field for its exercise seems differentiated. The conformity we observe now between the philosophical and ritual portions of the Śaiva texts results, in the Śaiva view, from this fundamental integrity.

The metaphysical unity of knowledge and action in Śaiva siddhānta provides the underlying theme and the end point of this study. I will follow an oscillating course throughout, back and forth between accounts of the philosophically constructed world of Śaiva *jñāna* and explication of Śaiva *kriyā* within that world, in an attempt to demonstrate and illustrate the integral relationship between these two modes of Śaiva religious consciousness. At the outset I can only point to the complex intertwining of knowing and acting in Śaiva siddhānta; in the course of the discussion to follow, it will take on a more definite shape and texture. In the end I hope to indicate that the "distinction" between philosophical knowledge and ritual action, while useful and necessary as a starting point for the study of Śaiva worship, becomes increasingly indistinct as we delve into it, much as the Śaiva philosophers themselves speak of the division between knowing and acting as only an "apparent" dichotomy of a fundamentally unified human capacity of consciousness.

Acknowledgments

AT THE COMMENCEMENT of daily worship, a Śaiva ritualist constructs a new "body of mantras" by superimposing onto himself a host of powers greater than his own. He is then able to make use of that augmented body in performing all subsequent acts of devotion. Writing this book has not exactly been an act of *pūjā*, but I too have benefited from and relied on the support and assistance of many powers beyond my own in the course of this study. I would like to invoke each here with the appropriate *namaskāra*.

My initial research in India, the *bīja* of all that follows, was facilitated through the Kuppuswami Sastri Research Institute in Madras, the Sarasvati Mahal Library in Thanjavur, and the Institut Français d'Indologie in Pondichéry. I was very fortunate to read Śaiva ritual texts with Dr. S. S. Janaki, Director of the Kuppuswami Sastri Research Institute, and philosophical texts with T. R. Damodaran, formerly with the Sarasvati Mahal Library. Both helped me in myriad ways during my stay in India, and I thank them for their friendship. I wish also to thank Śrī K. A. Sabharatna Sivacarya of Madras, whose command of *āgama*-based Saiva ritual, both practical and textual, is of a kind rarely encountered among Śaiva priests nowadays. His demonstrations and explications helped immensely in making the millenium-old *āgama* texts come alive for me. He was also kind enough to let me photograph his enactment of rites of daily worship.

Three scholars associated with the Institut Français d'Indologie deserve special mention: N. R. Bhatt, Hélène Brunner, and Bruno Dagens. Pandit Bhatt generously went over my early translations of the *Kāmikāgama*, patiently answering my endless questions, and Dr. Brunner sent me a valuable set of comments and suggestions on a *Kriyākramadyotikā* translation. Professor Dagens perceptively discussed the project in its early stages and later on made detailed suggestions on a written draft. More than this personal assistance, however, their careful and painstaking work in the field of *śaivāgama* studies over the past twenty-five years, collecting, editing, and translating, provides the foundation on which any future research rests. It would not be possible for me to cite all the places in this study where I have relied on their insights and authority.

At the University of Chicago, where the project germinated as a dissertation, I benefited greatly from day-to-day contact with a whole community of South Asian scholars. In particular, I would like to thank the members of my committee, A. K. Ramanujan and Bernard Cohn, for their support throughout. Ronald Inden, my adviser, has been especially important at every stage of this manuscript. He initially pointed me toward the study of

Śaiva siddhānta texts, and through numerous conversations he suggested new paths to explore in the material when I saw none. It is his combination of critical rigor and breadth of interest that I have sought, albeit imperfectly, to emulate in my study.

The Department of Religious Studies at Yale University, where the project made that difficult metamorphosis from dissertation to book, has provided a supportive and stimulating environment for research.

Truly the *mūlamantra* at the root of any research project in these times is funding. Support for research in India was provided by the U.S. Department of Education through a Fulbright-Hays fellowship. The USEF-I officers administering the grant in Delhi and Madras were always helpful to me. For writing up the dissertation, I enjoyed the support of the Mrs. Giles Whiting Foundation and the Committee on Southern Asian Studies, University of Chicago. Final preparations have been assisted through the grace of an A. Whitney Griswold Faculty Research Grant, the Frederick W. Hilles Fund, and the Morse Fellowship in the Humanities at Yale University.

Hank Heifetz transmitted some esoteric WordPerfect mantras to me at a crucial moment. Charles Bryan, a graphics student at the Yale School of Art, transformed several of my initial drawings into finished form. Several other persons read earlier versions of this study and helped remove many of its lingering faults: Charles Collins, Ginni Ishimatsu, Ralph Strohl, Cynthia Talbot, and two anonymous readers at Princeton University Press. Finally, I want to thank Rita McCleary, whose careful editing and countless suggestions are responsible for much of whatever clarity exists in this work.

Oṃ hāṃ sarvebhyo namaḥ.

Abbreviations

AĀ	*Ajitāgama*
AcĀ	*Acintyāgama*
ĀPV	*Ālayapraveśavidhi* of Samakaṇṭha
BhK	*Bhogakārikā* of Sadyojyoti
ĪP	*Īśānaśivagurudevapaddhati* of Īśānaśiva
JNP	*Jātinirṇayapūrvakālayapraveśavidhi* of Rāmakaṇṭha
KĀ	*Kāmikāgama, pūrvabhāga*
KālĀ	*Kālottarāgama* (*Sārdhatriśati KālĀ*)
KālĀV	*vṛtti* of Rāmakaṇṭha on *Kālottarāgama*
KārĀ	*Kāraṇāgama, pūrvabhāga*
KirĀ	*Kiraṇāgama*
KKD	*Kriyākramadyotikā* of Aghoraśiva
KKDP	*prabhā* of Nirmalamaṇi on *Kriyākramadyotikā*
LPur	*Liṅgapurāṇa*
ML	*Mudrālakṣaṇa*
MM	*Mayamata*
MPĀ	*Mataṅgapārameśvarāgama*
MPĀV	*vṛtti* of Rāmakaṇṭha on *Mataṅgapārameśvarāgama*
MṛĀ	*Mṛgendrāgama*
MṛĀV	*vṛtti* of Nārāyaṇakaṇṭha on *Mṛgendrāgama*
MṛĀVD	*dīpikā* of Aghoraśiva on *Mṛgendrāgamavṛtti*
MV	*Mahotsavavidhi*, a portion of Aghoraśiva's *KKD*
PĀ	*Pauṣkarāgama*
RĀ	*Rauravāgama*
ŚAC	*Śivārcanācandrikā* of Appayadīkṣita
SĀSS	*Sakalāgamasārasaṃgraha*
SDS	*Sarvadarśanasaṃgraha* of Mādhava
SP	*Somaśambhupaddhati* of Somaśambhu
ŚPbh	*Śaivaparibhāṣā* of Śivāgrayogin
ŚPM	*Śaivāgamaparibhāṣāmañjarī* of Vedajñāna
ŚPur	*Śivapurāṇa, Vāyavīyasamhitā*
ŚRS	*Śataratnasaṃgraha* of Umāpati
SS	*Siddhāntasārāvāli* of Trilocanaśiva
ŚSPbh	*Śaivasiddhāntaparibhāṣā* of Sūryabhaṭṭa
SSV	*vyākhyā* of Anantaśambhu on *Siddhāntasārāvāli*
SupĀ	*Suprabhedāgama*
SvāĀ	*Svāyambhuvāgama*
SvaT	*Svacchandatantra*

TP	*Tattvaprakāśa* of Bhojadeva
TPD	*dīpikā* of Śrīkumāra on *Tattvaprakāśa*
TPV	*vṛtti* of Aghoraśiva on *Tattvaprakāśa*
TS	*Tattvasaṃgraha* of Sadyojyoti
TST	*ṭīkā* of Aghoraśiva on *Tattvasaṃgraha*
TTN	*Tattvatrayanirṇaya* of Sadyojyoti
TTNV	*vṛtti* of Aghoraśiva on *Tattvatrayanirṇaya*
UKĀ	*Kāmikāgama, uttarabhāga*
VĀ	*Vīrāgama*
VŚĀ	*Vātulaśuddhāgama*

Ritual in an Oscillating Universe

Locating the Tradition

THIS IS a study of the inner world of the Hindu temple: the world, that is, constructed and acted upon by the priests who perform the liturgical rounds that animate and maintain a temple as a living place of worship. To comprehend this world, we will reenact the central ritual of temple Hinduism, seeking as we do to reconstruct as well the metaphysical setting within which this ritual makes sense and from which it derives its efficacy for those who perform it.

"Daily worship" (*pūjā*, *nityapūjā*) is the ubiquitous Hindu ritual form by which devotees of a divinity regularly offer tokens of their respect and adoration to that deity embodied in an image or icon. It is the most common and recurrent ritual action of Hindu temples, and in many respects it is paradigmatic for the entire system of temple ritual as it developed in medieval India. As a general ritual pattern, *pūjā* has myriad variations. Each Hindu order articulates its own version of *pūjā*, suitable for the particular god or goddess to whom it is directed and adapted to its own particular theological convictions.[1]

Here I will focus on the complex formulation of daily worship articulated by the Śaiva siddhānta school during the early medieval period, and recorded in a corpus of Śaiva *āgama* and *paddhati* texts compiled in roughly the eighth through twelfth centuries.[2] The Śaiva siddhānta texts offer without a doubt one of the most complete, detailed, and interesting descriptions of medieval Hindu liturgical practice, and one that is to some extent still authoritative today in South Indian temples.

More specifically, I will draw principally on two fundamental texts of this tradition: the *Kāmikāgama*, which provides a full discussion of public temple worship, and Aghoraśiva's *Kriyākramadyotikā*, a twelfth-century *paddhati* that gives the most influential Śaiva siddhānta account of private worship.[3] Concentrating on the ritual prescriptions (*vidhi*) for daily worship contained in these two texts will enable us to comprehend much of the metaphysical world of Śaiva siddhānta, for Śaiva *pūjā* acts as a virtual précis of Śaiva siddhānta theology, a daily catechism in action for worshipers who undertake it with diligence and mindfulness.

Before we enter the inner world of the medieval Śaiva masters and begin this imaginative reenactment of *nityapūjā*, however, it will be useful to locate the Śaiva siddhānta order outwardly, as a historical religious community that defined itself and formulated its theological and ritual system in a larger cosmopolitical setting. Śaiva siddhānta is nowadays a significant school of Hindu philosophy and religious practice prevalent only in the South Indian state of Tamilnad. However, in the early medieval period with which we will be primarily concerned, Śaiva siddhānta was a school of Pan-Indian scope enjoying close ties with the political order and often exercising decisive control over the principal religious and social institutions of the time. Let us begin not with the Śaiva priests and adepts themselves, but with one of the great patrons of medieval Śaivism, the Cola king Rājarāja I.

Rājarāja's Great Temple

In 985 C.E., when Rājarāja I became king, the Cola kingdom was a modest one. Under Rājarāja's great-grandfather Parāntaka I, it had expanded rapidly to include much of South India. But in 953 the Rastrakuta king Kṛṣṇa III marched from the north against the upstart Colas and defeated them decisively at the battle of Takkolam. Thirty-two years of retreat, dynastic confusion, and gradual rebuilding followed for the Cola royalty. By the time of Rājarāja's consecration, the Colas had reconsolidated their sovereignty in the Kaveri River basin of Tamilnad and had acquired some territories beyond their traditional regional center.[4]

Once he became king, Rājarāja began a series of military campaigns. As he explained in his inscriptions, he became convinced, "in his life of blossoming strength," that "the great goddess Earth, as well as the goddess of Fortune, had become his wife." Because of this conviction, he "graciously" conquered kings in every direction, extending his sovereignty until he was "so resplendent that he was worshiped everywhere."[5] These campaigns went on for nearly twenty years, until almost all of India south of the Tungabhadra, as well as parts of Sri Lanka and the Maldive Islands, owed homage to the Cola king. In his own terms, he accomplished a "conquest of the quarters" (*digvijaya*) and made all kings into his tributaries; he then returned to dwell in his own city, Thanjavur.

In 1003, the nineteenth year of his reign and near the completion of these military campaigns, Rājarāja began construction of an imperial temple in the capital. By the time of its consecration six or so years later, the Rājarājeśvara stood as the most massive temple in India: a granite tower of fourteen stories 190 feet high, with a base 96 feet square, set in a rectangular courtyard 500 feet by 250 feet. The primary icon of the temple was a colossal Śiva-liṅga, probably the largest such liṅga in existence. The octagonal dome at the top of the tower, directly above the central liṅga, was composed of a single huge stone, weighing about eighty tons, that according to tradition was conveyed to the top by means of a ramp four miles long. The temple was sometimes called the "Dakṣiṇameru," or World-Mountain of the South, and indeed it must have towered above the Cola landscape like a world-mountain.[6]

The purpose of this monumental structure was to provide a home for the divinity that Rājarāja and his retinue considered the preeminent overlord of the cosmos, so that the god would come to receive the homage and offerings of devotion presented by the king, his family, and his kingdom. The god was Śiva, referred to in the inscriptions variously as Rājarājeśvara ("Lord of Rājarāja"), Āḍavallān ("Master of Dance"), and Dakṣiṇameruviṭaṅkar ("Lord of the Southern World-Mountain"). Śiva typically dwells upon Mount Kailāsa, the Uttarameru or Northern World-Mountain. It is a measure of the ambition embodied in this imperial act that Rājarāja could portray himself as having offered Śiva a new home in the south, equal to Śiva's Himalayan abode.

To serve Śiva and the other divine inhabitants of the temple, Rājarāja and his royal entourage made extensive donations and endowments, many of which are recorded on the stone walls of the temple.[7] Rājarāja himself presented gold articles weighing almost five hundred pounds troy weight, silver objects of more than six hundred pounds troy, and myriad jewels. The king's elder sister Kundavai, the second most generous donor, gave about a hundred pounds of gold and almost two hundred pounds of silver and jewels. Rājarāja also gave land, making over the royal share of produce from numerous villages throughout his dominion and as far afield as Sri Lanka. These endowments yielded an annual income of roughly a quarter million bushels of rice paddy. To supply ghee for cooking and for burning oil lamps, livestock was donated to the temple. One inscription details 2,832 cows, 1,644 ewes, and 30 she-buffalos that were assigned to 366 cowherds, who were in turn required to supply ghee to the temple at the rate of one *ulakku* (roughly half a pint) per day for every 48 cows or 96 ewes. (An *ulakku* of ghee per day will keep a "perpetual lamp" burning continuously.) Arrangements were also made for the regular supply of such cooking ingredients and condiments as fruit, pulse, pepper, tamarind, mustard, cumin, sugar, curds, plantains, salt, greens, areca nut, and betel leaves. All of these were necessary for the regular offerings of worship on a suitably grand scale, and for the even grander special offerings made during the several "great festivals" held annually.[8]

A religious institution on such a scale of course required personnel as well as endowments. As the temple inscriptions record it, the king arranged for other temples throughout the realm to supply dancers, some four hundred in all, to entertain Śiva. Forty-eight musicians along with two drummers were assigned to the regular recitation of the *Tēvāram* hymns composed by the Tamil Śaiva saints. The assemblies of brahman settlements (*brahmadeyas*) were required to furnish young students to act as temple servants and accountants. Other villages were called upon to send people for carrying out such diverse services at the temple as holding the parasol (eleven persons), lighting lamps (eight persons), and sprinkling water on the deities (four persons); also required were potters, washermen, barbers, astrologers, tailors, jewel-stitchers, braziers, carpenters, and goldsmiths.

Priests (*ācāryas*) were brought in from all parts of the subcontinent to execute the liturgical program. One inscription details the provisions made for them: each year roughly forty-five hundred bushels of paddy were to be supplied for the head priest Sarvaśivapaṇḍita, his worthy students, and his students' students, who were natives of Aryadeśa (North India), Madhyadeśa (the Deccan), and Gauḍadeśa (Bengal).

While Rājarāja's imperial temple is one of the most impressive and best-documented medieval religious structures of South Asia, it is by no means unique. Throughout the subcontinent during the half millennium between 700 and 1200 C.E., and longer in the south, Hindu kings sought to outdo one another in the scale and lavishness of the temples they constructed. Calukyas, Pallavas, Rastrakutas, Pratiharas, Colas, Kalacuris, Candellas—a number of Hindu dynasties centered in various parts of the subcontinent staked claims to imperial status at some point during the early medieval period, and each sought to solidify and display its position through the construction of appropriately commanding stone monuments.

Even Rājarāja's son and successor, Rājendra I (1012–1044), performed a second *digvijaya*, extending still further the domain owing homage to the Cola crown, and then returned to construct thirty-five miles from Thanjavur a wholly new capital city, named Gangaikondacolapuram ("the city of the Cola king who took the Ganges"). In the midst of the new capital Rājendra built yet another imperial-scale Śaiva temple, to rival in its authoritative presence the edifice of his father.

Temple Hinduism

The ideological setting for Rājarāja's and Rājendra's building programs was a particular historical formation I will here simply call "temple Hinduism," which became the dominant religious and political order of South Asia in the seventh and eighth centuries, and which remained so for five hundred years.[9] Temple Hinduism consisted of a number of distinct schools of thought that nevertheless largely shared both a body of ideas about how the cosmos was organized and a set of practices that enabled followers to act most efficaciously in that cosmos. These practices not only sought to bring the agent personally into relation with God and to transform his or her condition, but they also collectively engendered the relations of community, authority, and hierarchy within human society. Though it drew upon earlier Indian formations such as the Vedic sacrificial system, temple Hinduism clearly distinguished itself from Vedism in several fundamental respects.

Temple Hinduism directs itself primarily toward two gods, Viṣṇu and Śiva. Each is viewed by his votaries as the highest overlord of the cosmos, the transcendent and encompassing divinity. The supreme character of the divinity is repeatedly expressed in appellations such as Puruṣa ("cosmic Person"), *parameśvara* ("the highest Lord"), and *viśveśvara* ("Lord of everything"). Yet, transcendent as they are believed to be, these gods are also fully immanent, pervasive throughout the cosmos, and capable of manifesting themselves visibly in the world through incarnation (*avatāra*), emanation (*vyūha*), or embodiment (*mūrti*) in order to enter into direct relations with other divinities and lesser beings such as humans. Schools might differ from one another as to which divinity is supreme, but they share the theological premise that, to be supreme, God must be both transcendent and immanent.

The other divinities who inhabit the universe recognize the superiority of Viṣṇu and Śiva. Narratives in the *purāṇas*, cosmogonic texts of temple Hinduism, often recount the events by which lesser gods such as Indra and Agni, who were paramount in the Vedas, have been brought to this recognition. Likewise, Śaiva *purāṇas* also feature accounts where Śiva's main contemporary competitors for supremacy, Viṣṇu and Brahman, assent to Śiva's preeminence. Accordingly, subordinate deities appear most often as acolytes and devotees, and occasionally as aspects, of the highest god.

Relations between the high gods and humans are, likewise and even more so, asymmetrical and hierarchical, not reciprocal as in the Vedas. The proper attitude for a person to take toward Viṣṇu or Śiva is that of *bhakti*: recognition of the god's superiority, devoted attentiveness, and desire to participate in his exalted domain. The god is in no way compelled by human devotion, nor by any ritual action humans may undertake (as the Vedic exegetes claimed of sacrificial ritual), but he may freely choose to grant favor (*prasāda*) or grace (*anugrāha*) to those humans who have properly recognized and served him.

Such acts of divine generosity of course have profound transformative consequences for their recipients. They bring one worldly benefits (*bhoga*), but much more important within this system of values, they lead one toward liberation (*mokṣa*), the highest state to which a human may aspire. (The Vedas, by contrast, may enable one to obtain worldly ends but do not envisage the superior goal of *mokṣa*, charge the advocates of temple Hinduism.) Liberation is conceptualized in various ways by the different schools of Hindu thought. *Moksa* always involves leaving behind the sufferings and fetters that constitute our normal worldly existence, but it may lead one, according to which school one follows, to a merging with the godhead, to permanent service at the feet of the Lord, to autonomous and parallel divinity, or to some other final and ultimate state. The character of liberation was one of the major points of contention among the theological schools that developed during this period.

The internal attitude of *bhakti* is most visibly externalized in temple Hinduism through ritual action, of which *pūjā* is the model. In this sense, *pūjā* replaces the Vedic sacrifice (*yajña*) as the paradigmatic ritual act of Indian religiosity during this period. In *pūjā*, a worshiper invokes or invites the deity into some material form, most often an image or icon visually and symbolically representing the deity, and presents to him both material offerings such as food and clothing and devoted services such as the recitation of his praises, music, dance, and songs. Texts classify all these material and performatory presentations to the deity as "services" (*upacāra*). Viṣṇu and Śiva, as gods simultaneously transcendent and immanent, enter into a variety of both anthropomorphic and aniconic objects so that their devotees may see them and make their offerings of homage.

In many respects, Hindu *pūjā* carries on the central ritual concerns of Vedic *yajña*. Both center on acts whereby humans offer food to the gods. Both require that the human participants attain a personal state of purity or godliness consonant with the solemnity of the ritual action, and both provide means through which divinities are summoned to be present at the ritual terrain. Once invoked, the divinities are treated with all the respect due them and presented with a repast of the finest order. In most cases the remainders of the meal are subsequently distributed among the community of human worshipers in a prescribed hierarchical order. Both, accordingly, involve an enactment of proper relations between humans and deities, as these are understood by each, and may articulate as well status relationships within the human community.

However, several fundamental features clearly distinguish *pūjā* from the Vedic form of worship. Vedic deities when invoked remain invisible. In *pūjā* deities are summoned to inhabit material embodiments and so make their presence evident even to humans of limited vision. Sacrificial offerings cannot be presented directly to the divinities; another deity, the fire god Agni, is required to act as intermediary, conveying the offerings to the other gods. Offerings of *pūjā*, by contrast, may be made directly to the highest god in the central image and to other subsidiary deities also present in their own individual embodiments. And as temple Hinduism seeks to render relations between humans and divinities more visible and direct, it also attempts to instantiate them more permanently. While Vedic public sacrifices are performed in temporary ritual settings constructed for the occasion, public *pūjā* (*parārthapūjā*) takes place in a durable structure, built to last out of stone or brick and elegantly decorated by sculptors and painters. Such a temple serves as an enduring home for the divine image and for the god himself who dwells within it.

During the early medieval period, the temple became the dominant religious institution of South Asia. Myriad temples of every scale were constructed and dedicated not only to the two primary divinities but also to the many lesser divinities who (at least in the view of Vaiṣṇavas and Śaivas) occupied lower rungs in the hierarchy of lordship. As the permanent residence of the deity in a particular community, the temple became much more than simply the site of *pūjā* offerings. It acted as host to a wide assortment of both personal and communal activities, ritual and otherwise. It provided the stage upon which performing and literary arts developed. As employer, landholder, and moneylender, it was often the major economic institution of the community. It occupied the social center of the community, and it was a primary arena in which relationships of authority and rank were constituted, contested, and displayed.[10]

To sponsor a temple was a central act of devotion. Because it made possible all subsequent offerings, it was considered a foundational and most efficacious ritual action. As offering public sacrifices had been in an earlier time, so during this period an essential act of rule was to sponsor and endow temples within one's dominion. This was true not just for independent and imperial kings, but also for subordinate regional chieftains and for local headmen or assemblies who exercised authority within their smaller and encompassed domains. Of course, at different levels of organization the resources available would also differ. Architectural texts gave directions for the construction of temples ranging from modest single-story shrines to vast towers of twelve or more stories, and liturgical texts like *Kāmikāgama* prescribed nine different gradations of *pūjā* offerings, ranging from "lowest of low" to "highest of high," that a temple should follow "according to its capacity." The size and wealth of a temple, accordingly, often served as the visible index not only of the degree of religious aspiration of its builders, but also of the scale of polity responsible for its construction and maintenance.

Building a temple, then, became a highly visible political act as well as one of devotion. For instance, only a "king of kings" whose kingdom included within it smaller, subordinated kingdoms, such as Rājarāja's did, was considered qualified to construct a "preeminent temple" (*mukhyaprāsāda*), which was said to include within itself the various types of smaller temples.[11] Rājarāja's imperial temple, in this light, was not simply a matter of a warrior turning his attention from military to religious matters in his dotage. He intended it rather as the completion of his "conquest of the quarters," a highly visible proclamation and embodiment of his political achievement, which at the same time located this earthly accomplishment in relation to Śiva's sovereignty over the entire universe. King over other kings, subject to no other human lord, Rājarāja yet proclaims his fealty to Śiva.

The Āgamas

A new genre of liturgical texts became prominent during the early medieval period, explicitly non-Vedic in origin and directed primarily toward the temple cults of Viṣṇu and Śiva. This genre comprises the Vaiṣṇava *samhitās*, the Śaiva *āgamas*, and somewhat later, the Śākta *tantras* centered on the Goddess. I will focus here on the Śaiva *āgamas*, but much of what I say applies equally to the *samhitās* and *tantras*. Like so many others in the field of Indian studies, this extensive body of literature was largely dismissed and left unexplored by scholars until recently. Yet it is a rich and diverse corpus of texts and offers one of the most important sources we have for understanding the formation and development of temple Hinduism.

A Śaiva *āgama* consists, ideally, of four "feet," or portions: knowledge (*jñāna*), ritual action (*kriyā*), proper conduct (*caryā*), and discipline (*yoga*). Together, these four parts constitute everything worth knowing from a spiritual point of view; the section on knowledge reveals how the cosmos is organized, and the other three sections fully instruct one who adheres to that view of the world in how to act in it. As the *Vāyusamhitā*, borrowing a trope from the *Mahābhārata*, puts it, "Whatever is said in the other treatises, one finds that in the Śaiva *āgamas*; and that which one does not find in the Śaiva *āgamas*, is not found anywhere else."[12]

The primary focus of the texts, however, is clearly on religious practice. The *āgamas* spell out in detail the organization of the temple cult, from the ritual procedures and architectural guidelines needed to construct and animate Śaiva temples, through the regular program of daily worship and subsidiary rites, to the much larger occasional festivals. Many of the texts elaborate a pattern as well for daily household ritual, which parallels the daily temple cult. They set forth a sequence of transformative rituals—initiations and consecrations—that progressively incorporate the subject into the Śaiva community, move him toward liberation, and empower him to act as a temple priest or adept. In this respect, the *āgamas* provide liturgical compendiums for Śaiva priests (*ācārya*), for renunciatory adepts (*sādhaka*), and for committed householders worshiping at home shrines. They are the primary ritual texts of medieval Śaivism.

According to the lists contained in nearly every text, the canon of Śaiva *āgamas* consists in 28 "root" treatises (*mūlāgama*) and some 197 "subsidiary" treatises (*upāgama*).[13] Despite this profusion, the texts repeatedly tell us that the system of knowledge (*śivajñāna*) they express is unitary. They view themselves as a single textual corpus. As the *Kāmikāgama* has it, each *āgama* represents a part of the body that is the whole of the *śivajñāna*: the *Kāmikāgama* is its feet, the *Yogajāgama* represents its ankles, and so on up to the *Kiraṇāgama* as its jewelry and *Vātulāgama* as its garments (*KĀ* 1.93–101).

They are fundamentally united, they claim, because all *āgamas* originate from a single source, namely from the highest god, Śiva. Initially, the texts say, the knowledge embodied in the *āgamas* exists not in any verbal formulation, but as "undifferentiated sound" or "pure thought," which has not yet assumed any apparent divisions, but which contains immanently all there is to know. During the process of emission (*sṛṣṭi*), by which all things become differentiated, Śiva divides this unitary and subtle knowledge into a number of versions, and in so doing transforms it into an auditory form (*śabdarūpa*) accessible to lower categories of beings. He emits it, according to some texts, in a series of "streams" (*srotas*) that issue from the five faces of Sadāśiva.[14] These differentiated verbal versions of the originally unitary *jñāna* are then passed on to a number of divine auditors, who in turn pass them on to others.

Eventually the *āgama*s reach the ears of humans, a momentous event. The first human auditors of the *āgama*s are always *ṛṣi*s, sages portrayed as the most highly accomplished of all humans. The instruction may take place at Śiva's dwelling on Mount Kailāsa or in a forest hermitage such as the famous Nārāyaṇāśrama. The sages approach the god and, desiring to hear the superior knowledge of a *śaivāgama*, humbly request the god to teach them. Here, for instance, is the setting in which Śrīkaṇṭha, a manifest form of Śiva, narrates the *Kāmikāgama* to an eminent coterie of pupils.

> On the southern peak of marvelous Kailāsa, veiled by the shade of full-grown fig trees, on a seat sparkling with jewels, clothed in the skin of a tiger, the great god Śrīkaṇṭha, lord of all, was attended by gods, demons, heavenly musicians, divine magicians, demigods, and still others.
>
> Kauśika, Kāśyapa, Agastya, Gautama, and Nārada, Sanatkumāra, Sanaka, Sanātana, and Sanandana, Bhṛgu, Ātri, Bharadvāja, Vasiṣṭha, and others—all these great sages desired to know the highest knowledge. They looked up at Śiva and Śakti, bowed at his feet, and addressed the Lord, Protector of Umā:
>
> "Blessed One, you are the Lord of the Gods of Gods. You untie the fetters that bind the soul. You are the cause of emission, preservation, veiling, reabsorption, and grace. You instantaneously set in motion the great *māyā*, made up of Ether and the other elements. You are joined with the highest Śakti, whose very form is complete intelligence. You are free from direction, space, and time. You bring joy to living beings. We have been ordered by you, O Lord of Gods, to perform the worship of Śiva. Out of compassion for your devotees, please deign to tell us, O Lord of Gods, the system of knowledge which came from Śiva's mouth, and its meaning in essence."
>
> Asked in this way by the sages, the Lord whose flag bears the bull and whose crown bears the gleaming half-moon answered in a deep voice.
>
> "You have asked well. So listen, you who have fulfilled your vows, to the highest system, which was extracted from the great text called 'Kāmika.' This system first appeared on Mount Meru, and has been passed on by Praṇava and others. It is the most complete system, containing ritual action (*kriyā*) and proper conduct (*caryā*) as well as discipline (*yoga*) and knowledge (*jñāna*)."
>
> The sages, addressed thus, fell to the ground and bowed. Having given them a command, Śiva now taught this unsurpassed text. (*KĀ* 1.1–14)

Śiva goes on to set forth his teachings with the serene authority of omniscience.

Śiva addresses his instruction to an audience of the converted: those gods, sages, and human followers who already recognize and accept his preeminence. As these teachings are handed down in distinct *āgama* texts, they remain the exclusive possession of Śaiva priests and initiates; others are, in fact, excluded from hearing them.

> If uninitiated members of the three twice-born classes, persons born in the *śūdra* class, persons born of mixed parentage such as the *savarṇa* group, architects (*śilpin*), artisans, and the like should study the Śaiva treatises, the king and kingdom will be quickly destroyed on account of that sin. So the king should prevent them. (*KĀ* 1.111–12)

For such a select audience there is little need for polemic directed at other religious groups or doctrines. There is, however, great need for practical instruction. Most of the contents of the *āgama*s concern ritual activity. Śiva sets forth, most often in the optative mood, those actions best calculated to lead his auditors to the highest states of attainment. Subsequent members of the Śaiva community have carefully guarded and preserved these instructions, regularly copying over the manuscripts and passing them on to new priestly generations over many centuries.

Because the *āgama*s consider themselves human recensions of what was originally uttered by Śiva, they do not lend themselves to precise dating. As divine revelations of a universal knowledge, the *āgama*s eschew all references that might tie them down to particular times and places. Further, their own theory of origination, involving a gradual emanation and successive transmission, implies an openness to textual emendation and accretion. As the *śivajñāna*, while remaining fundamentally one, has been differentiated and emitted over time, so human redactors of the *āgama*s have on occasion felt it necessary to add new formulations of Śaiva thought and practice insofar as they cohere with the basic unity of the teachings. The result, from a historicist point of view, is a corpus of texts that is maddeningly diverse in compositional chronology.

Undoubtedly many *āgama*s were in existence by 700 C.E. The Pallava king Narasimhavarman II (695–728) refers to himself as "one who has removed all his impurity (*mala*) by following the path of Śaiva siddhānta" in his foundation inscription on the Śiva Kailāsanātha temple of Kāñcipuram, the largest imperial edifice built by the Pallavas. Among his royal titles inscribed there, he styles himself a "follower of the *āgama*s" and "one whose means of knowledge is the *āgama*s."[15] The South Indian sage Tirumūlar mentions nine *āgama*s by name in his work of perhaps the seventh century, *Tirumantiram*. But the *āgama*s available to Narasimhavarman and Tirumūlar are not necessarily the *āgama*s that have been passed down to us.

One of the texts Tirumūlar refers to is the *Kāmikāgama*, often described as the "first" or "primary" *āgama*. This text is also mentioned by name in the *Sūtasamhitā*, which may also date from the seventh century. No doubt a *Kāmikāgama* existed at an early time. Yet most portions of the *Kāmikāgama* that we have undoubtedly reflect the much larger scale of temple construction and liturgy that developed in later centuries in South India. Its architectural portions, for instance, follow those of the *Mayamata*, which correspond to the Cola architecture of the eleventh century.[16] Ritual prescriptions are, in several cases, parallel to the prescriptions given in the digests of Somaśambhu (of the late eleventh century) and Aghoraśiva (twelfth century). (I speak here primarily of the *Pūrva Kāmikāgama*; the second division, the *Uttara Kāmikāgama*, is perhaps later still.)[17]

We must assume that a highly esteemed text like the *Kāmikāgama* would be subject to a complex process of revision, both reflecting and guiding developments and changes in the knowledge and practice of the Śaiva community. I would propose, as a tentative approximation, that the most significant recasting of the *Kāmikāgama* took place in Tamilnad during the eleventh century, in light of Cola-period temple culture, and under the strong influence of the Śaiva siddhānta school. Some of its contents are no doubt older than this, and some have been added since, but the weight of the text is grounded, it seems to me, in that period.

With some other *āgamas* we can be on surer chronological ground, at least as to their termini ad quem. The oldest extant *āgama* manuscript, of the *Kiraṇāgama*, was transcribed in 924 C.E.[18] The *Mṛgendrāgama* was commented upon by the Kashmiri Śaiva siddhānta author Nārāyaṇakaṇṭha in the late tenth or early eleventh century, and his commentary in turn was glossed by Aghoraśiva in the mid-twelfth century.[19] In cases such as these, we can be certain that the texts we have correspond to versions available in the tenth century, and perhaps earlier. Beyond this, however, scholars of the Śaiva *āgamas* have only begun to develop the means of distinguishing different chronological strata within the texts. Until such an internal archeology is more fully established, efforts to trace the development of pre–tenth-century Śaivism within the *āgamas* are premature.

As we have seen, the *āgamas* assert an overall coherence while recognizing at the same time the differentiation within the genre. "Like the sparkling gem Cintāmaṇi," says *Kāmikāgama*, "the Śaiva teachings appear as both one and many. Although they are unitary because of their speaker [Śiva], they are also multiple because they are divided into streams [as the gem, while a single object, glistens with many beams]" (*KĀ* 1.103). Indeed, within the *āgamas* is a diversity of teachings. They present neither a single philosophically consistent doctrine, nor a unified liturgical system; rather, they offer us a variegated, multiple body of Śaiva thought. On many basic matters, the *āgamas* appear in complete agreement. Yet within the corpus one finds fundamental points of disagreement as well. Some *āgamas* argue a monist metaphysics, while others are decidedly dualist. Some claim that ritual is the most efficacious means of religious attainment, while others assert that knowledge is more important. They advance different lists of the basic constituents of material being, the *tattvas*.[20] Such differences in the texts of course reflect the various "streams" of thought within a large and geographically extensive Śaiva community as it developed in the early medieval period.

If the *āgama* corpus, like Cintāmaṇi, was both one and many, the "schools" of Śaivism that formed themselves in the early medieval period took it as their task to formulate from this diverse canon a coherent doctrine, one that could hold up in philosophical debate. Yet, as it turned out, more than one unity subsisted within the *āgamas*. Different Śaiva schools articulated quite different philosophical viewpoints, yet each based its doctrines on the authority of the *āgamas*. The dualist Śaiva siddhānta, the strict monist Kashmiri schools of Trika and Pratyabhijñā, and the Vīraśaivas of Karnataka, to name the most noteworthy, all claimed allegiance to the Śaiva *āgamas*.[21] Of these, we are concerned here only with the Śaiva siddhānta.

Śaiva Siddhānta

The temple of Rājarāja reflects the teachings of one particular *āgama*-based school of Śaivism, the Śaiva siddhānta. Indeed, there are many reasons to suppose that this was the most prominent Hindu order in early medieval Tamilnad. Even today, Śaiva siddhānta is an important school of Hindu philosophy in Tamilnad, and temples in the region most often claim allegiance to Śaiva siddhānta liturgical texts.

It is difficult to be precise about the origins of Śaiva siddhānta as a distinct order. Sometime around the ninth century, it seems, Śaiva siddhānta appeared as part of a division within the larger Śaiva community. The works of the monist theologian Śaṅkara and his successors provide a useful index for this shift. Writing probably at the very beginning of the ninth century, Śaṅkara speaks in his commentary on *Brahmasūtra* 2.2.37 of a single order of Śaiva dualists, which he calls "Māheśvaras." The Māheśvaras are elsewhere called Pāśupatas. The mid-ninth-century commentaries of Vacaspati Miśra and Bhāskarācārya, by contrast, distinguish four categories of Śaivas: the Śaiva, Pāśupata, Kāruṇika, and Kāpālika orders. For these ninth-century observers, Śaivism was changing from a single and undifferentiated religious community to a group composed of several distinct orders or schools of thought. From the ninth century, it became conventional to speak of four Śaiva schools, though the names varied: most commonly they are called Śaiva siddhānta, Pāśupata, Kālāmukha, and Kāpālika.[22]

Within this new quaternity of Śaivism, Śaiva siddhānta attempted to portray itself as the "pure" (*śuddha*) Śaivism, the "fully completed" (*siddhānta*) Śaivism, or more simply as Śaivism par excellence. If Śaiva siddhānta is "auspicious" (*śaiva*), they claimed, the other so-called Śaiva orders are "inauspicious" (*raudra*). Not surprisingly, Śaiva siddhānta claimed to offer a more compelling and more efficacious formulation of the *śivajñāna*, particularly as regards human liberation, than the competing schools of Śaivism.[23] Yet we know very little about the actual doctrinal or practical disputes that brought about the division in Śaivism, nor do we know the context in which the division initially took place.

While the earliest moment of Śaiva siddhānta self-definition necessarily remains vague, the picture becomes clearer around 900 C.E. From this time on there exist a large number of dated inscriptions referring to Śaiva siddhānta priests and ascetics, furnishing much fuller information about their affiliations and spiritual lineages. Followers of Śaiva siddhānta turn up in Madhya Pradesh (especially the Dahala region), in Rajasthan, Gujarat, Maharashtra, Orissa, Andhra Pradesh, Tamilnad, and even in Southeast Asia. These epigraphical references coincide with the appearance of Śaiva monastic institutions (*maṭhas*), to which many of these Śaivas were attached, and with a heightened program of Śaiva temple construction throughout the subcontinent. The inscriptional and archeological evidence suggests that from the tenth through twelfth centuries a broadly extended network of interrelated Śaiva siddhānta lineages spread itself out over much of India, acting frequently as spiritual preceptors to kings, constructing and presiding over temples and monasteries, and propagating the teachings of the *āgamas*.[24]

Aghoraśiva, the twelfth-century South Indian author of many Śaiva siddhānta works, serves as an apt exemplar of this "stem with many widely spreading branches."[25] At the conclusion of his *Kriyākramadyotikā*, he specifies his lineage of twelve Śaiva preceptors reaching back to the legendary sage Durvāsas (*MV* pp. 424–27). Among his predecessors, he lists Uttuṅgaśiva, a Gujarati living at Kalyāṇanagarī (perhaps the capital of the later Calukyas, in Karnataka), and Brahmaśiva, also hailing from Gujarat; Pūrṇaśiva and Vidyāntaśiva, who served as royal preceptors in Varanasi; Sarvātmaśiva, who was "received hospitably" by the ruler of Great Puri, in the Northern Konkan near present-day Bombay; and Śrīkaṇṭhaśiva, "a bull among the Bengalis." Aghoraśiva's own preceptor also came from Bengal, apparently traveling south to Tamilnad. Several others in the succession lived and taught in the Cola dominions of South India.

During this period, the earliest independent Śaiva siddhānta treatises of explicitly human authorship were composed. From the tenth century on, Śaiva authors writing in Sanskrit produced an array of *āgama* commentaries (*vṛttis*), ritual manuals (*paddhatis*), and philosophical treatises. Here I will refer to this entire body of texts as the "*paddhati* literature." *Paddhatis* tread in the "footprints" of other texts, and this corpus of Śaiva writings, both ritual and philosophical, follows in the path set forth by the Śaiva *āgamas*. And since these texts, unlike the *āgamas*, do not profess to be the direct words of Śiva, the *paddhati* authors are not reticent about leaving clues that allow us to locate them historically. Thus, Aghoraśiva tells us in a colophon to his *Kriyākramadyotikā* that he completed this work in 1157 C.E. (*MV*

p. 433), and in his commentary to the *Tattvatrayanirṇaya* he extols himself as the guru ornamenting the Cola country (*TTNV* 32).

The primary task of the *paddhatis*, as their authors saw it, was to clarify the views of the Śaiva siddhānta school and to refute the wrong views of others, all in order to enhance the spiritual welfare of their audience. In light of the diverse teachings of the *āgamas*, it was important first of all to make the Śaiva teachings easily comprehensible. One of the earliest *paddhati* authors, Sadyojyoti says in the opening verse of *Tattvasaṃgraha*, "I will explain the *tattvas* concisely, so that even those of simple minds may understand" (*TS* 1). The *āgamas* themselves are sometimes too prolix to allow easy comprehension, but the *paddhati* authors claim to put matters simply, concisely, and clearly by virtue of their own comprehensive study and their lucidity. Īśānaśiva tells us that he wrote his *paddhati* only after extensive examination of the *āgama* texts (*ĪP* 1.1), while the eleventh-century Paramara king and author Bhojadeva praises his own clarity of mind: "The king Bhojadeva composed this matchless *Tattvaprakāśa*, containing the meaning of the *śaivāgamas*. In that lord's consciousness, the entire set of *tattvas* gleam as clearly as myrobalan fruits held in the palm of the hand" (*TP* 76). This effort at systematization of *āgama* teachings no doubt often had effects on the *āgamas* themselves, as texts like *Kāmikāgama* were revised to accord more closely with developing Śaiva siddhānta doctrine and practice.

The *paddhati* authors were inspired to set forth their system clearly and forcefully by other competing systems of thought. When Vidyākaṇṭha instructs his pupil Nārāyaṇakaṇṭha to compose a commentary on the *Mṛgendrāgama*, he explains the need for such a work: "Treatises are written time and again by adherents of other schools, while up to now the seal on this school has not been broken" (*MṛĀV vidyā* 1.1). Aghoraśiva gives a similar reason for commenting on Bhojadeva's *Tattvaprakāśa*: "I undertake this commentary because the text has elsewhere been commented upon by others who are filled with the tainted ideas of nondualism (*advaita*) and who lack the true knowledge of siddhānta" (*TPV* 1). These other systems, they claim, have led people astray. Confused by the welter of competing viewpoints, some people abandon the superior Śaiva view and follow other, inferior ones.

> Some have been won over by the Vedas, others by the views of Kaula, and still others by the Nyāya school. The willful elephant (*mataṅga*) has abandoned the path set out by Śaiva siddhānta and celebrated by the best gurus, and has been led on a bad route. Therefore, put to the test by these other scholars, we have sought to refute the wrong views by striking them with the goad of this commentary, and to return the elephant onto the correct path. (*MPĀV vidyā* 1.1)

Consequently there is a greater polemical dimension to the *paddhati* literature than to the *āgamas* upon which it was based. Sadyojyoti, for instance, directs his *Nareśvaraparīkṣā* chiefly against the Buddhists for their denial of the soul and against the Mīmāṃsakas, primary medieval proponents of the Vedic tradition, for their denial of the category of the Lord. Here, as in many *paddhati* texts, there is also a strong argument against nondualist positions such as those held by Kashmiri Śaivas and Advaita Vedāntins. A later text, Śivāgrayogin's *Śaivaparibhāṣā* takes it upon itself to summarize and refute the positions on *mokṣa* held by Cārvāka, Mādhyamika, Yogācāra, Sāṃkhya, Nyāya, Mīmāṃsa, Jainas, the *purāṇas*, and several competing Śaiva schools including the Mahāvratins, Pāśupatas, and Kāpālikas (*ŚPbh* pp. 335–52). *Paddhati* authors wrote consciously in a world of competing viewpoints, attempting to distinguish the Śaiva siddhānta route prominently from the many paths prescribed by others.

Their intellectual efforts, then, were directed at reestablishing a lost unity among the *āgama* texts and at guiding back to the right path a community of Śaivas who had wandered off. Yet through their efforts the *paddhati* authors created something as much new as old. They identified a central tradition within the more disparate corpus of the *āgamas*, articulated this tradition into a unified system of thought and action, and established it as the basis for a new community of priests, monks, and lay followers. So successful were the *paddhati* authors in this endeavor that they ended up nearly eclipsing the *āgamas* themselves as guides to Śaiva knowledge and practice.[26] It is to *paddhatis* such as Aghoraśiva's *Kriyākramadyotikā*, rather than to the *āgamas* upon which they are based, that later Śaiva practitioners have most often turned for ritual guidance.

Aghoraśiva stands at the culmination of this intellectual project, spanning two and a half centuries and encompassing many parts of India, that aimed at formulating from the Śaiva *āgamas* a coherent and systematic school of thought and practice.[27] Writing in South India in the mid-twelfth century, Aghoraśiva was one of the most prolific of all Śaiva siddhānta authors, composing commentaries on *āgamas*, an extensive ritual digest, several philosophical commentaries, and even a few works of belles lettres, unfortunately no longer available. He relied not only on the *āgamas* themselves but on the works of many other *paddhati* authors as well. He cited Uttuṅgaśiva, Bhojadeva, and Somaśambhu as among his teachers and influences; he wrote commentaries on the works of Sadyojyoti, Bhojadeva, Rāmakaṇṭha, and Nārāyaṇakaṇṭha; and in his writings he quoted from the works of many other Śaiva authors also. It is no exaggeration to say that his works offer the fullest, most cohesive articulation of the *āgama*-based Śaiva siddhānta system integrating philosophy and ritual.[28]

Within a century of Aghoraśiva's lifetime, two major events transformed the Śaiva siddhānta order. With the establishment of the Delhi sultanate in 1206 under Quṭb al-dīn Aybak, the balance of North Indian military power decisively shifted away from the independent Hindu dynasties that had supported temple Hindu orders like Śaiva siddhānta, and came to rest with iconoclastic Turko-Afghan Muslims. In this altered climate, Śaiva siddhānta seems to have quickly disappeared as an identifiable school in northern India. Compared with other, more ascetically oriented Śaiva orders such as the Kāpālikas and Kālāmukhas, Śaiva siddhānta was primarily an institutional school centered on temples and monastic networks, and consequently dependent on continuing royal patronage. As a result, it was particularly vulnerable to this transformation of the North Indian political order. When Śaivism did resurface as a public religion there several centuries later, regenerating itself under more tolerant Islamic regimes or within renegade Hindu clans, it was quite different in character from the medieval Śaiva siddhānta order. Meanwhile, the more aniconic school of Vīraśaivas became the dominant form of Śaivism in the Deccan. So from the thirteenth century on, Śaiva siddhānta has been largely a regional Hindu order of South India, and especially of Tamilnad, where it was largely unaffected by early Islamic attacks.

The second event was literary, not political. Around 1221, Meykaṇṭār composed the *Civañāṉapōtam*, the first and most important exposition of Śaiva siddhānta theology in Tamil.[29] This was soon followed by the extensive Tamil works of Aruḷnanti, Maṉavācakam Kaṭantār, and Umāpati, elaborating and extending Meykaṇṭār's core teachings. Even though these authors very largely and explicitly based their writings on the Sanskrit *āgama*s and the *paddhati*s, and even though Umāpati (as well as others) continued to compose works in Sanskrit as well as Tamil, the dominant language for Śaiva siddhānta theology (though not for ritual) shifted from Sanskrit to Tamil.

With this shift in linguistic preference also some changes in doctrinal emphasis. Most notable among these, from the perspective of this study, Tamil Śaiva siddhānta authors decreased the role of ritual in religious attainment, considering knowledge and devotion as sufficient for liberation.[30] At the same time, they sought to relate the teachings of Śaiva siddhānta to the earlier Tamil poetry of the *nāyanmār* poet-saints, a regional tradition of considerable popular bearing.[31] In some matters, such as epistemology and refutation of other schools, the Tamil authors clearly surpassed previous exponents of Śaiva siddhānta. However, the shift has also tended to cut off the ritual prescriptions of the *āgama*s and *paddhati*s (which are still to some extent authoritative in South Indian temples) from the theological moorings that the early medieval authors gave them.[32] In spite of this change, though, the Tamil version of Śaiva siddhānta is best seen as a philosophical continuation and extension of the earlier Sanskrit-based school.

These two events have also had a powerful bearing on the way scholars have characterized Śaiva siddhānta as a school of Hinduism. The importance of the Śaiva siddhānta order in Tamilnad and its relative or complete absence from other parts of South Asia have led most Indianists to view Śaiva siddhānta as solely a Tamil school, based on the Tamil-language texts of Meykaṇṭār and the other three "lineage founders." This tendency goes back at least as far as one of the pioneers of Tamil studies, G. U. Pope, who wrote:

> The Śaiva siddhānta is the most elaborate, influential and undoubtedly the most valuable of all the religions of India. It is peculiarly the Southern Indian and Tamil religion and must be studied by everyone who hopes to understand and influence the great South Indian peoples.[33]

Yet considerable inscriptional and textual evidence points to the Pan-Indian character of Śaiva siddhānta from the tenth to the thirteenth centuries, as I have indicated. The task of drawing these materials together into a connected historical account of Śaiva siddhānta as a coherent, widespread medieval Hindu order, however, remains to be accomplished.

Śaiva Siddhānta as a System

In this study, I take the notion of a Śaiva siddhānta "system" seriously. The texts themselves clearly envision the *āgamas* and *paddhati* literature as comprising a unity of thought and action, and accordingly I have chosen to portray Śaiva siddhānta as a coherent system of knowledge and practice.[34]

The work of developing and articulating Śaiva siddhānta as a ritual and theological system was, as I have indicated, a collective and historical endeavor, beginning in an early stage that is now largely unrecoverable (and will remain so until it is possible to establish a chronological segmentation of the *āgama* texts), evolving within the context of temple Hinduism as it became the dominant South Asian cosmopolitical formation, and receiving systematic treatment from Śaiva siddhānta authors who sought to derive from diverse *āgama* sources a coherent Śaiva dualism in knowledge and practice. This system was the special preserve of initiated Śaivites, for whom it represented a detailed depiction of the cosmos and a program for action within it. It was expressed more openly in the very public domain of the temple, for the participation of the larger community of Śiva worshipers.

In this reenactment of daily worship and explication of the Śaiva theological world, I will present the Śaiva siddhānta order, synchronically, at what appears to be the high point of Śaiva ritualism. The *Kāmikāgama* and *Kriyākramadyotikā* depict Śaiva siddhānta ritual as it was formulated (and, we can only presume, practiced by the most conscientious) in Tamilnad during the eleventh and twelfth centuries.[35] These two texts draw upon the work of several generations of Śaiva siddhānta *paddhati* authors as well as the unknown transmitters of the *āgamas*, and they clearly reflect the large-scale Śaiva temple cult of Cola-period Tamilnad.

In addition to these two basic treatises, I have found it necessary to use other Śaiva texts as well to supplement and contextualize the instructions of *Kāmikāgama* and *Kriyākramadyotikā*. In doing so I have tried to follow *Kāmikāgama*'s own directive concerning the use of primary and secondary texts in constructing a temple and performing worship in it.

> One should perform [the ritual construction and consecration of a temple], beginning with plowing and ending with establishment, according to a root treatise (*mūlāgama*) only; if performed according to a subsidiary treatise (*upāgama*), builder and sponsor will both be destroyed. . . . And temple rituals from plowing through worship itself should all be carried out according to the prescriptions of the text with which one began, not according to some other treatise. One may conduct a ritual according to the prescriptions of another treatise, however, if it is not discussed in the primary text. (*KĀ* 1.104–7)

The ritual reenactment here too follows the prescriptions of my two "root treatises" insofar as possible. But as predominantly ritual in subject matter, these two leave many matters implicit, particularly the theological background of the ritual. Such knowledge would have been tacitly supplied, of course, by the well-trained Śaiva initiate as he enacted the ritual, but we do not share this internalized knowledge.

Throughout this study, I make greatest use of *āgamas* and *paddhatis* that are most closely related in outlook to the two primary texts: philosophical treatises that Aghoraśiva commented upon, the *Mṛgendrāgama, Somaśambhupaddhati*, commentaries by Kashmiri Śaiva siddhānta authors, Nirmalamaṇi's commentary on the *Kriyākramadyotikā*, and so on. Certain texts in other genres of Sanskrit literature, such as *purāṇas* and *śilpaśāstras*, reflect a Śaiva siddhānta viewpoint, and I use several of these also.[36] With few exceptions, I refer only to texts that adhere to an identifiably Śaiva siddhānta perspective. (The most important exception to this is the monist Appayadīkṣita's *Śivārcanācandrikā*, which provides an unusally detailed guide to certain aspects of Śaiva *pūjā*.) Not only does this method enable us to avoid the "destruction" that *Kāmikāgama* predicts for those too promiscuous in their use of heterogeneous texts, but it also results in a portrait of early medieval Śaiva ritual and philosophy that is clear and systematic, just as the *paddhati* authors sought to make it.

There is of course a choice involved here, which should be noted at the outset. As a Śaiva order of priests and ascetics that developed over several centuries and in many regions of the subcontinent, Śaiva siddhānta was not a completely unified phenomenon. There were important doctrinal and procedural differences within the school.[37] For clarity of exposition, I choose to present one formulation of Śaiva siddhānta, one "stream" of the differentiated *śivajñāna*. Based as it is on several of the most esteemed and influential texts of the school, this version of Śaiva siddhānta was no doubt an authoritative one, especially in Tamilnad, in early medieval Kashmir, and probably in other regions as well. But I do not wish to suggest that all *āgamas* and Śaiva siddhānta texts completely cohere with it. When I speak of what "Śaivas say" or what "the *āgamas* tell us," it should be understood in this more particularized sense, as representing the views of an important, even central, group of early medieval Śaiva siddhānta masters who sought to articulate a compelling and coherent Śaiva worldview and to advance it as the highest form of knowledge, the *parajñāna*.

CHAPTER ONE

Ritual and Human Powers

Śaiva ritual is grounded in and grows out of the world that is known metaphysically through Śaiva siddhānta philosophy. It is within this world that the worshiper acts ritually. Accordingly, we must begin our reenactment of *pūjā* by comprehending in a preliminary manner how that world is fashioned: its fundamental constituents, the situation of human beings within it, the most important goals of human endeavor, and how purposeful action such as ritual may enable one to gain these goals. This preliminary description delineates a Śaiva "theory" of ritual, or, to put it more accurately, a matrix of propositions that constitute the world within which Śaivas conceptualize and practice ritual.

Let us start, then, where the Śaiva siddhāntins themselves start, with the three basic components of the world, as revealed by the *āgamas*.

The Three Categories

For Śaiva siddhānta philosophy, the entire universe is composed of three fundamental ontological categories (*padārtha*): *pati* (the Lord), *paśu* (bound souls), and *pāśa* (fetters). Although these three categories interact with one another in countless complex ways to constitute phenomenal existence (*samsāra*), they remain ultimately separate and distinct. Together, they include all that there is. "No other category at all," emphasizes Nārāyaṇakaṇṭha, "exists outside of *pati*, *paśu*, and *pāśa*" (*MṛĀV vidyā* 2.2).

Pati denotes Śiva, Lord of the Universe. The term *pati* in general usage refers to a relationship of lordship or mastery, in which one being commands the allegiance of others within some defined domain. As a householder (*gṛhapati*) is supposed to hold sway within his home, and a king (*bhūpati*, *narapati*) exercises dominion over a portion of the earth and its inhabitants, so too Śiva, Lord of All Creatures (*paśupati*), is the master of the created universe and all beings within it. The material worlds we live in are emitted and reabsorbed through his command. We are maintained in bondage and eventually granted grace by his activities.

Other entities as well are included in the category of *pati*: the multifarious Śakti, a group of eight Vidyeśvaras, Mantreśvaras, and assorted other divine lords. According to Śaiva theology, Śiva shares his sovereignty with these other beings. (I describe Śiva's segmentary overlordship more fully in

Chapter 4.) One crucial difference, however, distinguishes Śiva from all other lords, both human and divine. Lesser *pati*s rule over domains that are limited and always encompassed within other, larger spheres of lordship, and they are therefore subject to the commands of greater sovereigns. Śiva, by contrast, is completely autonomous (*svatantra*); there is no other sphere beyond that ruled by Śiva. Śiva commands other lords, but there is no other lord capable of commanding him. Śiva is the highest of all lords, the ultimate locus of all lordship. All movement in the cosmos takes place finally under his all-pervading direction.

Paśu designates the multiplicity of individual souls in their various states of bondage. In common usage, the term *paśu* denotes cattle or similar tethered domestic animals; it also refers to the victim of an animal sacrifice. Like these other fettered beings, human *paśu*s are considered by Śaiva philosophy to be creatures that are constrained by powerful forces restricting their freedom and that depend ultimately upon the good graces of their master, the Lord Śiva. As with the animal chosen to be a sacrificial victim, the culmination of the human soul's journey is to reach a divine state, freed of all earthly fetters, through ritual action. But unlike domesticated animals, as we will see below, the human *paśu* even in the state of bondage retains some capacity to alter his circumstances through his own efforts, and to help effect his own liberation.

Human *paśu*s are bound by a variety of *pāśa*s, or "fetters." *Pāśa* generally denotes a chain or rope used to catch something or to tie it up. A hunter's snare and a birdcatcher's net are both included in the semantic field covered by *pāśa*, as is the noose carried by Yama, god of death. According to Śaiva siddhānta, the human *paśu* is bound by fetters of a less obvious but much more tenacious sort. The body, the mind, and the world in which the body lives—in fact, the entire multifarious cosmos—all ensnare and imprison the soul in profound bondage. The fetters shackling a human soul are persistent, often lasting over many lifetimes. Fortunately, however, it is possible to remove or destroy them through human effort and divine grace.

Two fundamental dualities underlie these three ontological categories. First, everything that exists is either *cit* (consciousness) or *jaḍa* (inanimate substance). *Cit* denotes "consciousness" in the broadest sense, the principle of animation that distinguishes living, conscious, active entities from the inanimate and inert. Always inherent in *cit*, the *Mṛgendrāgama* tells us, are the two powers of knowing and acting (*jñānakriyāśakti*).[1] A conscious entity, then, is able to exercise agency through the innate capacities of its consciousness.

Jada, on the other hand, signifies real, material substance. In common usage, *jaḍa* is an adjective connoting torpor, dullness, inertia, apathy, coldness, stupidity. Śaiva philosophy uses this term to characterize the entire physical world. In fact, the *āgamas* include within the sphere of *jaḍa* many human faculties that we (with our very different, Cartesian-based ontology) would generally characterize as immaterial and mental or psychological: the ego (*ahamkāra*), the synthesizing mind (*manas*), the intellect (*buddhi*), and so on. In contrast to *cit*, *jaḍa* is inert. Substances may be altered or transformed by external forces, but they have no autonomous powers or initiative. They require consciousness to act upon or through them.

According to Śaiva philosophy, Śiva is composed solely and eternally of *cit*. The fetters, conversely, are entirely made up of inanimate substance. The ontological composition of these two categories is constant. However, the third category—the bound soul—is not so fixed. One constituent of the *paśu* is the individual soul (*ātman*), which like Śiva consists in consciousness. But unlike Śiva, a human soul is not altogether free from fetters and substance. The soul inhabits a body composed of substantive *jaḍa* and lives in a world that is substantive. Thus, the bound soul partakes of both *cit* and *jaḍa*, in an unstable and finally alterable mixture. This ambiguity and mutability inherent in the human situation are at the center of all Śaiva philosophy and ritual action.

The second basic dichotomy is between souls and Śiva. Both the soul and Śiva are characterized as *cit*; that is, both are conscious entities. Śiva exists always in a single state; he is "liberated without beginning" (*anādimukta*). The soul, in contrast, exists in one of two basic conditions. The normal condition of the soul is bondage (*bandhatva*), the state of a *paśu*, in which the soul is attached to fetters. In this condition, the fetters alienate the soul from Śiva. The other condition of the soul is liberation (*muktātman*), in which all fetters are removed from the soul once and for all. In liberation, the soul becomes equal to Śiva in almost all respects. Yet even then, according to Śaiva siddhānta, the soul never merges or becomes united with Śiva, as nondualist Śaiva schools would contend. The liberated soul is a separate, autonomous Śiva-like entity, but not one with Śiva. So the separation of souls and Śiva is not, for this school, based solely on the contingent presence in the soul of ignorance, fetters, or other alienating forces that may someday be overcome. Rather, it is a permanent and ontological distinction.

Fetters, Powers, and Human Effort

With this doubly dualistic metaphysical framework in mind, we can begin to see how the Śaivas understand the human condition and the possibilities of human attainment.

At the center of one's being lies the soul (*ātman*). The soul, for Śaiva siddhānta, is the irreducible essence of the person; other constituents are contingent and expendable. The soul animates and instigates all other ingredients making up the person; without the soul, these ingredients would remain an inert, torpid mass of substance. Sadyojyoti compares the relation of soul to other constituents with that of a king to his army.

> As a king commands his troops toward victory, so the soul (*aṇu*) commands the intellect and other faculties toward their proper purposes of cognition and the like. And so, while victory lies with the army, agency belongs to the king; here also, while cognition and the like are located in the intellect and other faculties, their agency belongs to the soul. (*BhK* 50–51)

The soul is eternal, while other parts of the person have a beginning and an end. When its current body passes away, the soul transmigrates to another one. Even when the entire world is reabsorbed during the cosmic dissolution, the soul remains, patiently awaiting the next creation. And when final liberation is attained, it is the soul that attains it.

The soul possesses consciousness. To put it more precisely, the innate form (*svarūpa*) of the soul *is* consciousness. Consciousness, we have seen, entails the twin powers of knowing and acting, and so these powers too inhere in the soul. As humans, we are empirically aware that we possess the capacities to know things and to initiate action, of course, but that empirical recognition gives us only a partial view of the true situation. In fact, say the Śaivas, the soul's powers of knowing and acting are potentially infinite, amounting to omniscience and omnipotence, just like those of Śiva.

Unfortunately, in the ordinary human condition, our unlimited powers are not available to us because they are constrained by fetters. As a tether impedes a cow's power of movement, the fetters subdue the soul's own inherent powers. The fetters are said to "cover over" (*āvaraṇa*) the soul's qualities; they "suppress" (*rodhana*) its powers of knowledge and activity. Bhojadeva compares one particular fetter, *mala* ("primordial stain"), to the tarnish that blackens a copper pot (*TP* 18); Aghoraśiva uses the analogy of a cataract covering the eye to indicate the "blindness" caused by *mala* (*TPV* 9). In addition to *mala*, Śaiva texts speak of two other types of fetters that bind the soul: *karman*, the residue of past actions, and *māyā*, the constituents of the material cosmos. Together, these three impediments overpower the soul's innate capacities, reducing it to its "normal" state of bondage.

The intrinsic powers of the soul and the extrinsic fetters attached to it therefore stand in opposition to one another. Each person is an arena of struggle. The powers of knowing and acting tend toward their own fuller expression, while the obdurate forces of the fetters aim to subdue them. It is a contest not between good and evil, nor precisely between life and death, but rather between empowerment and suppression, animation and torpor.

The conflict of these forces in every living person accounts for the variations we observe in the capacities of different humans to know and to act.

Some persons are evidently wise, while others are clearly foolish. Some are powerful and others weak. The Śaivas envision a vast hierarchy of beings, divine as well as human, arranged on the basis of the relative distribution of powers and fetters. At the highest level of this hierarchy stand Śiva and those souls who have attained liberation (*muktātman*)—beings whose powers of knowledge and action are entirely unimpeded by any fetters. Below them is a group of divine beings classified as Vijñānakevala, which includes the eight Vidyeśvaras and the seventy million mantras. The Vijñānakevalas have removed certain categories of fetters (*karman* and *māyā*) but continue to be affected by one fetter, *mala*. Because of their relative freedom from fetters, they enjoy vast—though not yet infinite—powers, and they use these powers to carry out Śiva's commands. Next comes another group of divinities, the Pralayakevala, who are free from *māyā* but not from *karman* or *mala*. They too use their lesser but still immense powers to act as Śiva's lieutenants throughout the cosmos. Finally, at the bottom of this hierarchy, are beings such as ourselves (termed *sakala*s), whose innate powers are largely suppressed by all three types of fetters.

	mala	*karman*	*māyā*
Śiva	–	–	–
muktātman	–	–	–
Vijñānakevala	+	–	–
Pralayakevala	+	+	–
sakala	+	+	+

Among humans as well there are differences. As in any battle, the balance of the opposing forces may shift. While all humans are in thrall to all three fetters, the degree of their hold over us can change. In some persons, due to bewilderment and imprudent conduct, fetters gain the upper hand. As a result, such a person becomes increasingly unable to understand the true state of things, and his behavior becomes more and more controlled by fluctuating desires and insatiable craving. Śivāgrayogin classifies him as a *prākṛta*, commenting that his thought, "like dream-knowledge," is a confusing mixture of knowledge and ignorance, and that he is proud of his "self," which he mistakenly identifies with his body, senses, and other impermanent derivatives of the material world (*ŚPbh* pp. 152–53). Fetters stifle the innate powers of his soul, and he spirals ever deeper into bondage.

In other persons, fetters "ripen" (*pāka*) or are "consumed" (*bhoga*) through a combination of well-directed human action and divine grace. As a result, the grip of the fetters on such a person's soul loosens, and his innate powers are able increasingly to emerge. The emergence of powers, in turn, serves as the basis for further effort aimed at removing fetters, which reciprocally allows the person still greater access to his own formerly suppressed powers. According to Śivāgrayogin's classification, this is the path followed by the *vainayika*, the one who is "purified in mind, speech, and body" by following the Śaiva teachings, and who becomes truly knowledgeable both in worldly matters and in the Śaiva system (*ŚPbh* pp. 152–53).

The end point of his increasing empowerment, when the fetters are completely removed and the soul's capacities are fully manifest, is liberation (*mokṣa*). This is the "victory" toward which the soul ought to direct all its efforts. At this point, the soul recovers its inherent omniscience and omnipotence and becomes fully equal in its powers to Śiva.[2]

Clearly, from the Śaiva perspective it is desirable to tilt the scales in favor of the soul's innate powers. But how is this to be done? In contrast to some nontheistic Hindu schools, Śaivas insist that it cannot be done entirely through human agency. Nor does it happen of its own accord. As Aghoraśiva puts it,

> Souls are not able to attain worldly pleasures or liberation themselves, since their own powers are not free due to bondage, just as a bound animal (*paśu*) like a ram cannot free itself. And fetters will neither act nor cease acting by themselves just for the sake of the soul, because they are inanimate (*jaḍa*), just as a rope or the like will not untie itself. (*TST* 50–51)

If neither *paśu* nor *pāśa* can decisively shift the balance, the task must be left to *pati*. Ultimately, it is only through Śiva's grace (*anugrāha*) that souls may escape fetters and realize their full powers. In the *Śivapurāṇa*, Vāyu uses the analogy of refining metal: "This soul, which must be purified, is purified only through contact with Śiva. When a metal rod is placed in fire, it is the fire alone, not the metal, that brings about the burning" (*ŚPur Vāyavīya* 1.31.46). Aghoraśiva concludes, "So therefore, Śiva himself is the one who brings about worldly pleasures and liberation for souls" (*TST* 50–51).

Nevertheless, the Śaivas also grant an important role in this battle to human effort. Strict adherence to a doctrine of divine grace could easily lead to an attitude of quietism, while Śaiva siddhānta texts always prescribe a rigorously active program of study, proper conduct, yogic discipline, and ritual action. One must, in Vāyu's metaphor, manage to place oneself in Śiva's purifying fire, and that requires initiative. For instance, at the completion of his initiatory ceremony, the initiate is informed by his guru of his new responsibilities as a member of the Śaiva community. Īśānaśiva arranges these under eight rubrics. Some of these responsibilities are simple interdictions:

> This is the first rule: one should not revile Śiva, the preceptor, or Śiva's devotees. Nor should one tread on the shadow of a temple, a preceptor, a liṅga, or even a cow marked with the Śaiva insignia. . . . The third rule is this: one should not

> allow those who have not been initiated to copy or to hear the practices, the common rules of conduct, or the texts of the Śaiva school. (*ĪP kriyā* 18; vol. 3, pp. 185–86)

Others involve regular ritual observances:

> The fourth rule is: one should eat only after first worshiping Śiva and the preceptor twice, thrice, or at least once. . . . One should practice all the restraints and duties prescribed by yoga. On the fourteenth and eighth days of the fortnight, the conjunctions of planets, and other auspicious days, one should worship at a pure shrine or the like following the rules for special occasions. One should make a vow, and eat only once a day, either at night or during the day.

In other texts, the obligation to develop one's knowledge through teaching and study is also emphasized.

> Members of the Śaiva community should get up at dawn. When they have completed their daily rites, they should bow to their preceptor and carry out the duties that the guru orders. Those who live with the guru and depend on him should go over their lessons and listen to the Śaiva texts that he teaches, abandoning all feelings of pride, jealousy, hypocrisy, and passion. (*MṛĀ caryā* 66–67)

Clearly the Śaiva texts do not disregard the usefulness of activity in attaining human ends.

The efficacy of human action derives ultimately from the opposition of innate capacities and suppressing fetters. Precisely by exercising the powers of consciousness in a clearly directed and appropriate manner, a person is able to contribute to the removal of his bondage and thereby to his own empowerment. For instance, by studying his lessons and listening to the *āgama*s taught by his guru, a Śaiva neophyte helps eradicate many of the erroneous notions he may have held concerning the true nature of things. Increasing knowledge may persuade the aspirant to be more diligent in his practice of ritual, which for Śaivas is the most efficacious mode of action, and will enable him to perform it with a deeper understanding of its metaphysical foundations. Ritual, in turn, helps destroy fetters resulting from prior action, thereby increasing his capacities both to know and to act, which reciprocally informs his study of the *śivajñāna*, and so on. (I will trace out the path of increasing empowerment and final liberation in greater detail in Chapter 3.)

Human effort, then, is important and can accomplish real and significant changes in a person's situation. One should not derive from this, however, the arrogant conclusion that human effort alone suffices for the highest levels of attainment. According to Śaiva siddhānta, Śiva's grace is the basis for all truly efficacious human actions. But this grace acts through many channels. The *āgama*s contain Śiva's own teachings, emitted by him at the beginning of creation as an act of grace toward bound souls. Śaiva rituals all involve the employment of Śiva's own mantra powers, and in the most important liberating ritual in the Śaiva system, Śiva himself intervenes through the intermediary of the initiating guru to destroy the initiate's fetters and to help recover his long-suppressed innate powers, an act of supreme grace.

Knowing

Just as human beings can be ranked according to their capacities to know, so too various kinds of knowledge differ hierarchically. Bodies of knowledge may be more or less comprehensive in scope and offer greater or lesser illumination. Of the many systems of knowledge in the world, some, such as the sciences of medicine and astrology, are adapted to useful but limited worldly affairs, while others, such as Buddhism or Pāñcarātra Vaiṣṇavism, are aimed at comprehending the fundamental organization of the world and enabling one to act in accord with this. Of all bodies of knowledge, however, the Śaivas claim that the system emitted by Śiva and collected in the *āgamas* is the highest, most complete form. The texts refer to it as *parajñāna*, the "superior knowledge."

Śaivas give three main reasons why *śivajñāna* is superior: its authorship, its appropriate audience, and its illuminating power. First of all, the knowledge contained in the *āgamas* comes originally from the mouth of Śiva, who knows all. The *āgama* texts as they exist today take pride in tracing their own lineages back to an initial emission from Śiva. By an act of grace, Śiva transmits the various *āgamas* to appropriate divinities, who in turn allow the most eminent human sages to hear the teachings, and these sages then pass the *āgamas* on to other human auditors. Śaivas call this the *tantrāvatāra*, the "descent" of the *āgama* texts from Śiva to the Śaiva community. Moreover, according to *Kāmikāgama*, it is Śiva's highest, upraised face that emits the *āgamas*, while his other four, hierarchically inferior faces are responsible for other forms of knowledge like the Vedas (*KĀ* 1.17–27). Systems of knowledge like Buddhism that are created by human beings, who are necessarily limited in their knowledge, can hardly compare with those produced by Śiva. Therefore the superiority of the Śaiva system of knowledge over all other systems results originally from the omniscience of its source, Śiva.[3]

Śiva intends the Śaiva system for the most highly qualified persons, those most capable of exercising the power of knowing. Other systems are proper for those at lower levels of aptitude. As *Mṛgendrāgama* says, "Śiva ... revealed this [*śivajñāna* contained in the *Mṛgendrāgama*] to those fit to receive it, for their attainment; to others [not fit to receive the *śivajñāna*], he revealed a teaching adapted [to their capacities]" (*MṛĀ vidyā* 1.26). Commenting on this passage, Nārāyaṇakaṇṭha explains that the ones fit to receive the highest knowledge are "those who wish to achieve the highest state, on account of the ripened state of their impurity." On the other hand, "to those who, because of the unripened state of their impurity, follow the systems of bound souls," Śiva has revealed teachings "congenial" to their inferior capabilities and lesser aspirations (*MṛĀV vidyā* 1.26). What one is capable of knowing is a matter of one's degree of bondage. Inferior systems of knowledge are suitable for those who are dominated by fetters and may offer them some limited spiritual assistance. When a person's fetters become ripened and his power of knowing begins to emerge more fully, however, the *śivajñāna* becomes the only appropriate system. Only that knowledge can lead him to the highest levels of attainment.

Because it is meant for an audience of those who are most accomplished and aspire to the highest states, the content of the Śaiva system is more comprehensive and illuminating and covers a greater range of topics than any other system.

> This knowledge is authoritative because, while it elucidates matters accessible to other systems, it also enables the comprehension of matters to which these systems do not give access. As it is said, "[A science] which enables the comprehension of unknown things [as well] is authoritative."[4]

While inferior systems like the Vedas elucidate the categories of soul and fetters, according to the *Kāmikāgama*, the Śaiva system alone adequately clarifies the category of *pati*, the Lord Śiva. The greater comprehensiveness of the Śaiva system results, as one would expect, from the greater comprehension of its author. "Because the authors [of other systems of knowledge] were not omniscient, they do not describe clearly the totality of things. . . . But in the Śaiva system all this is present in its most complete form" (*MṛĀ vidyā*. 2.10–11). Since among authors only Śiva knows everything, only the knowledge spoken by him can claim to be truly complete.

A system of knowledge is not simply a passive body of contents. In the Śaiva view, correct knowledge *does* something: it destroys ignorance (*ajñāna*, *avidyā*) by illuminating the true nature of things. Śiva himself reflects on this elucidating capacity of knowledge when he is about to emit the *āgamas*: "When the light consisting of the sound [of these texts] shines, no longer will the worlds be covered in thick darkness and ignorance" (*AĀ* 1.33–35). Without *śivajñāna*, the world is obscured by the darkness of ignorance. Śiva's teachings in the *āgamas*, however, dispel ignorance as sunlight does the darkness of night, enabling one to see things as they are. The *Kāmikāgama* uses a related image to describe the difference between the Śaiva system of knowledge and other systems: "One should consider the distinction between superior and inferior systems of knowledge like the difference at night between the eyes of a cat and those of a man" (*KĀ* 1.16–17).

One who knows the *śivajñāna* has the feline ability to see the true nature of things even in a darkened world.

Higher forms of knowledge disclose a previously hidden order of things. Metaphors equating ignorance with darkness and emphasizing the ability of knowledge to dispel or penetrate this obscurity remind us once again of the limited human power of knowing without *śivajñāna*. Fetters suppress our capacity to recognize the truth, and we tend to mistake the impermanent for the permanent, the impure for the pure, and sorrow for pleasure (*TPV* 39). The Śaiva system of knowledge communicated to us through the *āgama*s dispels such ignorance by revealing what is truly permanent and what is not. It uncovers an underlying order to the world, more real, more permanent, and—when translated into action—more effective in attaining the highest goals.

Acting

Purposeful action, like knowledge, is a basic capacity of the human soul, and like knowledge, action takes many different forms in the world, some superior to others. Some actions rely on limited worldly knowledge, use instruments of limited efficacy, and aim at accomplishing limited, everyday results. In contrast, other actions may be based on more comprehensive knowledge of the world, make use of more powerful means, and aim at attaining more far-reaching results. For instance, an Ayurvedic physician attempting to recover the bodily health of his patient uses a system of largely empirical knowledge concerning the human organism; he treats the patient with dietary and medicinal concoctions that have a therapeutic effect on the patient's body. For some maladies such action is entirely adequate, while for others a more penetrating intervention may be necessary. A patient suffering from the bite of a poisonous snake, for example, requires stronger treatment than Ayurveda can offer. She must quickly seek out a healer adept in the use of the GARUḌA mantra, who can employ this more powerful method to cure snakebite and thereby effect a result not obtainable through conventional medical treatments.[5] (Here and throughout this study, I adopt the convention of designating mantras by capital letters, serving to set them apart from normal discourse, as they deserve.)[6]

To treat the condition of the human soul in its profound bondage, action of a much greater efficacy still is required. In this case, only Śaiva ritual action is able to make a significant impact.

Ritual, in the Śaiva view, is not different in kind from other forms of practical activity. It is not, for instance, distinguished as "expressive" or "symbolic" activity in contrast to "pragmatic," nor as "sacred" action in contrast to "profane." The two terms most often used to denote "ritual action" in the *āgamas*, *kriyā* and *karman*, both derive from the common Sanskrit root *kṛ* (to do, to make), and both signify "action" in the very broadest sense. Like all intentional activity, ritual action is an expression of the soul's power of consciousness, which directs instruments and forces toward accomplishing some aim. However, Śaivas do posit a hierarchical distinction between Śaiva ritual and other modes of action. Among all forms of human action, they say, Śaiva ritual is preeminent in the scope of knowledge upon which it is based, in the efficacy of the instruments it employs, and in the levels of attainment to which it allows access.

The superiority of Śaiva ritual as a mode of action derives, not surprisingly, from Śiva. Śaiva ritual is a part of the *śivajñāna* revealed by the Lord who is both omniscient and omnipotent. Nārāyaṇakaṇṭha puts it this way:

> The superiority of the knowledge presented here [i.e., in the *jñānapāda*] derives from its author; it is taught by Paramaśiva who himself knows and accomplishes all objects, who transcends bound souls and fetters, and who is himself unsurpassed. So too all the practical methods such as initiation taught here are also superior, because they concur with what is known. (*MṛĀV vidyā* 2.11)

Just as Śiva's authorship insures the superiority of Śaiva knowledge over other systems of knowledge, so that same origin determines that Śaiva ritual will be superior to any other form of practical action.

Further, as Nārāyaṇakaṇṭha's comment makes clear, Śaiva ritual action "concurs" with the highest philosophical knowledge. There exists an originative "conformity" (*anuga*) between the sections in the *āgamas* discussing knowledge and those discussing action. Since the *śivajñāna* discloses the most fundamental order of things, actions that accord with this order are bound to be more successful in accomplishing their ends. Superior, comprehensive knowledge leads to superior, efficacious action.

All action, say the Śaivas, necessarily involves the use of "instruments" (*kāraṇa*). Animating consciousness (*cit*) cannot act in and through itself; it must employ palpable objects or forces to carry out its intentions. Śiva, for instance, engages a host of self-arising energies or powers (*śaktis*), mantras, and subordinate deities acting as agents (*adhikārins*) to fulfill his commands. Souls embodied in human forms likewise depend on instruments to perform their much more restricted actions. Conventionally, Śaiva texts speak of the primary human instrumentalities as those of "mind, speech, and body." As humans, we carry out all our ordinary human actions using one or more of these fundamental apparatuses.

In ritual, one employs the same three instruments, but in a more focused and powerful manner. Sūryabhaṭṭa specifies that a worshiper should perform the acts of worship "with faith, and accompanied by activities of mind, speech, and body, such as especially meditation, mantra repetitions, and *mudrās*" (*ŚSPbh* p. 37). Meditation (*dhyāna*) is a particularly potent mental activity, learned through the practice of yoga, by which the mind undistractedly centers itself on a visualized divine form or some nonvisual reality, making that entity present to a high degree.[7] Similarly, *mudrās* are ritually prescribed hand gestures, bodily activities with more far-reaching results than normal movements or gestures of the body. The *Kāraṇāgama* makes clear the efficacy of such ritual gestures with an etymological definition: "It gives delight (*mudā*) to the gods and drives away (*dravayati*) the demons. Because of its power to delight and to drive away, it is called a Śaiva *mudrā*."[8] Normal bodily gestures and hand movements may affect material objects close at hand; only *mudrās* have the power to influence gods and demons beyond one's ordinary reach.[9]

Of all instruments available to humans, however, the mantra is most significant. Mantras more than anything else distinguish Śaiva ritual from everyday action.

> From the first plowing [to establish a temple], all rites are accomplished with mantras. In consequence, since mantras are intended for ritual, [an action] is not ritual without mantras. One establishes the deity with mantras, and one worships him with mantras. One bathes him with mantras, and one offers him oblations with mantras. Expiatory rites are done by mantras, and initiation through mantras also. With mantras one acquires supernormal powers, and with mantras one attains the place of Śiva.[10]

To begin with, mantras are speech acts; one speaks a mantra, just as one speaks ordinary sentences. But mantras are not simply human utterances or formulas. They are also, more fundamentally, powerful divine beings or forces that exist independently of any human usage. The speech act is the signifier (*vācaka*), the divine being is the signified (*vācya*); the mantra may be thought of as the sign in which the two are intimately—and not arbitrarily—united.

> A mantra is recognized as having a dual form, resulting from a division of signified and signifier. The signifier has the form of speech, while the signified is the referent (*artha*). However, it is also acknowledged that the signified and signifier are essentially identical (*tadātmya*). (*KĀ* 2.3–4)

The *āgamas* speak of seventy million mantras that are emitted by Śiva at the beginning of creation and that Śiva then commands to carry out his lordly functions in various parts of the world. Thus, mantras are first and foremost the instruments of Śiva himself. By properly articulating the "sonant form" of a mantra (as signifier), the Śaiva ritualist is also able to summon and to channel those same powers (as signified) into the sphere of ritual, to accomplish his own ends. In Śaiva ritual, one gains access to Śiva's own instrumentality by using Śiva's mantras.[11]

Since the knowledge on which it is based is more comprehensive, and the instruments it employs more powerful, Śaiva ritual is bound to lead to superior results. But the rituals of other systems are useful, the Śaivas concede, at least for accomplishing lesser goals. "Those who are purified through Vedic rituals like Agnihotra and Candrāyana attain joy in the three worlds. Those who offer a hundred sacrifices gain the abode of Indra." Joy and heavenly abodes are, of course, legitimate and worthy aims for aspiration. Yet such attainments pale before those of the Śaiva devotee. "However, the place attained by those devoted to Śiva, even when [Śaiva rituals] are improperly performed, cannot be achieved [by non-Śaivas] even with a thousand sacrifices" (*MPĀ vidyā* 26.11). Vedic rituals, say the Śaivas, at best result in worldly enjoyments (*bhoga*); Śaiva rituals yield such enjoyments too but lead ultimately to liberation (*mokṣa*). And liberation, in the Śaiva scale of values, is the highest possible human attainment.

Even the rituals of other systems that claim to lead to liberation in fact take the aspirant only to an inferior level of *mokṣa*. Nārāyaṇakaṇṭha for one speaks of these as "phantom" liberations: "The liberation in the Śaiva system is superior because it is beyond the purview of all other systems . . . since the liberation which other systems teach is only a phantom of liberation" (*MṛĀV vidyā* 2.11). He goes on to quote another text, which asserts that those supposedly "liberated" according to methods other than the Śaiva are in fact released only from the three "attributes" (*guṇas*), not from the three fetters. Other Śaiva authors of a more conciliatory bent distinguish between incomplete, lower (*apara*) liberation and complete, higher (*para*) liberation. "There are seven grades of *mokṣa*," asserts Vedajñāna, and of them only one is subtle, transcendent, fully achieved, and completely autonomous; the other six leave one still heteronomous, subordinate to another lord (*ŚPM* 7.34–35).[12] Only Śaiva ritual offers the highest form of release, the *paramokṣa*.

Knowing and Acting

The Śaivas, then, pugnaciously assert the superiority of their system over all others. The revealed knowledge in the *āgamas* is more comprehensive than any other form of knowledge; the ritual action prescribed by the *āgamas* is more efficacious than any other mode of practical activity. But one might still ask which of these is more important, knowledge or ritual action?

One can find supporters of both positions within Śaiva siddhānta. Some texts clearly grant a greater role in the attainment of liberation to knowledge. "Devotees gain liberation solely through knowledge," argues the *Ajitāgama* (18.3–4). "As for a ritual like worship, it gives only worldly results such as divine status (*indrapada*)." Others by contrast stress the necessity of ritual action. Aghoraśiva uses the analogy of a cataract covering the eye to support this position. Because the cataract is a physical affliction, recognition alone is not sufficient to remove it; physical action in the form of medical treatment is required. So too the fetters that cover the soul are substantive, and one must remove them through ritual activity, not through knowledge alone (*TPV* 15).

The most common stance taken by Śaiva siddhānta texts acknowledges the necessity of both knowledge and action for attaining the highest goals. Śivāgrayogin (who himself emphasizes knowledge) quotes an unnamed text to this effect:

> Knowledge devoid of activity is not the preeminent means of attainment (*pradhāna*), nor is activity devoid of understanding the preeminent means. Therefore, successful attainment of liberation arises only through both of them together, just as a bird does not fly without two wings. (*ŚPbh* pp. 311–14)

Or, to use another analogy: "Like rice mixed with honey, or like honey mixed with rice, ritual austerities and knowledge combined make an excellent medicine" (*ŚPbh* pp. 311–14). Whether it is a matter of rising like a bird to a higher level of attainment or of medically treating the malady of bondage, the Śaiva aspirant needs to make full use of both his conscious powers of knowing and acting. These are not two separate pathways leading to the same end, but two interrelated and complementary constituents of a single path.

Even those texts that emphasize knowledge concede that ritual action is also crucial, because it gives rise to knowledge. As the *Ajitāgama* continues, "When Śiva the Lord of All Gods is worshiped, he grants knowledge and devotion" (*AĀ* 18.4). Without ritual practice, the requisite knowledge might never arise. Conversely, those who focus on action recognize that correct knowledge is required for the proper comprehension and practice of ritual. While Nārāyaṇakaṇṭha holds that the ritual of initiation (*dīkṣā*) is the singular key to liberation, he adds this proviso:

> It is not possible to perform initiation without knowledge, because knowledge provides the means of determining the inherent form of bound souls, fetters, and the Lord, indicates how to accomplish all paths of attainment, and reveals the greatness of the Mantras, the Mantreśvaras, and others. (*MṛĀV yoga* 1)

Without correct knowledge, one's ritual practice will be shaky and finally fruitless.

The mutual implication and necessity of both knowledge and ritual action as modes of religious praxis have for the Śaivas an ontological basis, as we have seen. The two powers of knowing and acting are ultimately unitary, the integral power of consciousness directing itself toward what is to be known (*jñeya*) and what needs to be done (*kārya*). So in the contest between the soul's innate powers and the fetters, a Śaiva aspirant must exercise both powers if he is to alter his own condition of bondage to a significant degree.

The Śaiva Ritual System

Considering the importance Śaivas grant to ritual action, it is not surprising that the scope of the Śaiva ritual system described in the *āgamas* is extremely broad. The *āgamas* give detailed directions for rituals large and small, public and private, optional and obligatory; for rituals one may perform directly and those that require the mediation of a Śaiva priest; for rituals performed with external actions and substances and those performed internally through meditation and visualization; and for rituals that confer worldly benefits and those that lead to liberation.

For instance, the published *Kāmikāgama* discusses only *kriyā*—the other three *pādas* of this *āgama* are fragmentary or lost—and requires some twelve thousand verses to do so.[13] In the course of this text, one finds extensive instructions for the construction and ritual establishment of Śaiva temples and other religious structures, beginning with the selection and preliminary plowing of the site, up through the culminating consecration, which transforms the man-made edifice into a divine habitation. The text also specifies rituals for establishing (*pratiṣṭhā*) the central liṅga of a temple and various divine icons, in order to render them suitable supports for the presence of Śiva and other divinities. A temple once activated maintains a schedule of celebrations on auspicious occasions ranging from special fortnightly bathings (*snāpana*) of the liṅga to major annual calendrical festivals (*mahotsava*) like Dīpāvali and Śivarātri; *Kāmikāgama* gives directions for a complete round of such occasional rituals. Further, it describes a set of sixteen major gift-giving ceremonies (*mahādānas*) such as the *hiraṇyagarbha* (the "golden womb" ceremony) that a Śaiva ruler or wealthy patron may optionally choose to have performed.

In addition to this temple-oriented ritual program, the *Kāmikāgama* also specifies a sequence of what one might call "spiritual life-cycle" rituals oriented toward the individual Śaivite: first a series of three initiations (*dīkṣā*) that incorporate persons into the Śaiva community and alter their spiritual status, then several consecrations (*abhiṣeka*) that empower initiated Śaivites to act in special capacities such as priest or mantra-adept, and finally cremation (*antyeṣṭi*) formulated as a final liberating ritual. There are discussions of ritual austerities for expiating (*prāyaścitta*) previous acts of wrongdoing or ritual omissions, and of ritual pacifications (*śānti*) employed to placate threatening forces. The text also gives instructions for a sequence of daily observances that every initiated Śaivite concerned with his spiritual welfare ought to perform regularly: morning ablutions (*snāna*), worship of the sun, daily worship of Śiva, a fire oblation (*homa*), worship of Caṇḍa and others.

Of all rituals in the Śaiva system, the most recurrent and pervasive is the daily worship (*nityapūjā*) of Śiva. *Āgamas* speak glowingly of its far-reaching effects. The *Kāmikāgama* tells us, simply, that daily worship "yields the fruits of both worldly pleasure and liberation" (*KĀ* 4.1). More extravagantly, the *Suprabhedāgama* cites many results the worshiper may accomplish through his worship:

> Now I will describe the order of rules for Śaiva worship, which destroys every sin, produces happiness in all the worlds, grants the benefits of all gifts and all sacrifices, removes stains resulting from the murder of a brahman and all other crimes, grants the benefits of the horse sacrifice, gives victory, creates prosperity, expands one's territory, and destroys one's enemies. There has never been merit equal to that of worshiping Śiva, and never will be.[14]

The texts advise all eligible members of the Śaiva community to perform *nityapūjā* every day, without exception. The *Kāmikāgama* stresses this imperative with hyperbole:

> The one born in self-deception who fails to worship the Lord Śiva will long sink in an ocean of unhappiness in this world. It is better to stop breathing or even cut off your head than to eat without worshiping the Three-eyed Lord. Recognizing this, one should worship Sadāśiva with perseverance. (*KĀ* 4.12–14)

A diligent Śaivite should offer such worship privately and on his own behalf (*ātmārtha*), in a home shrine or some other auspicious place, one or more times a day. In addition, daily worship is also performed in every Śaiva temple, by a duly consecrated Śaiva priest, publicly and on behalf of others (*parārtha*).[15] The benefits of public *pūjā* are not confined to the priest but extend throughout the community.

> Worshiping in a village, town, or city, beside a river or on a mountain, at the sixty-eight great holy sites or some other beautiful divine abode of Śiva where there is a liṅga—whether it be self-arising, divine, a liṅga-shaped stone, or one put up by a sage, or at a liṅga established by humans—is regarded as worship on behalf of others. Worship on behalf of others should be performed to increase the longevity, health, victory, and prosperity of the ruler, and to make the villagers and others thrive. (*KĀ* 4.3–6)

Depending on their size and resources, temples may offer worship once, twice, thrice, or up to eight times daily; quantities of food and other substances offered may range from rather meager amounts to large-scale feasts requiring many bushels of rice. These daily offerings, however large or small, form the liturgical backbone of all Śaiva temples.

In addition to its regular performance as an independent ritual, daily worship also figures frequently as an element in other, larger Śaiva rituals. For instance, a priest offers *nityapūjā* intact at the commencement of the annual offering of the expiatory *pavitra*. In initiation, the initiating guru makes three offerings of daily worship at the outset. Moreover, important rites from daily worship are employed as building blocks to construct more complex rituals. The invocation used to summon Śiva in daily worship, for instance, is found repeatedly embedded within other rituals. When a text directs the ritualist to "perform invocation," it generally means that he should carry out invocation according to the method employed in daily worship. Because of this paradigmatic quality, many *āgama*s and *paddhati*s begin their discussion of *kriyā* with daily worship. Thus, one may view daily worship as a unity of constituent syntactic parts that, both as a whole and as parts, are repeatedly embedded within other ritual compositions in the Śaiva system.[16]

Looked at from another angle, daily worship contains a synopsis of the entire Śaiva system of ritual. Within this single ritual one finds condensed enactments of many other Śaiva rituals. The rite of self-purification in daily worship, for instance, is a compressed version of liberating initiation. A brief offering of the *pavitra* in daily worship is an abbreviated recapitulation of the annual *pavitrārohana*. There are many more examples: *vāstupūjā*, *abhiṣeka*, *nityotsava*, and other rites enacted daily within *pūjā* replicate in abbreviated form larger counterpart rituals. And just as Hindu *pūjā* historically replaced the Vedic sacrifice even while maintaining many of its central concerns and features, Śaiva worship includes within its regular liturgical program a brief fire sacrifice (*homa*), subordinated to the more central act of liṅga worship but nevertheless present. As daily worship pervades all other Śaiva rituals, so also all other rituals are immanent within daily worship.

Because daily worship so permeates the ritual practice of Śaiva siddhānta, it offers a privileged point of entry into the Śaiva world. We need then to ask what makes it so important. Why do the Śaivas make daily worship the paradigmatic ritual in their system of action? What happens in daily worship that gives it such centrality?

Daily Worship and the Worshiper

The dominant scholarly viewpoint has regarded *pūjā* as an undifferentiated ritual form. If you've seen one *pūjā*, according to this perspective, you've seen them all. In this study, I take the opposite approach. It is in the very specificity of the Śaiva siddhānta formulation of *pūjā* that its primary significance lies.

During the early medieval period, the various schools of temple Hinduism formulated and reformulated their own versions of *pūjā*, appropriate with suitable modifications for both public and domestic practice. Vaikhānasa, Pāñcarātra, and later Śrī Vaiṣṇava schools devoted to Viṣṇu as supreme god developed forms of daily worship suitable to the theological personality of Viṣṇu, while Pāśupata and Śaiva siddhānta groups addressed parallel rituals of *pūjā* to Śiva. Forms of *pūjā* were developed to reflect differing philosophical propensities: monist and dualist *pūjā*s, idealist and realist *pūjā*s.

Some versions of *pūjā* emphasized the efficacy of devotion, while others stressed knowledge, and still others ritual action itself. *Pūjā* became a common ritual form in which contesting schools of thought could enact, display, and (they each hoped) constitute the shared world of medieval India in ways consonant with their own metaphysical premises and soteriological aims. As a central ritual of temple Hinduism, *pūjā* acted as a ceremonial arena for philosophical as well as ritual debate.

In carefully elaborating *pūjā* as a distinctive Śaiva siddhānta liturgy, the Śaivas attempted to present *pūjā* not simply as a set of ritual injunctions, but as a condensed practical catechism of the world as it was known through Śaiva philosophy, and as an implicit argument for the superior comprehensiveness and efficacy of their system of knowledge and action.

In simplest outline, the daily worship of Śiva consists in three main sequences of ritual actions. The first sequence is a set of preliminary rites, termed the "five purifications" (*pañcaśuddhi*), in which the worshiper makes himself, the ritual substances, the place of worship, the mantras, and finally the liṅga suitable for the reception and service of Śiva. The second sequence, termed "invocation" (*āvāhana*), summons Śiva into the liṅga. The worshiper constructs an elaborate throne and embodiment as a support for Śiva's presence in the ritual and then conveys Śiva there. In the third sequence the ritualist offers a series of "services" (*upacāra*) to Śiva, as an expression of his homage. Through his services, the worshiper treats his chosen deity as a divine guest. After these services have been completed, the worshiper allows Śiva to depart from the liṅga and *nityapūjā* ends.

Reduced in this way to a formal scheme, such an account gives little indication of the significance of Śaiva worship. A similar pattern of worship, with a few variations, can and does underlie the regular *pūjā* of Hindu schools directed toward many Hindu divinities, and a similar pattern is employed by worshipers adhering to various philosophical persuasions. At this level, we have perhaps located the least common denominator of *pūjā* as a form of Hindu worship, but we have learned almost nothing of the particular role daily worship plays within the Śaiva siddhānta system, nor the meaning it holds for Śaiva adherents. As we look more closely, however, we find that the Śaiva texts expand on each element in this outline, developing from the simple scheme a highly detailed set of prescriptions for daily performance. Through these expansions, Śaiva siddhānta distinguishes its own version of Śaiva *pūjā* from all other forms. Moreover, following the principle of conformity between *jñāna* and *kriyā*, Śaiva texts formulate this ritual action as one fully imbued with Śaiva knowledge.

Within the course of *nityapūjā* the worshiper puts into action all the major categories and themes of Śaiva siddhānta philosophy. In our reenactment of Śaiva *pūjā*, we will also explore each of these central Śaiva topics. As we have seen, Śaiva metaphysics recognizes three fundamental and irreducible ontological categories: fetters (*pāśa*), souls (*paśu*), and Śiva (*pati*). The basic cosmological processes of the manifest cosmos (i.e., *pāśa*)—the cyclical emission (*sṛṣṭi*) and reabsorption (*saṃhāra*) of the oscillating universe—serve as an ordering principle for ritual procedures throughout daily worship. This organizing logic of emission and reabsorption is the focus of Chapter 2. The soteriological passage of the soul (*paśu*) from bondage to Śiva-ness, a passage requiring many lifetimes of active endeavor, is recapitulated daily in the rite of self-purification (*ātmaśuddhi*), by which the worshiper purifies himself for *pūjā*. The process of becoming a Śiva is the subject of Chapter 3. Invoking Śiva into the liṅga (*āvāhana*), the worshiper instantiates through his actions a portrait of Śiva (*pati*) as he is known to Śaiva theology. In Chapter 4, we will also formulate a theological depiction of Śiva, based on philosophical description and the ritual procedures of invocation. Finally, when offering purified substances and "services" (*upacāras*) to Śiva embodied in the liṅga, the worshiper brings all three categories of Śaiva metaphysics into active relationship with one another. So too we will examine the interrelationship of the three categories in Chapter 5.

Through his daily practice, the Śaiva worshiper enacts the knowledge of Śaiva metaphysics, reviewing it regularly and making it present in and through his mind, speech, and body. But who is this prototypical worshiper?

He is, first of all, an initiated member of the Śaiva community, whether householder, ascetic, or priest. To perform *nityapūjā*, one must at the minimum undergo *samayadīkṣā*, the "general initiation" that confers, according to most accounts, the competence to perform worship on one's own behalf (*ātmārthapūjā*). For many Śaiva householders, this is sufficient. A temple priest who is responsible for offering worship on behalf of others (*parārthapūjā*), however, must undergo additional ritual preparation: a "liberating initiation" (*nirvāṇadīkṣā*) and then a "priestly anointment" (*ācāryābhiṣeka*) that infuses him with the powers necessary to officiate in public liturgy. Since the pattern of Śaiva worship is largely the same for domestic and temple worship, I will treat the two as a single ritual format in this study, noting a few important deviations between them along the way.

Second, he is a male. The performance of *nityapūjā*, both public and private, is in effect restricted to males because only males are eligible to receive the general initiation "with seed" (*sabīja*) that enables one to offer worship oneself. "For men is performed initiation with seed, which binds one to the common code of conduct (*samayācāra*), while for those not capable [of receiving this initiation] is performed initiation without seed, which does not confer the common code of conduct" (*SP* 3.1.9). Those "not capable" of receiving the more fruitful *sabīja* initiation, specifies the *Svatantra*, are "children, simpletons, elderly persons, women, hedonists, and disabled persons."[17] The participation of women in worshiping Śiva, as these texts prescribe it, always requires a mediating male, either an initiated husband performing domestic *pūjā* or a consecrated priest administering temple worship. Accordingly, in this book, I will refer to our paradigmatic worshiper throughout as a gender-specific "he."

The worshiper may belong to any of the four classes (*varṇas*). Unlike the Vedas, which exclude *śūdras* from learning or participating in the sacrificial program, the *āgamas* insist that *śūdras* also are eligible to receive initiation and thereby become "twice-borns" according to Śaiva reckoning. As such, they may—indeed, must—study the *śivajñāna* and perform the round of daily rituals prescribed as the common code of conduct for initiated Śaivas. The priesthood is more restricted. To become a Śaiva priest, according to the *āgamas*, one must belong to one of the five *ādiśaiva* clans of Śaiva brāhmaṇas. The texts distinguish the Śaiva brāhmaṇas from other, "ordinary" brahmans and specifically forbid ordinary brahmans, as well as those belonging to other classes, to perform temple worship.

By performing ritual, such a worshiper participates actively and consciously in the world that is revealed in the *śivajñāna*, and in the process he should come to know that world ever more fully. By following this prototypical Śaiva worshiper in his daily *pūjā*, we too can aim to reconstitute in our own minds that Śaiva world within which he acts.[18]

CHAPTER TWO

Oscillation in the Ritual Universe

THE UNIVERSE oscillates. It comes and goes, emerges and disappears. This is a basic cosmological tenet for many schools of Hindu thought: the universe as we know it undergoes an endless cycle of creations and destructions. Within each cycle, the cosmos begins as an undifferentiated "something" from which evolves, in orderly sequence, the multiplicity of creation that we see all around us. In time the cosmos exhausts itself, and all this multiplicity merges once again into its undifferentiated source. A period of cessation or sleep follows, and then the cosmos begins its evolution again in the next cycle. In this way, our universe oscillates between moments of creation and destruction, evolution and involution, activity and quietude, expansion and contraction.

For Śaivas, this pulsation does not confine itself to cosmogonic motion. Rather, it is a ubiquitous principle of a dynamic universe, governing all creation. Cyclical phenomena such as the alternation of day and night, the recurring phases of the moon, and the annual succession of the seasons all exemplify the cosmic pattern of oscillation. So too the sequence of bodily births and deaths through which each human soul transmigrates forms part of the larger cycle of creation and destruction that characterizes the Śaiva world.

Śaiva daily worship also echoes the rhythm of the oscillating universe. The paired concepts of "emission" (*sṛṣṭi*) and "reabsorption" (*saṃhāra*), with which Śaivite cosmology describes the movements of the oscillating universe, are embedded as an organizing logic in the patterning of worship. As I will show in this chapter, the Śaiva worshiper repeatedly enacts in his ritual performance the motions of emission and reabsorption, which are at the same time the activities Śiva himself performs to animate the cosmos.

EMISSION AND REABSORPTION

According to Śaiva philosophy, Śiva performs five fundamental activities (*pañcakṛtya*) that shape and activate the universe. Of these, the two highest activities relate primarily to the soul: he "veils" (*tirobhāva*) the true nature of things from bound souls, and he grants "grace" (*anugrāha*) to souls when they are ready for it, liberating them from their bondage. (I will focus on these activities in the next chapter.) His other three activities—emission, maintenance (*sthiti*), and reabsorption—bring about the complex evolutions and involutions of the substantive worlds in which souls reside. Maintenance denotes an activity of stabilization or stasis, whereby Śiva enables things to stay temporarily as they are. As such, it does not figure prominently in the dynamic cosmology of Śaiva siddhānta. Śiva acts on substance primarily through his paired activities of emission and reabsorption, which set in motion the oscillations of our ever-fluctuating world. Through these interventions, Śiva acts as the ultimate instrumental cause (*nimitta*)—though not as material cause (*upādāna*)—of all cosmic movement.

Śiva's five fundamental activities are made most visibly apparent to a human audience in the famous iconic form of Śiva as the Dancing Lord (*naṭarāja*), developed by South Indian artisans during the Cola period and heavily patronized by Cola rulers.[1] (Rājarāja made the Dancing Lord Śiva the central processional deity of his great temple in Thanjavur, for example.) Here Śiva elegantly dances within a flaming hoop, his matted hair swirling outward as he crushes underfoot a demon and raises his other foot aloft. (See Plate 1.) As Tamil exegetes have explained, the demon below is Apasmāra, ignorance, and Śiva's raised foot grants grace. His right hand extended in the gesture of "fear not" indicates his activity of maintenance or protection. The circle with its flames represents the material cosmos, ontologically separate from the Lord, which Śiva keeps in perpetual oscillating motion with his two hands holding the drum of emission and the fire of reabsorption.

Movement brought about through emanation is said to follow the "path of emission" (*sṛṣṭimārga*), while the converse movement follows the "path of reabsorption" (*saṃhāramārga*). Movement or transformation (*pariṇāma*) along these paths can be described by various terms. The path of emission denotes a movement from unity to differentiation, from one to many, from pervasiveness to increasing particularity. By contrast, the path of reabsorption reintegrates that which has become separated; it reinstates the unity lost through differentiation.

The notions of emission and reabsorption embody an ontological principle at the same time as they describe a cosmological process. The character or inherent nature (*svabhāva*) of a thing is in an important sense determined by its position within a path of emission. Within any domain, that which is more proximate to the emitting source enjoys an ontological priority over that which is further removed from it.

This principle has several important ramifications. Emission indicates a general movement from subtle (*sūkṣma*) and relatively intangible to gross (*sthūla*) and relatively tangible; reabsorption the reverse. Emission moves from pure to impure, while reabsorption moves from impure to pure. Because of their relative subtlety and purity, less differentiated objects are superior to highly differentiated ones. Emission follows a path of diminishing rank, reabsorption the opposite.

Emission and reabsorption relate as well to the disposition of things in space. The path of emission is most often represented visually as a descending motion from high to low, or as a radiating movement proceeding outward from a center toward peripheries. Reabsorption ascends or moves inward toward a center. The representation of emission as centrifugal movement and reabsorption as centripetal is a common convention in Indian visual arts, and as we will see, it is an important spatial principle in Śaiva ritual. Since emission involves a movement from what is pervasive to what is particular, the center in such representations does not simply denote one element among many. As the emitting source, it encompasses or includes within it all peripheral elements; it represents the whole of which the peripheral elements are subsidiary parts.

The notions of emission and reabsorption, then, govern a bundle of contrastive terms, interconnected by two converse paths of movement:

unity		differentiation
integration		disintegration
subtle	——— emission ———→	gross
pure		impure
superior		inferior
high	←——— reabsorption ———	low
center		periphery
encompassing		encompassed

The rhythm of the manifest universe is an oscillation back and forth between these opposite poles, under the direction of Śiva, the ultimate instrumental cause of all transformation.

The linked movements of emission and reabsorption are fundamental processes of the cosmos, and we may observe them in many domains. Most important, the emission and reabsorption of the *tattvas* (the "such-nesses" or constituent units of manifest being) from and into their source-substances *māyā* and *mahāmāyā* are the basic cosmological processes creating the manifest worlds in which we live. For Śaiva cosmology, *māyā* is the material cause of our world. It is real and substantive (*vastutā*), not illusory, and it is ontologically separate from Śiva. (In this respect, Śaivas accept a Sāṃkhya-like dualism and reject the monism of schools like Advaita Vedānta and Kashmiri Śaivism.) At the outset of each creation, *māyā* is undifferentiated and pervasive. Śiva then agitates *māyā* with his appointed powers and causes it to emit, in orderly sequence, the differentiated thirty-one *tattvas* of the impure cosmos. (See Figure 1 for a mapping of the *tattvas*' evolution.) While *māyā* is subtle, its derivative *tattvas* become increasingly tangible until we reach the five material elements (*bhūta*), among which Earth is the most highly differentiated and gross of all *tattvas*. These differentiated *tattvas* enter into multiple combinations with one another, to-

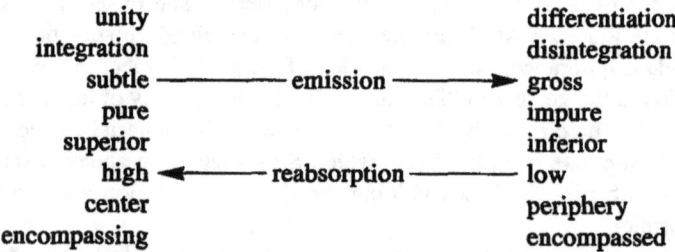

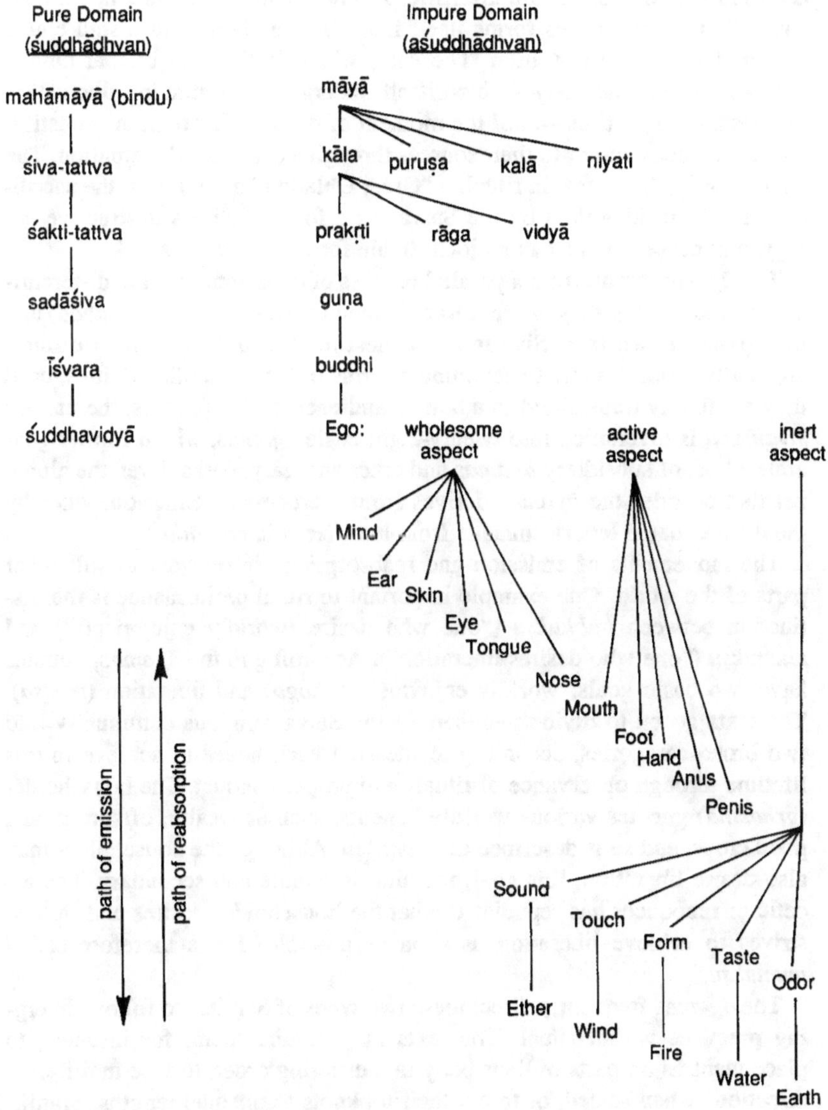

Fig. 1. Emission and reabsorption of the *tattvas*

gether constituting what we recognize as our ever-fluctuating world of *samsāra*. At the time of reabsorption (*pralaya*), each *tattva* remerges into its source, until all are reintegrated into *māyā*. Quiescent, unitary *māyā* then awaits another emission.[2]

Such an emission and reabsorption of constituents take place as well for each individual soul, in life after life. Human creation occurs when a concatenation of substances forms itself into a human body and a soul enters into that material substratum. The soul, which is the core of that human person, inhabits the body—which itself undergoes a continuing fluctuation of substance over time—until the moment of death. After that, the constituents of the body return to their sources through a ceremonial cremation. The soulless body becomes, in ritual, a "Great Oblation" offered into the sacrificial fire Agni, identified by the Śaivas as a form of Śiva's destructive energy, and ceases to exist as an identifiable form.

The *āgamas* result from a parallel process of emission. From undifferentiated sound (*nāda*), they are first transformed into audible sound (*śabda*) and then passed down from Śiva in his highest form through a number of hierarchically inferior, more differentiated forms of Śiva and other deities, until they are finally transmitted to a human audience. In the process, the unitary *śivajñāna* is diversified into twenty-eight basic *āgamas*, which further generate a host of subsidiary *āgamas* and other ancillary works. Even the alphabet that encodes the *āgamas* derives from a process of emission, whereby the differentiated letters emanate from undifferentiated *nāda*.[3]

The movements of emission and reabsorption are relevant to still other parts of the world. One example important to ritual performance is the distinction between *bubhukṣu* ("one who desires worldly enjoyments") and *mumukṣu* ("one who desires liberation"). According to the *āgamas*, humans have two basic goals: worldly enjoyment (*bhoga*) and liberation (*mokṣa*). The texts go on to divide members of the Śaiva religious community into two broad categories, according to the goal each hopes to achieve in this lifetime through observance of rituals and proper conduct. The householder (*gṛhastha*) pursues various worldly benefits, such as wealth, offspring, and good crops, and so is described as *bubhukṣu*. Although the householder may also desire liberation, this goal, for him, is remote and secondary. The ascetic or renouncer has repudiated what the householder desires and instead strives to achieve liberation as soon as possible. He is therefore called *mumukṣu*.

The *āgamas* frequently direct these two types of Śaivites to follow diverging practices within ritual. The texts may require them, for instance, to place mantras on parts of their body in a differing order, to face in different directions when seated, or to cut their topknots to unequal lengths. Significantly, the *bubhukṣu* is consistently directed to follow a procedure that represents the path of emission, while the *mumukṣu* must always follow the path of reabsorption. Why should this be the case? Although the texts do not explicitly tell us, it is not difficult to postulate a satisfying explanation. The householder seeks worldly benefits, things that come about through the differentiation of the cosmos. The renouncer pursues liberation through a purification of himself, a decreasing involvement with the material aspects of his being, and a reunification of his soul as similar to Śiva. Thus the householder and the renouncer mirror, by their own actions and the purposes with which they undertake them, Śiva's activities of emission and reabsorption, respectively. So too in ritual their actions recapitulate these fundamental principles of the cosmos in accord with their own purposes.

The movements of emission and reabsorption appear throughout daily worship, and all Śaiva ritual, as basic organizing principles. They order elements and actions within the ritual, and in so doing they bring this ritual order into accord with the fundamental order of the cosmos. As Śiva causes the constituents of the manifest world to be emitted and reabsorbed, the worshiper himself, acting as a Śiva, causes the elements of the ritual domain to follow the same pattern of emission and reabsorption. Let us examine how he does so.

Metamorphosis of the Hands

Near the beginning of daily worship, at the commencement of self-purification (*ātmaśuddhi*), the worshiper is directed to "impose mantras on his hands" (*karanyāsa*). This simple rite is an important preparation for the acts that follow, many of which require use of the hands for their performance. "Ritual actions such as imposing mantras are done with the hands," explains *Mṛgendrāgama*, "so the hands must be impregnated with mantras beforehand" (*MṛĀ kriyā* 3.2). By imposing mantras on them, the ritualist "transforms the hands into a Śiva" (*śivīkaraṇa*) or "permeates the entire hand with Śakti." *Karanyāsa*, then, is a rite of metamorphosis, by which the worshiper temporarily transforms his hands from their normal state to a divine one, a condition in which they are capable of performing all subsequent rites.

To metamorphose his hands, the worshiper must do two things: first purify them, and then impose onto them a series of powerful mantras. He purifies his hands by rubbing each hand and reciting the ASTRA ("weapon") mantra, which (Nirmalamaṇi tells us) with its fiery form burns off all impurities up to the wrists (*KKDP* p. 25). He next inundates them with the ŚAKTI mantra. Once this purification is completed, the worshiper may begin to reconstruct his hands as Śiva-like instruments by imposing mantras.

"Imposition" (*nyāsa*) of mantras is one of the most basic and frequent ritual actions in the Śaiva system. One imposes a mantra onto some object simply by touching that object and reciting the mantra. In some cases, the texts also direct the worshiper to visualize (*bhāvanā*) the form of the deity referred to by the mantra as he imposes it. The power of the mantra and of the deity with which it is identical infuses the object, and the object is thereby transformed.[4]

In transforming his hands, as in many other ritual operations, the worshiper imposes two primary groups of mantras, the five *brahmamantras* and the six *aṅgamantras*. Because these two sets, along with the MŪLA mantra, are the most frequently employed and efficacious of all Śaiva mantras, it is necessary to consider briefly just what they are.

When Śiva performs the five fundamental activities, he employs the five *brahmamantras*. In simplest form they are:

Oṃ hoṃ, I bow to Īśāna.
Oṃ heṃ, I bow to Tatpuruṣa.
Oṃ huṃ, I bow to Aghora.
Oṃ hiṃ, I bow to Vāma.
Oṃ haṃ, I bow to Sadyojāta.

Each mantra effects a particular action: IŚĀNA grants grace, TATPURUṢA veils, AGHORA reabsorbs, VĀMA stabilizes, and SADYOJĀTA emits. Since these mantras are, in effect, the instruments with which Śiva acts in the world, they are said to constitute his "body." "Śiva's body, beginning with the head, is composed of the five mantras that are appropriate for the five activities: IŚĀNA, TATPURUṢA, AGHORA, VĀMA, and SADYOJĀTA" (*MṛĀ vidyā* 3.8–9). In a similar fashion, the five mantras make up the five faces of Sadāśiva, the most complete manifest form of the divinity. IŚĀNA, in this case, is the upraised face of Sadāśiva, TATPURUṢA the eastern face, and so on in a generally circumambulatory order.

brahmamantra	*activity*	*face of Sadāśiva*
IŚĀNA	grace	upraised
TATPURUṢA	veiling	east
AGHORA	reabsorption	south
VĀMA	maintenance	north
SADYOJĀTA	emission	west

In Śaiva ritual, the performer most often imposes the five mantras as a hierarchical set onto some entity to give that entity the powers of Śiva, to enable it to act as a Śiva.[5]

In his cosmic activities, Śiva employs still other mantras, most important of which are the six *aṅgamantras* ("limb-mantras"). "Just as fire and the sun are powerful because of their rays," *Kāmikāgama* tells us, "Śiva is likewise invincible and all-performing because of his limbs (*aṅga*), which arise from his inherent nature" (*KĀ* 4.362–63). Śiva's six limb-mantras are NETRA (eye), HṚD (heart), ŚIRAS (head), ŚIKHĀ (topknot), KAVACA (armor), and ASTRA (weapon).[6] The worshiper often uses these mantras individually to effect particular ritual transformations: KAVACA, for instance, is particularly suitable for protecting things, while HṚD is the mantra appropriate for filling or pouring something into something else. The *aṅgamantras* may also be imposed as a set, granting still more of Śiva's own mantra powers to the

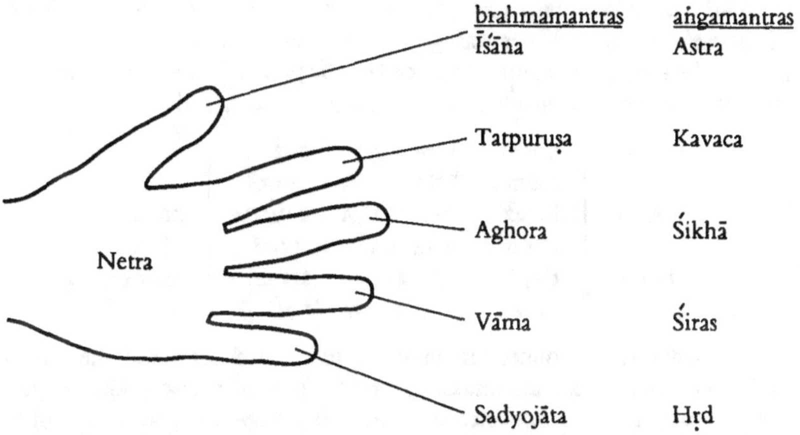

Fig. 2. Imposition of mantras onto the hand (*karanyāsa*)

recipient.[7] So by imposing the *brahmamantras* and *aṅgamantras* onto his hands, the worshiper literally makes them similar to Śiva.

The texts specify the fingers on which the *brahmamantras* are to be imposed. ĪŚĀNA is to be on the thumbs, TATPURUṢA on the index fingers, AGHORA on the middle fingers, VĀMA on the ring fingers, and SADYOJĀTA on the little fingers. Similarly, the worshiper imposes the *aṅgamantras* onto specific places. NETRA is placed on the palms, ASTRA on the thumbs, KAVACA on the index fingers, ŚIKHĀ on the middle fingers, ŚIRAS on the ring fingers, and HṚD on the little fingers. (See Figure 2 and also the photograph sequence of *karanyāsa*, Plate 2.) Once the connection between particular mantras and fingers is established, it is maintained throughout the ritual. Whenever the *brahmamantras* are imposed later in the ritual, the appropriate fingers are to be used (*AĀ* 20.81–84).

The locations of the mantras on the fingers do not vary. However, depending on whether one is a householder or a renouncer, the order in which they are to be placed does. The *Kāmikāgama* spells this out clearly:

> The householder should impose mantras on his hands according to the path of emission. For forest-dwellers and ascetics [i.e., *mumukṣus*], imposition according to the path of reabsorption is recommended. Imposing the *brahmamantras* ĪŚĀNA through SADYOJĀTA on the five fingers beginning with the thumb and ending with the little finger, respectively, is termed imposition according to emission. Placing SADYOJĀTA to ĪŚĀNA on the fingers beginning with the little finger and ending with the thumb is called imposition according to reabsorption. (*KĀ* 4.43–45)

The text then adds, as if to make sure we observe the connection: "The order here is the same as the order of emission and reabsorption of the world."

Similarly, the *aṅgamantras* are placed beginning with the thumbs in the case of householders, and beginning with the little fingers for renouncers. NETRA, the sixth *aṅgamantra*, is placed on the palms. The hands of the ritualist, now infused with mantras, can be diagrammed as follows:

		finger	*brahma*	*aṅga*		
	↓	thumb	IŚĀNA	ASTRA	↑	
order		index	TATPURUṢA	KAVACA		order
of		middle	AGHORA	ŚIKHĀ		of
emission		ring	VĀMA	ŚIRAS		reabsorption
(*bubhukṣus*)		little	SADYOJĀTA	HṚD		(*mumukṣus*)

Having establish a connection between the householder and the path of emission, and between the renouncer and the path of reabsorption, one must now ask why each is connected with parallel yet opposing sequences of fingers and mantras. The logic to the choice of these two sequences can be uncovered with a closer look.

No intrinsic connection links the various fingers and the mantras placed on them. Nothing about the index finger in itself, that is, makes it an appropriate location for TATPURUṢA.[8] We must attend instead to a series of associations between the two sets of mantras employed in this rite and other realities. As shown already, the five *brahmamantras* are connected with Śiva's five fundamental activities and with the five faces of Sadāśiva. But the Śaiva texts do not stop there. Rather, they establish a whole series of associative connections linking the *brahmamantras* to the five *kalās*, the five elements, the thirty-six *tattvas*, the parts of the body, the worlds, and so on: in short, to all basic constituents of the cosmos. In addition, the five *brahmamantras* are related to the five *aṅgamantras* used in this rite. This connection corresponds to the way they are placed together on the fingers here. IŚĀNA is associated with ASTRA and both are imposed on the thumb, TATPURUṢA and KAVACA are on the index finger, and so on.

The order of placement may become clearer by looking at two sets of associated realities, the five material elements and five bodily parts, as they are related to the *brahmamantras* and *aṅgamantras*.

brahma	*aṅga*	*element*	*body part*
IŚĀNA	ASTRA	Ether	head
TATPURUṢA	KAVACA	Wind	face
AGHORA	ŚIKHĀ	Fire	heart
VĀMA	ŚIRAS	Water	genitals
SADYOJĀTA	HṚD	Earth	feet

The set of material elements certainly follows the path of emission as we read the chart downwards—Ether is more subtle and pure than Wind, Wind than Fire, and so on. Similarly, the parts of the body descend according to the path of emission. And so too the two sets of mantras are arranged in an order of ontological priority, with IŚĀNA considered more subtle than TATPURUṢA, and so on.

In no case are the elements of the sets directly linked in a chain of emission. Ether does not emit Wind, and the head does not emit the feet; nor does IŚĀNA emit TATPURUṢA. Rather, the elements of each set are positioned toward one another according to criteria (purity, subtlety, etc.) that are comprehended by the concepts of emission and reabsorption. Ether is to Wind as IŚĀNA is to TATPURUṢA—higher on the scale of emission. Thus, a common principle—that of cosmic movement—relates multiple sets to one another.

This ranking of the five *brahmamantras*, identical with Sadāśiva's faces, is further supported by their association with the five activities. The Īśāna face of Sadāśiva undertakes the activity of grace, the highest of the five, while the Sadyojāta face performs emission, the lowest. In the view of *Kāmikāgama*, it was the Īśāna face that emanated the *śaivāgamas*, while the other faces produced inferior systems of knowledge. Similarly, in any circumambulation of a liṅga, Īśāna is honored first, then Tatpuruṣa, Aghora, Vāma, and Sadyojāta, following their order of rank.

We are now in a position to summarize the logic of the two converse sequences of imposing mantras onto the hands. In transforming the hands so that they are suitable for subsequent rites, the ritualist is directed to follow one or another order of placement, according to whether he is a householder or a renouncer. The order of placement corresponds to either the path of emission or the path of reabsorption.

The connection between Sadāśiva's five faces and the parts of the body reminds us that the logic of emission and reabsorption extends to the body as well. The higher portions of the body correspond to the higher elements, the superior faces of Sadāśiva, and thus to the more subtle, pure, unified range of things. The lower body portions similarly coincide with the less subtle, more differentiated. Such a vaulation of the upright human body, in which the head is superior and pure while the feet are inferior and impure, will be familiar to all students of Indian culture; the Śaivas have simply adapted it to their own cosmological premises. As the *Kāmikāgama* summarizes: "Beginning with the head is called the order of emission; beginning with the feet would be the order of reabsorption" (*KĀ* 4.48). This correspondence between movements within the body and the paths of cosmic movement is crucial to the rite of self-purification.

Transformation of the Body

The body of the worshiper is one of the two material focal points of daily worship. (The liṅga is the other.) Accordingly, procedures relating to the worshiper's body within the ritual are quite complex, worthy of a separate study in themselves. Like Śiva, the god who encompasses apparent contradictions, the body must serve seemingly contrary purposes during worship. The body is both actor and acted upon; it performs the myriad ritual actions and is also the object of many of these actions. The disposition of the body within the ritual space must always be taken into account, and yet the body itself becomes a ritual terrain in "internal worship." The worshiper transforms his body into a Śiva-like form, invokes Śiva into several locations in his body, worships those manifestations of Śiva within himself, and then uses his Śiva-body to perform services for a Śiva apart from himself.

The most important ritual process involving the worshiper's body is the rite of self-purification (*ātmaśuddhi*). Self-purification is one of the "five purifications" (*pañcaśuddhi*) necessary to transform the entire ritual domain into a suitably pure condition: purification of self, of the place (*sthāna*), of the mantras, of the liṅga, and of the substances (*dravya*) to be offered. The worshiper performs *ātmaśuddhi* early in *pūjā* in order to render his body fit for subsequent parts of the ritual.

"Only a Śiva can worship Śiva," say the texts. Yet in his normal condition the worshiper is unlike Śiva in two fundamental respects: he is immersed in impurities, and he lacks Śiva's powers. Before he may worship Śiva, he must deal with both these deficiencies. First, with a set of purificatory actions he empties his body of its impure material constituents; then he superimposes mantras invoking Śiva's powers onto all parts of his body. In this way his body is made over into an unfettered "divine body," a pure body composed of mantra powers. As Śiva acts through mantras that constitute his body, so the worshiper is now able to act in ritual with his body reconstituted as a mantra-body.

The relevance of emission and reabsorption to this rite may be stated very briefly. Upward movements on or within the body follow the path of reabsorption, while descending movements follow the path of emission. Ritual actions aimed at removing things from the body follow an ascending course, and actions that impose or add things onto the body move downward. The movement that the ritualist follows in transforming his body is therefore cyclic: first ascending as he reabsorbs all bodily impurities, then descending as he imposes mantras on it. In the process, he fundamentally alters the constituents of his body, replacing impurities with the powers of mantras.

Purification

The worshiper removes the impurities from his body in two steps. He first reabsorbs all the *tattvas* of his subtle body (*sūkṣmaśarīra*), and then he collapses and burns the elements of his gross body (*sthūlaśarīra*). These processes result in a profound emptying out of the body, leaving it a kind of tabula rasa to be filled subsequently with mantras. Although the texts offer a variety of methods for achieving this aim, I will focus here on the two most common techniques, as described by Aghoraśiva.

The purification of the subtle body is an explicit application of the notion of reabsorption. The subtle body, for the Śaivas, is made up of the thirty-six differentiated *tattvas*, dispersed throughout the body. In their differentiated state, these *tattvas* are inherently impure. The Śaivas do not view impurity as a "pollution" that infects normally pure matter. There is no attempt here to distinguish pure from impure *tattvas*, or to identify and counteract particular sources of impurity in the subtle body. Rather, everything in a state of differentiation is impure. Accordingly, the entire constitution of the subtle body—all the *tattvas* that form the manifest cosmos—must be reabsorbed into the two undifferentiated source-substances, *māyā* and *mahāmāyā*. Purity exists only in the state of integration, where all material constituents are unified within their sources.

The method of purification, therefore, follows the order of reabsorption. Says Aghoraśiva: "In order to purify the subtle body, the worshiper should cause the *tattvas* to be dissolved (*laya*), each into its own source (*kāraṇa*), in an inverse order [to that of their emission] ending with *mahāmāyā*" (*KKD* p. 57). His commentator, Nirmalamaṇi, glosses *laya* as "reabsorption" and explains that each *tattva* "goes within" the source-substance that gave birth to it. The worshiper carries out this reabsorption through internal visualization. "Accordingly, he should visualize Earth reabsorbed into Odor, Water into Taste, Fire into Form, Wind into Touch, Ether into Sound, and these perceptible qualities (*tanmātra*) into the inert aspect of the ego (*tamasāhamkāra*)" (*KKD* p. 57). And so on, reversing the order of emission, until the thirty-one *tattvas* of the impure domain (*aśuddhādhvan*) are unified in *māyā* and the five *tattvas* of the pure domain reintegrated within *mahāmāyā*. (See Figure 1, reading the chart upward.) In this integral state, *māyā* and *mahāmāyā* are completely without impurity.

By absorbing all the *tattvas* of the subtle body into their two sources, the worshiper is able to remove a large part of the impurities that distinguish his body from that of Śiva. Yet other impurities still bind the worshiper's soul. There are also impurities of the gross body, identified with the five material elements (*bhūtas*), Earth, Water, Fire, Wind, and Ether.

To purify the body of these elements, the worshiper must imagine each of them as a "domain" (*maṇḍala*). Then from each domain he expels all its attributes or inherent perceptible qualities (*tanmātra*) with an expulsion of breath and imagines each element to have assumed the form of its opposing element. Once these elements have been collapsed into one another, the worshiper uses an imagined fire to consume finally all impurities arising from his body.

I will consider two features of this rite in greater detail: the visualization of the domains for each element, and the procedure for expelling the attributes.

Each material element has a domain, which the worshiper is required to represent visually to himself. The texts describe the features of each domain

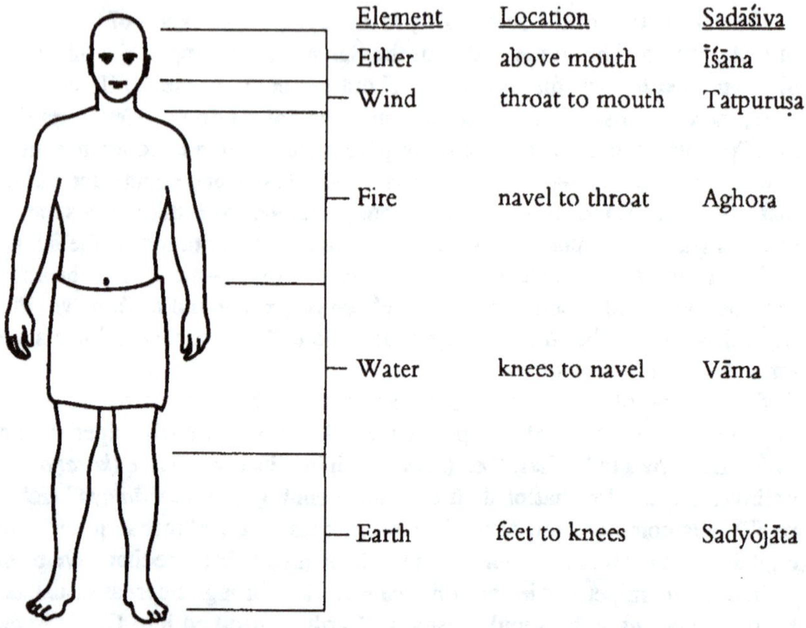

Fig. 3. Locations of domains (version 1)

succinctly, as an aid to visualization. Aghoraśiva, for instance, lists the color, character, form, insignia, governor (*adhisthātṛ*), seed-syllable, Kāraṇeśvara, and *kalā* of each domain.

> He should visualize the Earth *maṇḍala* as yellow, firm, square, and decorated with a thunderbolt; it is presided over by its governor Sadyojāta; it is connected with the seed-syllable of Earth, HLĀṂ, and with Brahman as its Kāraṇeśvara, and it has the form of *nivṛttikalā*; it extends from the feet up to the head. (*KKD* pp. 57–58)

And so on, with each ascending domain.[9]

Each domain is situated in a particular part of the body. *Kāmikāgama* reports two differing traditions, one relating the domains to the parts of the body, the other to the five "subtle centers" (*granthi*). Both locate the domains in an ascending order of reabsorption. Each also relates them to deities that form a part of the visualization. Version one, illustrated in Figure 3, relates the regions to the five faces of Sadāśiva, as described in the preceding section. Version two relates them to the locations of the subtle centers, presided over by the Kāraṇeśvaras.

The Kāraṇeśvaras are important because they govern the body's breath channels, and these channels are crucial in the many ritual acts involving the breath. The Śaivas, as do other yogic schools of Hinduism, envision the human organism as having a "subtle anatomy" of breath channels in addition to its more evident, "gross" physique. The subtle anatomy is called into play whenever controlled yogic breathing (*prāṇāyāma*) is employed in ritual, for it describes the inner conduits along which the breath flows. (This "subtle anatomy" is not directly related to the "subtle body" of the thirty-six *tattvas* discussed above.)

Aghoraśiva describes it this way:

> The worshiper should then visualize the *suṣumnā*: it is a hollow tube, double from the two big toes up as far as the abdomen, and single above that up to the *brahmarandhra*, connected at the heart, throat, and other subtle centers with the *iḍā* and *piṅgalā*, and fastened [at each center] with upside-down lotus buds. (*KKD* p. 56)

The body contains three tubes or subtle channels (*nāḍi*) through which the breath flows—the *iḍā*, *piṅgalā*, and *suṣumnā*. These tubes are connected at five subtle centers (*granthis*, literally "joint"), located at the heart, throat, palate, eyebrows, and *brahmarandhra* (the "divine aperture" at the top of the head). The *granthis* are visualized as lotus buds that bind the tubes, often restricting the breath's passage through them. Each *granthi* has a "lord" whose duty it is to preside over it. These lords are the Kāraṇeśvaras: Brahman presides over the heart, Viṣṇu the throat, Rudra the palate, Īśvara the eyebrows, and Sadāśiva the *brahmarandhra*. As with the five parts of Sadāśiva, they are hierarchically ordered in the body, with Brahman the lowest and Sadāśiva the highest. (See Figure 4.)

Above the *brahmarandhra* the Śaivas envision one more center still: the *dvādaśānta*, twelve thumb-widths above the worshiper's head. It is here, outside the body and yet close by it, that Śiva resides in his highest, formless aspect, as Paramaśiva (*KKD* p. 5). And because this is the ritual "location" of Paramaśiva (who, as we will see, is pervasive and limitless), the *dvādaśānta* acts as an important target for many ritual operations.

Each domain has a number of attributes, corresponding to the number of perceptible qualities present in each material element. The element Earth contains all five sensory qualities—Sound, Touch, Form, Taste, and Odor. Water has four qualities (omitting Odor), Fire has three, and so on. Accordingly the worshiper must expel all five attributes from the visualized Earth domain, four attributes from Water, and so on for each domain. Each attribute must be expelled by an individual "expulsion" (*udghāta*).

> Beginning with an inhalation, he sets his breath in motion along the *suṣumnā* up to *dvādaśānta*, reciting: "Oṃ hlāṃ hlāṃ hlāṃ hlāṃ hlāṃ, to *nivṛttikalā*, haḥ huṃ phaṭ." He returns his breath, and exhales it through the right channel. When he has thus evicted the perceptible qualities Odor, Taste, Form, Touch, and Sound with five such expulsions he should visualize the element Earth subdued by its own opponent, Wind, and resembling it. (*KKD* pp. 57–58)

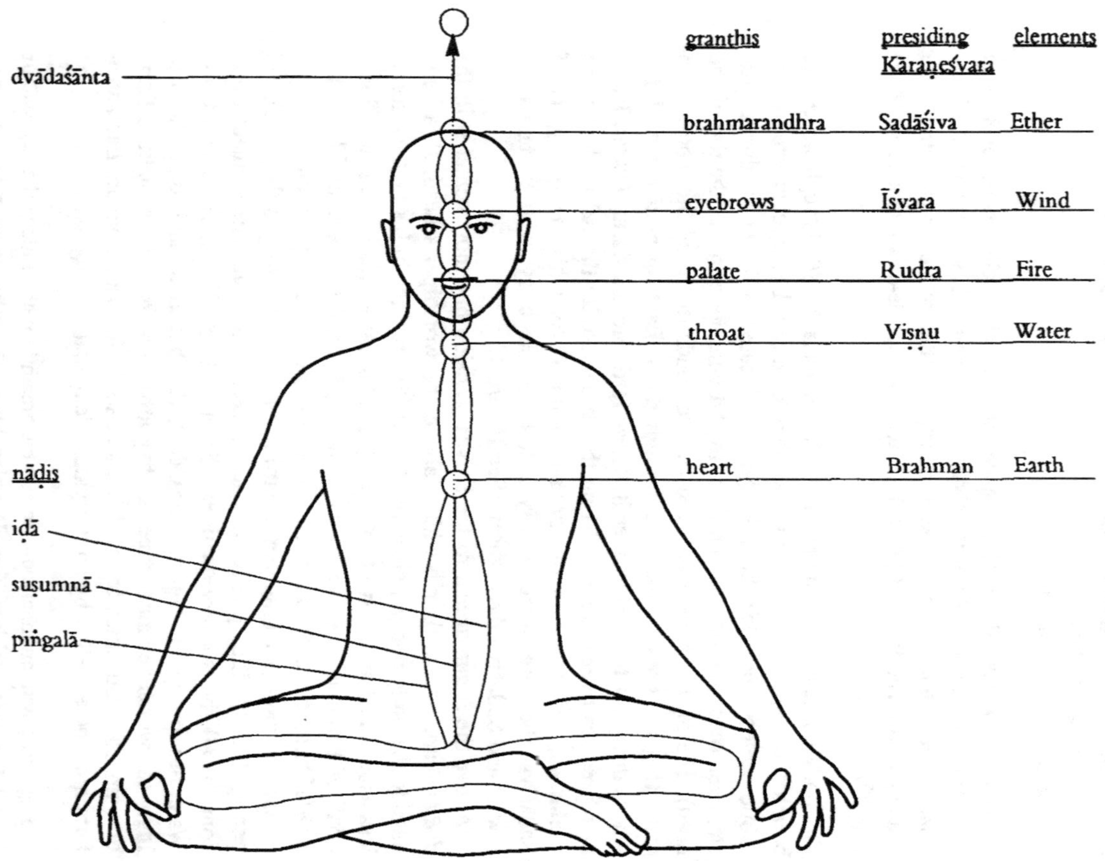

Fig. 4. Subtle anatomy and domains

(The mysterious *nivṛttikalā* appearing in the mantra here will be explained in the next chapter.)

The ejection that expels each attribute is a breath that ascends in the worshiper's body, flowing along the *suṣumnā*, the central channel, all the way to the *dvādaśānta*. (See photographs of *udghāta*, Plate 4.) Several other ritual procedures require that the breath be directed along the *suṣumnā* in the same way. For example, in order to protect the soul from the annihilating fire used in self-purification, the worshiper transports it along the *suṣumnā* to the *dvādaśānta*, where it merges with Śiva. He first uses a mantra to force open the *granthis*; then,

> he casts his breath upward while giving the *mudrā* of reabsorption (*samhāramudrā*) and reciting, "Oṃ hūṃ hāṃ haṃ hāṃ hūṃ, I bow to the soul," and with one ejection discharging the Kāraṇeśvaras in order beginning with Brahman, he joins his soul with Śiva in the *dvādaśānta*. (*KKD* p. 57)

After he has purified the body, the worshiper leads the soul back into it with an inhalation, "descending according to the order of emission" (*KKD* p. 59). Similarly, the PRĀSĀDA mantra, used in purifying the mantras and in the invocation of Śiva, is directed along the *suṣumnā* until it merges with Paramaśiva in the *dvādaśānta*, as I will describe in Chapter 4.

In all these cases, one uses ascending movements of breath along the *suṣumnā* to remove things from the body. They either expel impurities from the body or transport more subtle things (such as the soul or mantras) to a more pure location outside the body. The yoga-controlled breath follows the path of reabsorption upward.

When the worshiper has expelled the attributes of each elemental *maṇḍala* using the upward ejection of breath, he visualizes that each element has taken on the form of, and been neutralized by, its contrary element. The element Wind subdues Earth, and is in turn subdued by it. Water conquers and is conquered by Fire. Ether takes on the form of Highest Ether (*paramākāśa*). With the obstructive forces of the elements thus curbed, the worshiper is now able to annihilate them fully. "Then, with the fire arising from his right big toe, and with the ASTRA mantra, he burns the impurities of the elements located in the body, which is the product of *karman* whose consequences have begun (*prārabdha*), and then inundates it" (*KKD* p. 58). The imagined fire, following the path of reabsorption upward from his toe, purifies his gross body, as the visualized reabsorption of *tattvas* into their source-substances purified his subtle body. And so, with both aspects of his material form suitably cleansed of all impurities, the worshiper pictures it to himself as a pure, empty frame.

> Imagining it completely emptied of all that has the form of a fetter, the worshiper should bathe his entire body, inside and out, with streams of nectar flowing from

the upside-down lotus at the top of his crown, penetrating the openings of every capillary, using MŪLĀ ending in VAUṢAṬ. (*KKD* p. 59)

All impurities that normally distinguish the worshiper's body from that of Śiva have now been ritually extirpated.[10]

Reconstruction

The purifications completely empty the worshiper's body of impurities. The subsequent rite, which imposes mantras onto the body, reconstructs the body. Since mantras replace the impure constituents that were removed through purification, the worshiper's rebuilt body exists at a higher state of being than before. The texts refer to it as a "divine body" and as a "body of mantras," a Śiva-like instrument that enables the transformed worshiper to perform all the ritual operations of *nityapūjā* to follow. (The body of mantras the worshiper imposes onto himself is exactly parallel to the divine body he later imposes onto the liṅga, into which Śiva is invoked.) And, as purification follows the path of reabsorption, this reconstruction, which adds powers to the body, follows the path of emission.

A minimal reconstruction of the body requires only that the worshiper impose five *aṅgamantras* (omitting NETRA) onto suitable parts of the body. Aghoraśiva prescribes this method for worship on one's own behalf. The worshiper begins by imposing the HṚD ("heart") mantra, appropriately, onto his heart, using his thumb and little finger, onto which HṚD has previously been imposed during *karanyāsa*. Next he imposes ŚIRAS ("head") onto the crown, using thumb and ring finger, and so on.

aṅgamantra	*body placement*	*fingers*
HṚD	heart	thumb & little
ŚIRAS	crown	thumb & ring
ŚIKHĀ	topknot	thumb & middle
KAVACA	throat & chest	two index fingers
ASTRA	palms	two ring fingers

While the order of placement here does not follow a clearly descending bodily course, indicating the path of emission, it might be better characterized as a movement from the center outward: beginning with the heart, the innermost bodily constituent, where the soul is sometimes localized, and ending with the external adjuncts of armor covering throat and chest and weapons held in the hands. Emission, too, follows this route.

The *Kāmikāgama* prescribes a much more elaborate method of reconstruction for a priest performing *pūjā* on behalf of others. Not only must the priest impose the *aṅgamantras* onto his body; he should also impose the *brahmamantras*, the thirty-eight *kalās*, the mantras of the fifty-one letters of the alphabet, the "limbs" of the alphabet, nine unspecified *tattvas*, and the VYOMAVYĀPIN ("space-pervading") mantra. Of these seven sets, five follow a clearly descending bodily arrangement. The remaining two, the *aṅgamantras* and the alphabet *aṅgamantras*, follow a course that moves from inside out. Thus all, in this sense, are imposed onto the body according to the order of emission.

The priest begins his mantra impositions by placing the five *brahmamantras* on five segments of the body, starting with ĪŚĀNA on the head and continuing with TATPURUṢA on the mouth, AGHORA on the heart, VĀMA on the genitals, and SADYOJĀTA on the feet. (See photograph sequence on *brahmamantranyāsa*, Plate 3.) As with the placement of the *aṅgamantras*, the worshiper here uses for each imposition the finger onto which the corresponding mantra has already been placed: the thumb, already impregnated with ĪŚĀNA, imposes ĪŚĀNA onto the head, and so on. The five *brahmamantras* constitute the active body of Sadāśiva, sometimes visualized as Sadāśiva's five faces. As an alternative, *Kāmikāgama* tells us, the worshiper may prefer to impose the five *brahmamantras* onto his own five "faces": ĪŚĀNA on his upraised face (i.e., the top of his head), TATPURUṢA on his easterly face (his actual face, since he is facing east), and so on around his head in circumambulatory order. In either case, it is clear, the priest is invoking onto his own body the most fundamental powers of Śiva himself; he is reconstructing his body as a Sadāśiva.

If the five faces of Sadāśiva represent Śiva's active power differentiated into five fundamental activities, the thirty-eight *kalās* represent a further particularization of Śiva's power. The term *kalā* in general usage denotes a portion of some larger unity, such as the sixteen "digits" of the moon or the interest accruing on the principal of a loan. Śaivas use the term to refer to several different partitioned wholes, as we will see in succeeding chapters. Here, the thirty-eight *kalās* are *śaktis*, portions of the unitary energy whereby Sadāśiva acts in the world, and they are grouped in sets pertaining to each of his five faces.[11] Thus, ĪŚĀNA has five related *kalās* (Śaśinī, Aṅgadā, Iṣṭā, Marīci, and Jvālinī), TATPURUṢA has four, AGHORA eight, and so on. After imposing the five *brahmamantras*, the worshiper may place the thirty-eight *kalāmantras* on appropriate parts of his body, again following the order of emission. He begins with the five *kalāmantras* of the ĪŚĀNA group, imposing them onto his five faces: ŚAŚINĪ on his upraised face, AṄGADĀ on his easterly face, and continuing in circumambulatory fashion. The four *kalāmantras* of TATPURUṢA are to be placed, again, on the four mouths, omitting the upraised one; the eight *kalās* of AGHORA are imposed onto the middle of the body, from neck to abdomen, where AGHORA has already been placed; and so on to complete the full set. Each group of *kalāmantras* further empowers the portion of the worshiper's body where the corresponding *brahmamantra* is located.

After several more sets of mantras, *Kāmikāgama* tells us, the worshiper should complete the construction of his divine body with the VYOMAVYĀPIN mantra: "Then he should impose VYOMAVYĀPIN on his body from the head to the toes" (*Kā* 4.176). This is the final mantra imposition in the process of reconstruction. For the *Mataṅgapārameśvarāgama*, VYOMAVYĀPIN is the womb of all mantras (*MPĀ kriyā* 1.60), a śakti who is the veritable body of Śiva (*MPĀV vidyā* 7.31), a goddess of eighty-one words. In its eighty-one parts are contained, according to this account, the five *brahmamantras*, the *aṅgamantras*, the eight mantras of the Vidyeśvaras, GĀYATRĪ, SĀVITRĪ, mantras pertaining to Caṇḍa, the eight World Guardians, and others still. In other words, it is a comprehensive mantra, a mantra that contains condensed forms of a great many other mantras. In fact, according to Viśvanātha, the mantra evokes the entire world of Śiva.[12] As with other sets of mantras, VYOMAVYĀPIN is reversible: one may recite it either according to the order of emission or to that of reabsorption. Here, employing the mantra to help empower his body for ritual, the worshiper imposes VYOMAVYĀPIN according to the order of emission and places its eighty-one portions from his head down to his toes.

So, covering his body repeatedly with groups of mantras, following the path of emission for each group, the worshiper builds his divine body. After a purificatory reabsorption of all worldly constituents, he imposes onto every part of his frame mantras that instantiate the very powers with which Śiva acts, until he attains a "state of mantra" (*mantratva*). When the metamorphosis is complete, the worshiper has emitted for himself a body similar to that of Śiva, a divine body saturated with mantra powers. With this divine body he also may act as a Śiva within the sphere of ritual.

Construction of Ritual Spaces

Daily worship performed on behalf of others takes place in a temple. The temple itself has been constructed in accord with *āgama* prescription and has been ritually constituted through a series of rites beginning with the initial plowing of the earth and ending with the final establishment (*pratiṣṭhā*) of the central liṅga. The temple has its own geography, its own disposition of structures, and its own organization of images. The priest performing *pūjā* must move within and through this preexisting structure. Moreover, during the course of temple worship, he is called upon to construct new ritual spaces within the temple.

Temple space, like the worshiper's body, is organized in Śaiva ritual according to cosmological principles. The primary organizing logic of each of these structures—permanent temple and temporary ritual constructs—is that of emission and reabsorption.

In the preceding section, the primary visual point of reference was the human body as a vertical axis. Actions following the path of emission took a descending course, and those following reabsorption an ascending one. In considering ritual spaces, however, the most apt visual image is a two-dimensional horizontal diagram with a distinct center. The diagram may be a circle, a lotus design, a square, or a rectangle. What is important is that it have a center and outer elements constituting its peripheries, arranged as concentric "circuits" of locations. Objects and deities are located within these spaces according to their relation to the emitting center of the space. Movements within such spaces must participate in the same logic: movement from the center outward follows the path of emission, while movement from the peripheries inward toward the center follows the path of reabsorption.

Topography of the Temple

The temple where one performs *pūjā* is, first of all, a place on earth where a divinity may dwell. In this sense, it is homologous with human homes; both are termed *vāstu*, "dwelling sites." A Śaiva temple is a dwelling for Śiva. Śiva resides there in the liṅga, the lord (*īśvara*) of the manor. But Śiva is not the only divinity to live there.

As Lord of the Cosmos (*viśveśvara*) and Ruler over all other gods (*devadeveśa*), Śiva is typically surrounded by hosts of gods and assorted other spirits who act as his attendants, guardians, devotees, and agents. Śaiva texts often envision the Himalayan mountains, where Śiva sits in state, as the scene in which the various *āgamas* were first taught.

> That most excellent mountain, the pleasing, sweet-caverned Mandara was frequented by all the eighteen groups of beings: by gods, titans, celestial musicians, demons, and troops of divine women, by Yakṣas, fiends, snake-lords, spirits, ghosts, and ghouls, by Mothers and dwarves, by sprites and eagles, by Vidyādharas as well as by centaurs and sages. . . . It was filled with various herds of animals, such as rutting elephants, lions, bears, deer, and monkeys, all free of hostility. And there the moon-crested lord Śiva, husband of Umā and lord of all the gods, sat on his divine throne made up of the four throne-powers beginning with Dharma. Brahman, Indra, Kubera, Sūrya, Candra, Varuṇa, Yama, and Vāyu, the Vasus, the Ādityas, and the Rudras—all the gods were honoring him. Viṣṇu approached him respectfully, and asked the Teacher of the World a question. (*AĀ* 1.1–10)

The discourse with which Śiva answers Viṣṇu's inquiry is the first revelation of the teaching handed down to us as the *Ajitāgama*.

In such assemblies of Śiva's court, deities who appear in the teachings of other schools as independent high gods are incorporated and hierarchized. They observe the etiquette of the subjugated: they bow, they wait with folded hands, and they sing the praises of their superior. In Śaiva *āgamas*, they are classified most generally as *adhikārins*, "agents" whom Śiva employs to carry out his various lordly activities. Ten of them (including many of those listed as auditors on Mandara Mountain) act, under Śiva's order, as "World Guardians" (*lokapāla*) protecting the world in all eight cardinal and intermediate directions as well as above and below. In this way, these other divinities participate in Śiva's sovereignty, but in a subordinate and dutiful fashion. Śiva alone is autonomous; all other gods, lords of encompassed domains, are dependent upon his command.

As in these mountain scenes, gods throng the ritually constructed dwellings of Śiva, which are themselves often compared to Mandara, Kailāsa, and other preeminent mountains. From the very first, they live in the *vāstumaṇḍala*, a diagram employed as a ground plan when constructing the temple.[13] They cover the outer walls of the temple. They inhabit their own subsidiary shrines arrayed in the courtyards surrounding the main shrine and its *śivaliṅga*. A Śaiva temple complex is permeated not just by the presence of Śiva, but by all the beings who accompany him and share in his sovereignty.

The gods do not dispose themselves randomly around the temple, like the "wild mob" Western visitors to Indian temples have sometimes seen.[14] In the world of Śiva, location is too important to leave to chance. The temple complex forms a structure of hierarchically ordered spaces, and Śaiva texts carefully prescribe which divinities should occupy which positions. As in the court of a human king, subordinates must arrange themselves around their overlord in a definite and determinate order, expressive of their political relations of respective inferiority and superiority. For this reason the Śaiva temple, viewed as a community of divinities, acts as a topography of Śiva's cosmic lordship.[15]

At the emanating center of the temple complex is the liṅga, Śiva's "mark" (*liṅga*), a smooth, cylindrical shaft set in a pedestal (*pīṭha*) identified with Śakti. This is the primary icon of the temple, for Śiva in his highest form inhabits it. Significantly, the liṅga is nonpartite, undifferentiated (*niṣkala*) in form, in contrast to anthropomorphic images, which are differentiated (*sakala*). Not only does this icon occupy the geographical center of the central shrine, but it is also considered to be, in some sense, the generative source of the entire temple complex. As the *Ajitāgama* puts it, "During reabsorption, all beings are reabsorbed (*laya*) into it, and [during emission] they emanate out from it—for that reason it is called liṅ-ga. When that liṅga is worshiped, all the gods are worshiped" (*AĀ kriyā* 3.17–18).

The liṅga in its pedestal resides in the "womb-room" (*garbhagṛha*), which in turn is the innermost chamber of the "root-temple" (*mūlaprāsāda*), the primary structure of the complex. This central shrine serves, in the architectural prescriptions of the *āgama*s and related texts, as the reference point for all else. Other structures are located prescribed distances from this center and are sized in proportion to it.

From the central icon, the structure extends in the four directions and upward as well, creating the familiar pyramidal form of the Hindu temple. On the outer walls of the shrine, manifest gods appear, as if emerging from the walls in every direction. Here the worshiper may see Śiva in his more anthropomorphic aspects and other important divinities who are part of his court.

> At each level of the temple, [the temple architect] should place divinities in the cardinal directions, in due order. One should locate the two door-guardians Nandin and Mahākāla to the east, Dakṣiṇamūrti [Śiva as teacher] to the south, Viṣṇu or else the Liṅgodbhava form to the west, and Brahman to the north [on the first level]. . . . One should place Indra or Skanda in the east, Vīrabhadra [an angry emanation of Śiva] would be in the south, the Man-lion incarnation of Viṣṇu to the west, and Brahman the creator or Kubera the giver of wealth on the second level. On the third level is the host of Maruts. At every level one should place additional gods, *siddhas*, celestial musicians, and preeminent sages, such that there be sixteen manifest images (*pratimā*) at each. (*MM* 19.39–46)

Mayamata's prescriptions for locating deities here correspond particularly to the Cola-period Śaiva temples of the late tenth and eleventh centuries.

One or as many as five courtyards and protecting walls (*prakāra*) surround and enclose the central shrine. The term *prakāra* designates the wall, and also by extension the interior space defined by that wall. According to *Mayamata*, these outer courtyards and walls serve three functions: they protect the main temple, embellish it, and serve as dwelling places for Śiva's attendant divinities (*parivāradevatā*) (*MM* 23.1). Throughout the courtyards small shrines, mirroring the central one but on a diminished scale, face the primary temple. And in them, occupying partite images, reside the attendant deities who form Śiva's outside entourages (*bāhyāvaraṇa*) Or these minions may be placed in the cloister against the *prakāra* walls, so as to face the main shrine.

The number of attendants may vary according to the grandeur of the complex. For *Mayamata*, "those who are knowledgeable in the *śāstras* say that there should be eight attendants, or twelve, or sixteen, or even thirty-two attendants" (*MM* 23.36–37), and the text goes on to state that one wall and eight attendants only are recommended for modest temples. For larger structures, *Ajitāgama* specifies that the entourages increase in number as they proceed outward: eight attendants in the "inner circle" (*antarmaṇḍala*), sixteen in the "inner garland" (*antarhāra*) or second enclosure, and thirty-two in the "middle garland" (*madhyahāra*), the third surround (*AĀ* 39.1–3). As the groups become more differentiated, they decrease in stature. Among Śiva's inner circle of attendants are his family members (Gaṇeśa, Skanda), his most devoted followers (Nandin, Caṇḍa), and divinities who have their own substantial followings (Brahman, Viṣṇu, Durgā). In the second entourage, the eight World Guardians—the once-powerful Vedic deities now employed to watch over the directions—are joined by a mixed group of eight more attendants, including human sages, the consorts of Brahman and Viṣṇu, and others. The third courtyard contains four groups of eight divinities: the eight Vasus, the eight Maruts, the eight Mahānāgas, and the eight Pramathas. While *Ajitāgama* does give these lesser gods individual names, it must be admitted that they are rather insignificant members of Śiva's assembly.[16]

The topography of divinity established in the Śaiva temple complex suggests radiating projection, outward from a central undifferentiated unity, gradually becoming more and more particularized as it extends toward the periphery. From the nonpartite liṅga, anthropomorphic or partite images in increasing numbers and decreasing importance seem to proceed. Yet despite the appearance of emanation from a central point, it is important to remember, these attendant deities are not portrayed in Śaiva siddhānta theology merely as projections of Śiva's being. Śiva is not the material cause of these other divinities, as monist schools might contend. Rather, they are distinct beings who recognize Śiva's overlordship and participate in his sovereignty by acting as his agents. What emanates through the temple, in the siddhānta view, is Śiva's lordship (*aiśvarya*); what brings these other deities to be present in the Śaiva temple is their shared, hierarchized participation in his rule.

Bathing Pots and Śiva's Entourages

Daily worship does not call for an elaborate reconstitution of the temple, as it calls for the worshiper to reconstruct his own body. The priest does offer a brief *vāstupūjā* ("worship of the site") upon entering the temple, which recapitulates in abbreviated form the much more elaborate *vāstupūjā* performed during the establishment of the temple. He must also purify the place of worship (*sthānaśuddhi*) as one of the five purifications, but this too is a relatively simple procedure aimed primarily at protecting the ritual terrain from intruders. For the most part, the priest takes the temple as a given, a structure within which he moves and acts.

Yet there are other ritual spaces that the worshiper must create anew during *nityapūjā*. When he sets up pots of water for anointing the image (*abhiṣeka*) later, he carefully prepares a large flat surface, draws a diagram on it, fills the diagram with water-pots in a specified order, and then invokes a deity into each container. The resulting array of divinely infused pottery is a temporary ritual construct, created and used by the worshiper in his bathing of the deity. Similarly, when offering services to Śiva, he builds another temporary ritual structure, using visualization (*bhāvanā*) rather than material substances. The worshiper visualizes five "entourages" (*āvaraṇa*) or circles of deities around Śiva and offers worship to each one. Śiva is imagined as the divine lord surrounded by a royal court of lesser divinities in attendance on him.

The *Kāmikāgama* describes the consecration of pots in considerable detail.[17] In an auspicious part of the pillared hall, the priest clears a space, smearing it with cow dung and other purifying substances and imposing mantras onto the space. He then constructs a diagram, beginning with the central square. The text relates methods of construction for diagrams containing 5, 9, 25, 49, 108, 208, 508, and 1,008 spaces. The larger diagrams are more appropriate for the more elaborate, occasional rituals; for daily worship, 25 pots should be used, or as many as 108 pots if the temple is offering the "highest among high" type of worship. The resulting diagrams always appear as symmetrical projections from a center, expanding outward in every direction. (See Figure 5.)[18]

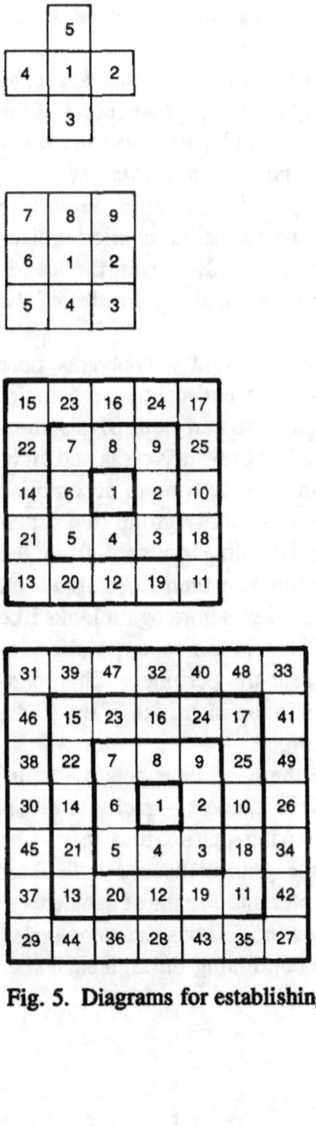

A. Five-Pot Bath
1. Śiva and Śakti
2. Tatpuruṣa
3. Aghora
4. Vāma
5. Sadyojāta

B. Nine-Pot Bath
1. Śiva and Śakti
2–9. Vidyeśvaras: Ananta, Sūkṣma, Śiva, Ekanetra, Ekarudra, Trīmūrti, Śrīkaṇṭha, Śikhaṇḍin

C. Twenty-five-Pot Bath
1. Śiva and Śakti
2–9. Vidyeśvaras (as above)
10–17. Mūrtīśvaras: Bhava, Śarva, Īśāna, Paśupati, Ugra, Rudra, Bhīma, Mahādeva
18–25. Eight Rudras (not named)

D. Forty-nine-Pot Bath
1. Śiva and Śakti
2–9. Vidyeśvaras
10.–17. Mūrtīśvaras
18–25. Eight Rudras
26–33. Gaṇeśvaras: Nandin, Mahākāla, Gaṇeśa, Vṛṣa, Bhṛṅgin, Skanda, Ambikā, Caṇḍa
34–41. Anguṣṭha and seven unnamed deities
42–49. Krodha, Caṇḍa, Saṃvartaka, Jyotiḥ, Piṅgalaśūraga, Pañcāntaka, Ekavīra, Śikheda

Fig. 5. Diagrams for establishing pots

The worshiper then places water-pots in the spaces of the diagram and begins to fill them. First he fills the "Śiva-pot" (*śivakumbha*) in the central square, using from four to forty quarts of water. He next fills the "Śakti-pot" (*vardhanī*) with half the amount used in the Śiva-pot and places it in the central square to the left of the Śiva-pot. Then he proceeds outward, following a circumambulatory order within each concentric circuit of squares, filling the remaining pots with one to four quarts of water. The priest must also place a variety of substances in the pots, including jewels in the two central ones, and properly dress the pots of Śiva and Śakti.[19]

When the pots have been prepared, he invokes deities into them. He begins with the central Śiva-pot and performs in condensed form the rite of invocation that he will later use to bring Śiva into the liṅga. He does the same with the Śakti-pot, and then, proceeding outward again, he invokes deities into all the peripheral pots.[20]

The pots of Śiva and Śakti must always be placed in the central space, as the Śiva liṅga and Śakti pedestal always occupy the conceptual center of the temple. And as the surrounding deities of the temple, here too the other deities are "agents" (*adhikārin*) of Śiva, appointed by him to exercise all his activities within some specific domain. Consequently, the lesser deities are placed in the outer circuits surrounding Śiva, their specific location indicative of their inferior degree of competence and power. However, the identities of these lords are not entirely parallel to those of the divinities of the temple.

In the innermost circuit are placed most often the eight Vidyeśvaras, pure beings who are assigned by Śiva to reign over the entire impure domain. They are the first and most direct agents delegated to carry out Śiva's commands. In the next circuit are invoked groups of eight Mūrtīśvaras and eight Rudras, manifest forms that Śiva assumes from time to time to accomplish particular purposes. Other groups, including Śiva's family group (the Gaṇeśvaras), occupy more peripheral positions. Proceeding outward from the center, the deities become less pure, more limited in their dominion, and lower in the order of emission. The resulting ritual structure again looks like a map of Śiva's dominion: an encompassing Śiva in the center, and an increasingly differentiated group of his agents near the periphery. This mapping differs from the topography of the temple in the identities of the lords, but not in the principle by which they are arranged.

As the worshiper invokes these deities into the pots, he enacts the emission of Śiva's sovereignty. At every stage of the process—tracing the diagram, placing the pots, filling them, and invoking deities into them—he moves from the center outward. He treats the pots in accord with their status, filling the central pots with the most water and the finest substances. When he later uses these pots to bathe the liṅga, he follows the same order, beginning with the pots of Śiva and Śakti and continuing through each suc-

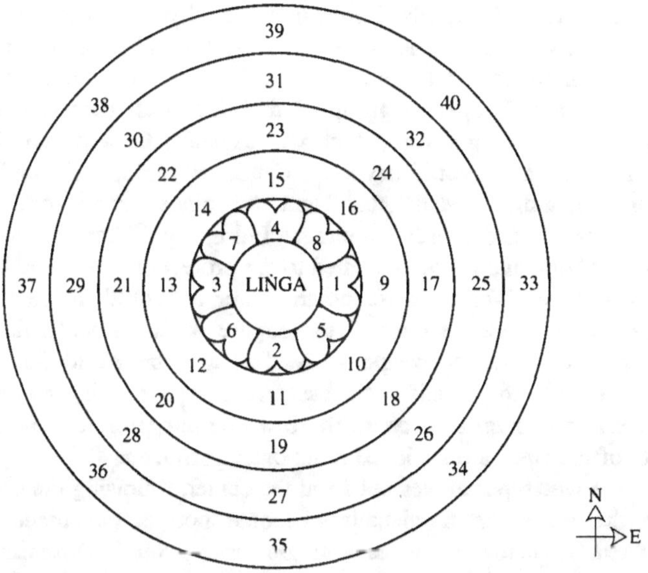

Center: Liṅga
First Entourage (1–8): *brahmamantras* and *aṅgamantras*
Second Entourage (9–16): Vidyeśvaras
Third Entourage (17–24): Gaṇeśvaras
Fourth Entourage (25–32): World Guardians
Fifth Entourage (33–40): Weapons of the World Guardians

Fig. 6. Śiva's entourages

ceeding circuit of pots (*RĀ* 1 p. 96). He thereby inundates the liṅga with the whole extent of Śiva's sovereignty, embodied in the bathing pots.

Similarly in the rite of the entourages, the worshiper follows the patterning of temple topography. Here the worshiper must imagine Śiva seated at the center of a royal court made up of one, three, or five groups of deities in attendance. He visualizes each deity according to an appropriate meditation verse, invokes the deity into this mentally constructed form, and then worships it with all the proper offerings. If the deities in subsidiary shrines outside the sanctum constitute Śiva's "exterior entourages," the envisioned divinities here make up his "interior entourages" (*antarāvaraṇa*), the court within. In both, the attending divinities are located in a series of concentric circles facing the central liṅga.

Once again, the entourages are located in an order of priority with respect to the center. (See Figure 6.) In the innermost circle, termed the *garbhāvaraṇa* ("womb-entourage"), the worshiper visualizes the *brahmamantras* and the *aṅgamantras*, direct emanations of Śiva's own body. The divinities of this interior entourage, the *Kāmikāgama* tells us, "are to be drawn out (*ānetavya*) from Śiva, [the *brahmamantras*] from his chest etc., and [the *aṅgamantras*] from his heart etc." (*KĀ* 4.456). The worshiper places the Vidyeśvaras in the second entourage. In the third are found the Gaṇeśvaras, "Lords of the Troops," a group of divinities best described as forming Śiva's household: his wife, Ambikā; his sons, Gaṇeśa and Skanda; his mount, Vṛṣa; his favored devotees, Caṇḍa, Bhṛṅgin, and Nandin; and his primary guardian, Mahākāla. Next he places the World Guardians (*lokapālas*) in the fourth entourage: Indra, Agni, Yama, Nirṛti, Varuṇa, Vāyu, Kubera, and Īśāna. Assigned to the protection of the ten directions of this world, the World Guardians are lower in rank than the Vidyeśvaras, whose domain extends over all the impure worlds. Finally, the outermost entourage contains the weapons (*āyudha*) that the World Guardians bear: Indra's thunderbolt stands in the east, Agni's spear in the southeast, and so on. As in a human royal court, those whose duty it is to protect the attendants of the court are stationed at its outer perimeter.

As the worshiper moves out from the center, following the path of emission, the deities that he visualizes become more particularized, more individuated. *Kāmikāgama* gives a single description for visualizing all the *brahmamantras*: they are "five-faced, ten-armed, wearing crowns adorned with the moon, and carrying excellent weapons" (*KĀ* 4.450–51). Similarly, a single composite description serves for all the *aṅgamantras*, and another for the Vidyeśvaras. But in the third entourage, the worshiper must visualize each of the Gaṇeśvaras as an individual, distinctive deity. The World Guardians and their weapons are also differentiated, each from the other, and the worshiper visualizes each one distinctively. The deities also become less like Śiva away from the center. *Brahmamantras* and *aṅgamantras* all have five faces and ten arms as Sadāśiva has. The Vidyeśvaras have "ten arms like Śiva" but just four faces, and in the outer entourages deities tend to have just one face and two arms. The Gaṇeśvaras are distinguished from the World Guardians by their third eyes; only Īśvara (i.e., Śiva) among the World Guardians shares this Śiva-like trait.

After they have been invoked in this way, the entourages of Śiva's court must be treated with due hospitality. During the services of worship, the worshiper feeds and makes other offerings to each of these deities, in proper hierarchical order beginning with Śiva at the center and proceeding outward. And then, at the close of worship, the divine attendants must be dismissed. The worshiper, says *Kāmikāgama*, "makes the gods surrounding the liṅga get up with ASTRA and the *mudrā* of reabsorption, and joins them such that they are united in the embodied form, using the MŪRTI mantra" (*KĀ* 4.518–19). The entourages are once again reabsorbed into the central figure of Śiva.

The rites of the bathing pots and of the entourages create spaces that are geometrically distinct but conceptually parallel. In both, the worshiper constructs ritual diagrams consisting of an array of deities located in concentric order around Śiva. They are arranged in an order of priority, with those who are most like Śiva (in purity, in domain of rule, in visible form, and so on) placed closest to the center. The worshiper successively invokes the deities, following the path of emission. The deities are, in fact, emissaries of the encompassing lord Śiva—subordinate sharers in his sovereignty and attendants at his divine court. They are "drawn out" from Śiva, and after enjoying a brief period of independent embodiment, they are rejoined into Śiva.

The organization of the temple and its divinities serves as the paradigm for these other, ritually created structures of divinity. Yet the priest during *pūjā* does not simply re-create the map of Śiva's lordship substantiated in the stone and metal images of the temple complex. Rather, he creates new topographies that involve the participation of other powers and divinities as well. While the agents in each case differ, the logic of their placement does not. Temple, bathing pots, and visualized court all portray Śiva's sovereignty as an emanation outward from the center, creating a concentric hierarchy of spaces that other sharers in Śiva's lordship inhabit in accord with their status and dominion.

Ritual Movements in Space

A priest must move physically within the temple during the course of worship, and the central deity in a sense does also. Their movements are informed by the same logic of emission and reabsorption that governs the more static dispositions of divinities stationed within the temple complex.

The temple, as we have seen, is an emanated structure, unfolding from its center, and space within the temple is organized as a concentric hierarchy, with the most exalted areas located at or nearest the center. To approach the preeminent deity in the liṅga, the worshiper necessarily begins outside the temple walls and gradually approaches the inner sanctum, moving from the periphery to the center of the ritual space. Hence he follows the order of reabsorption. His movement within the temple goes contrary to the movement by which the temple has been emitted, returning as it were to its source.

Not everyone can accomplish this approach. Only those persons who are qualified, within the Śaiva hierarchy of spiritual attainment, may enter the most sacred precincts of the temple. The *āgama*s make specific provisions concerning who may and may not perform temple worship on behalf of others. "Worship on behalf of others must always be done by a Śaivabrāhmaṇa. A pious *ādiśaiva*, best among the brahmans, does worship regularly, but if others should perform worship other than for their own behalf alone, the worshipers will be destroyed" (*KĀ* 4.6–7). One criterion is that of birth: a priest must be born as a brahman, and moreover in one of the five *ādiśaiva* ("primary Śaiva") or Śaiva-brahmana clans.[21] Other brahmans are disqualified.

> Those who are born from Brahman's mouth but without Śiva's emission [i.e., brahmans not of the five *ādiśaiva* clans] are common brahmans. They are not competent to offer worship for others. If by some mistake they do, king and country will be destroyed. If those common brahmans worship Śiva for hire, they will be ruined within six months. Therefore one should avoid them. (*KĀ* 4.7–9)

Not only must a priest be born in the proper brahmanic clan, but he must also be qualified ritually. Only a member of the Śaiva community who has undergone both liberating initiation (*nirvāṇadīkṣā*) and a priestly anointment (*ācāryābhiṣeka*) may act suitably as temple priest, worshiping on behalf of the community. "No stain attaches to worship undertaken for others' benefit that is offered by an intelligent Śaiva-brāhmaṇa who has received initiation and anointment, since he will be obedient to the order of Śiva" (*KĀ* 4.10). The two rituals necessary to priestly competence, as I describe in the next chapter, transform the condition of the initiate's soul so that it is similar to Śiva, and then imbue him with the lordly powers of Śiva. In other words, only one who has been made into a virtual Śiva himself may approach Śiva in his highest form, embodied in the liṅga, to offer worship on behalf of others.

Other texts, such as the *Suprabhedāgama* and Rāmakaṇṭha's *Jātinirṇayapūrvakālayapraveśavidhi*, suggest a more far-reaching relationship of temple space to human access. A series of gradations of purity within the temple as an emanated space correspond to gradations of capacity to approach the center among various categories of Śaiva worshipers.

> Śaiva-brāhmaṇa priests worship in the *garbhagṛha*. Initiated non-*ādiśaiva* brahmans worship in the entry-passage (*antarāla*). Common brahmans reciting the Vedas worship in the fore-pavilion (*ardhamaṇḍapa*). Sacrificers, ascetics, and renouncers worship in the main pavilion (*mukhamaṇḍapa*). Kings [i.e., *kṣatriyas*] and *vaiśyas* worship in the door pavilion (*dvāramaṇḍapa*). *Śūdras* who have received liberating initiation worship in the outer pavilion. *Śūdras* who have received common initiation worship in the dance pavilion. And initiates of other castes should worship at the door of the entry-tower (*gopura*).[22]

And these limits on entry are not to be transgressed, Samakaṇṭha tells us, for there are stiff consequences.

> The one who, out of perversity, leaves his own place and goes [too far into the temple], although he has been told not to, will certainly go to hell, tossed there by Śiva. And even if one goes too far out of ignorance, there will nevertheless be some disturbance in the kingdom.[23]

Earlier I showed that the *mumukṣu*, the seeker of liberation, characteristically follows the path of reabsorption in his guiding aim and in his ritual action, while the *bubhukṣu* treads the path of emission in ritual and in everyday aspiration. Here the distances that different Śaivas have traversed on the spiritual path of reabsorption reappear, indexed topographically by the extent to which they are judged suitable to approach the central icon of the shrine, along the temple path of reabsorption.

Corresponding to these hierarchies of spaces and persons, Rāmakaṇṭha points out, is a hierarchy of texts. The worship performed in the sanctum by *ādiśaiva* brahmans employs the Śaiva *āgamas* and their distinctive Śaiva mantras as primary text. Common brahmans reciting the Vedas and their Vedic mantras are stationed farther out from the center, in the fore-pavilion. And good *śūdras* are authorized to recite the Tamil hymns (*draviḍastotra*), the devotional praise poems composed by the Tamil *nāyanmār* saints, in the great pavilion, still farther from the center that is Śiva himself (*JNP* 29–35).

Priestly qualifications alone are not sufficient to allow a worshiper to penetrate into the central sanctum. As the priest moves from outside the temple toward the central liṅga, he must also transform his own state of being. Before entering the temple, the worshiper first reaches a state of personal purity through performing his daily ablutions and bath. Such bathing, *Mṛgendrāgama* tells us, engenders the capacity to undertake auspicious rituals like *pūjā* (*MṛĀ kriyā* 2.1). He then enters into its outer precincts, offering worship to the various deities who inhabit the door frame and protecting the temple against "intruders" (*vighna*). Next he must transform himself with a more thoroughgoing purification and the construction of a divine body, as we have seen. Only then may the priest enter the central abode of the liṅga, again worshiping the deities of the sanctum's door frame and protecting it against intruders as he enters.

The worshiper thus reaches the liṅga and also transforms his body into one similar to Śiva. But worship cannot take place until Śiva is induced into approaching and entering the liṅga. For Śiva, this requires a descent into form, from the unmanifest into manifestation. The worshiper visualizes an elaborate throne for Śiva and then prepares for him an "embodied form" (*mūrti*) to reside in. Finally he invokes Śiva into this form, and the services of worship may commence. (This procedure will be described in detail in Chapter 4.)

Two approaches from different directions meet in the act of worship. The worshiper follows the path of reabsorption toward the center of the temple, congruent with the transformation of his body. Śiva follows the path of emission by descending from his absolute state into the visualized form that the worshiper has constructed for him. The temple is the ritual terrain upon which both these approaches may occur, and the sanctum the place in which they may meet.

Even though only properly consecrated Śaiva priests are eligible to enter the sanctum in temple worship, others do gain access to Śiva at one point during worship. Extending his descent into form, Śiva regularly ventures forth from the *garbhagṛha* to tour the temple domain of which he is lord. Śiva makes such a "procession" (*yātrā*) daily as part of a "daily festival" (*nityotsava*), and much more dramatically during the occasional "great festivals" (*mahotsava*) celebrated at prescribed times during the year. He does so, says the *Kāraṇāgama*, to benefit all beings: "for those rogues, birds, and animals who are not initiated, as well as for initiates and devotees."[24]

To make his daily tour, Śiva enters a special mobile image placed on an ornamented palanquin. Temple attendants take the litter on their heads and proceed out from the center. Śiva takes along the accoutrements of his lordship, such as canopy, parasol, and chowrey-fans, and he is accompanied on his rounds by a processional throng of musicians, singers, dancers, priests, and devotees. In larger processions, other deities of Śiva's court might also accompany him, each embodied in its own image and carried on its own palanquin. Śiva and his retinue typically make three circumambulations: the first circling the main shrine, the second visiting each of the subordinate deities of the exterior entourages, and the third going still farther afield to circle the outer walls of the temple or even parade through the town. Then they return from the peripheries to the sanctum, and Śiva resumes his customary position, where he is once again worshiped by the priest.

According to the *Kāraṇāgama* definition, the festival (*utsava*) of Śiva's procession is an "emission outward" (*udbhūtasṛṣṭi*).[25] Śiva's movement here follows the path of emission in several senses. In space he proceeds from the center to the outer precincts of the ritual terrain. In form he transfers his presence, most often, from the immobile, undifferentiated "root" liṅga to a portable, differentiated image (*pratimā*) representing Śiva in manifest aspect. And, most important, as he visits those subordinate deities with whom he shares lordship, he also emanates his lordship, extending his grace outward to the larger community, for whom, due to birth or insufficient ritual preparation, entry into the central shrine is proscribed.

The Ritual World and the "Real" World

The Śaiva cosmogonic vision of an oscillating universe finds itself reflected in the patterned actions of ritual. The paired dynamics of emission and reabsorption govern everything, it would seem, from the disposition of divinities in the temple complex to the order in which a worshiper should impose mantras onto his fingers. The worshiper's hands, his body, his movements in the temple, and even Śiva's movements all follow a common logic, which Śaivas would claim is the basic organizing logic of the manifest cosmos itself.

All this certainly evokes the notion, familiar to all historians of religion, of interrelated macrocosmos and microcosmos. The Śaiva worshiper's repetition of certain cosmological principles, graphing them onto diverse portions of a ritual domain set apart from everyday life, suggests that Śaiva ritual is an attempt to construct a microcosm reflecting a particular macrocosmic conception of the way things are.

While the use of such a model as a convenient shorthand to comprehend Śaiva ritual is not erroneous as such, it does suggest a misconception, at least insofar as the Śaiva self-understanding goes. It implies that the world constructed and acted upon within ritual is a representation of a larger and distinct world, and that the ritual world, as a symbolic construct or a reflection, exists at a lower order of ontological reality. To suppose that Śaiva ritual "mirrors" microcosmically a real world that exists apart from it, however, would seriously misconstrue the Śaivas' basically realistic and integral sense of what they are doing. Other metaphors of mimesis implying a separation of real and ritual domains, such as "play," "theater," and the like, are equally misleading. To put it as directly as possible: Śaiva daily worship is understood to be real action, employing real forces, directed at real recipients, and accomplishing real effects. Ritual is not a metaphor for Śaiva cosmology, for it participates in that same world.

Since Śiva is all-pervading, it should not be surprising that the universe revealed through Śaiva knowledge and acted within during ritual appears multiply embedded within itself, rather like the computer images generated by fractal geometrists. Śiva's determining activities of emission and reabsorption, as we have seen, reproduce themselves at various scales, so that the worshiper's hand, his body, a pot diagram, a temple layout, and much more all appear to be projections of the same universal dynamic.

If anything, the ritual world holds a privileged ontological status for the Śaivas, in much the same way that the knowledge revealed in Śaiva texts promotes itself as a privileged episteme. As we have seen, Śaiva knowledge claims to reveal a normally hidden, and more fundamental, order of things existing within the world, underlying and determining the phenomenal world ordinarily accessible to our powers of knowing. These two types of knowledge—Śaiva knowledge and ordinary knowledge—are not directed at distinct domains, but rather are two levels of apprehension of a single complex world, the first more penetrating and encompassing than the other. Śaiva ritual bears an analogous relation to ordinary, worldly action: it is efficacious action based on the underlying principles of organization of the world, the axiomatic forces revealed by Śaiva philosophical texts.

For this reason, too, ritual discloses knowledge through action, in a condensed, reiterative, and compelling way. The ritual world is a synecdoche by which one may be able to perceive more immediately, with less interference, the fuller state of things. (So too, although Śiva is all-pervasive, the *āgamas* assert that he becomes "specially present" in the ritual terrain during daily worship.) The worshiper is called upon to focus, over and over, day after day, on the primary principles of the Śaiva world as he acts with and through them in ritual. What he sees, directly, as they animate his own actions, are the multiple projections—theoretically infinite, since pervasive—of the cosmological and theological foundations of the single world, Śiva's world.

Plate 1. Naṭarāja (Rajaraja Museum, Thanjavur)

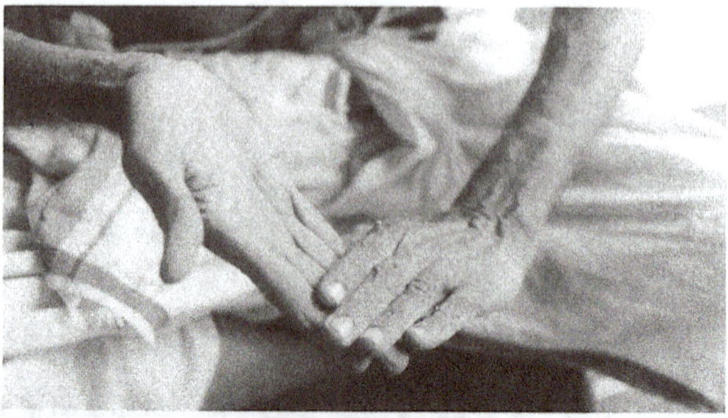
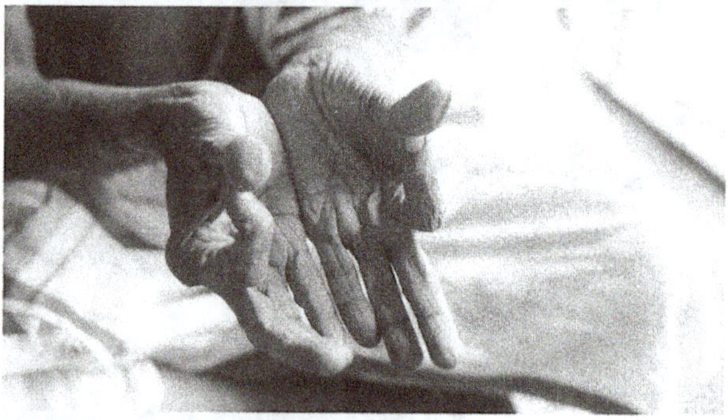
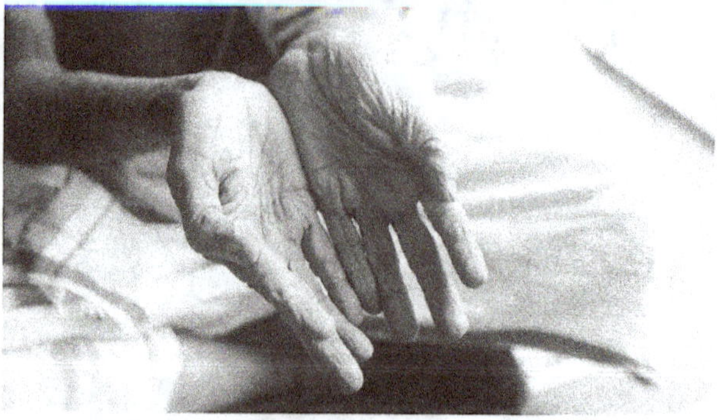
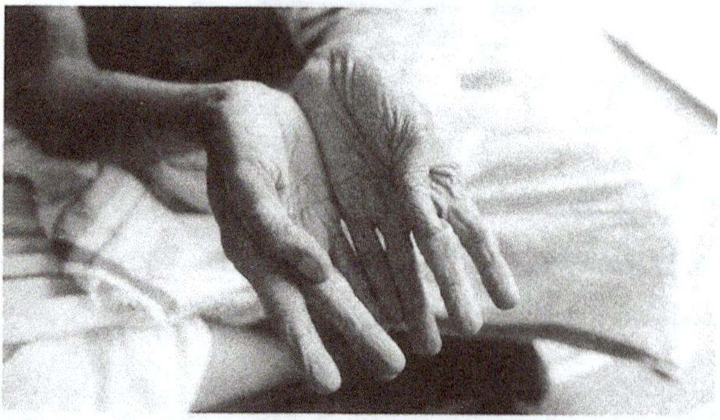

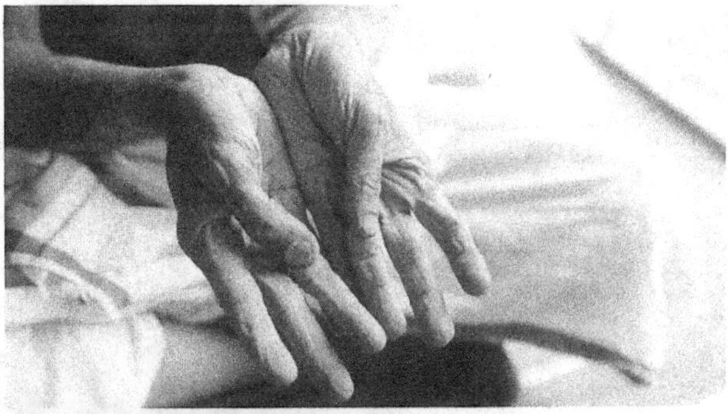

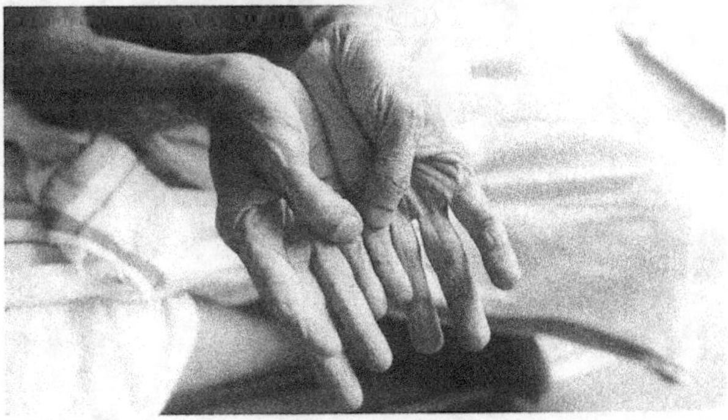

Plate 2. Imposition of *brahmamantras* onto the hands (*karanyāsa*), following order of emission

a. Purification of the hands
b. Īśāna imposed onto thumbs
c. Tatpuruṣa imposed onto index fingers
d. Aghora imposed onto middle fingers
e. Vāma imposed onto ring fingers
f. Sadyojāta imposed onto little fingers

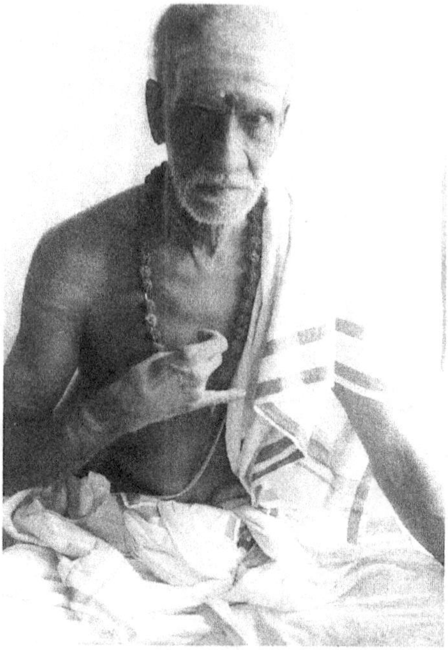

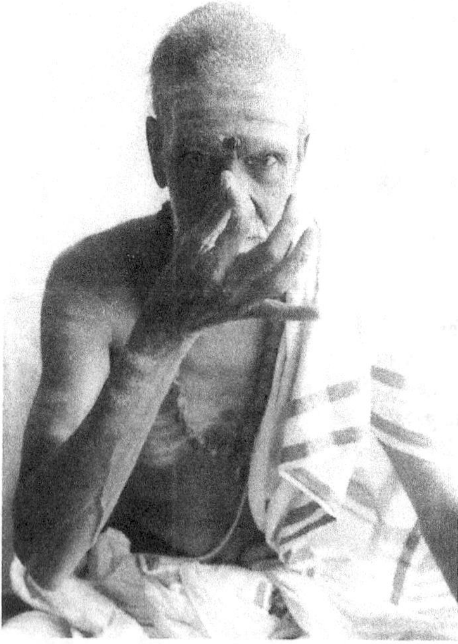

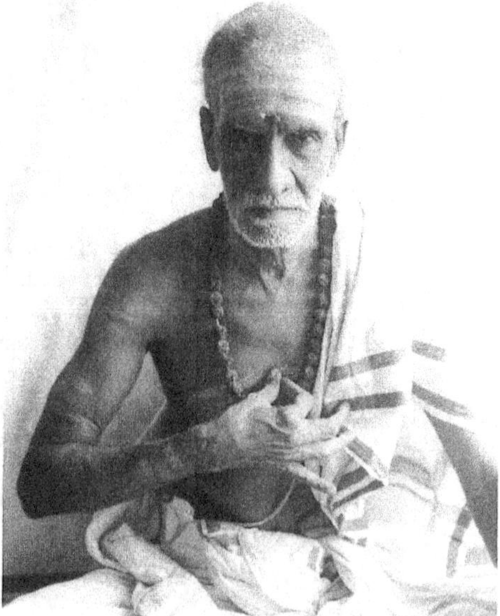

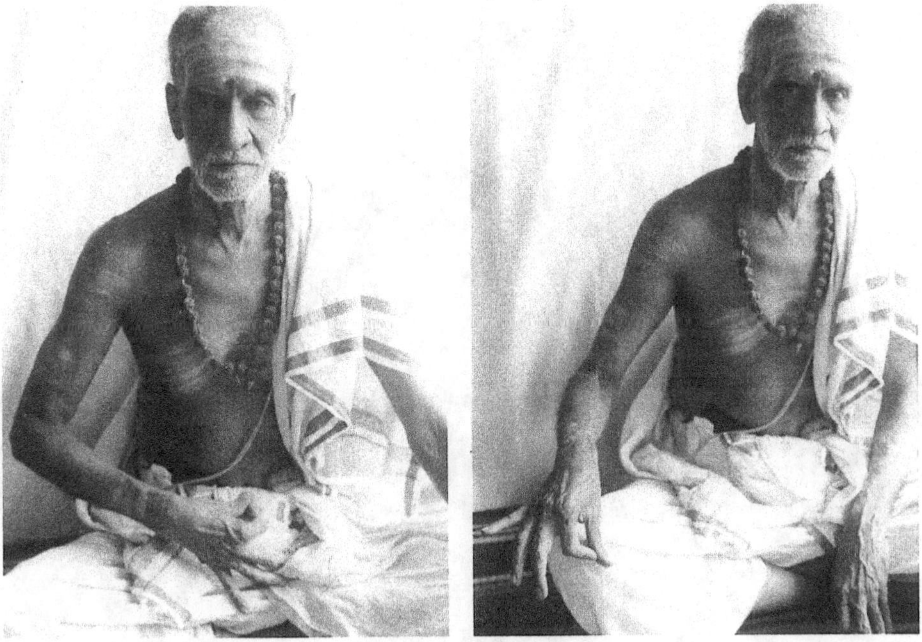

Plate 3. Imposition of *brahmamantras* onto the worshiper, following order of emission

a. ĀSANA and MŪRTI imposed onto heart
b. ĪŚĀNA imposed onto crown
c. TATPURUṢA imposed onto face
d. AGHORA imposed onto heart
e. VĀMA imposed onto genitals
f. SADYOJĀTA imposed onto feet

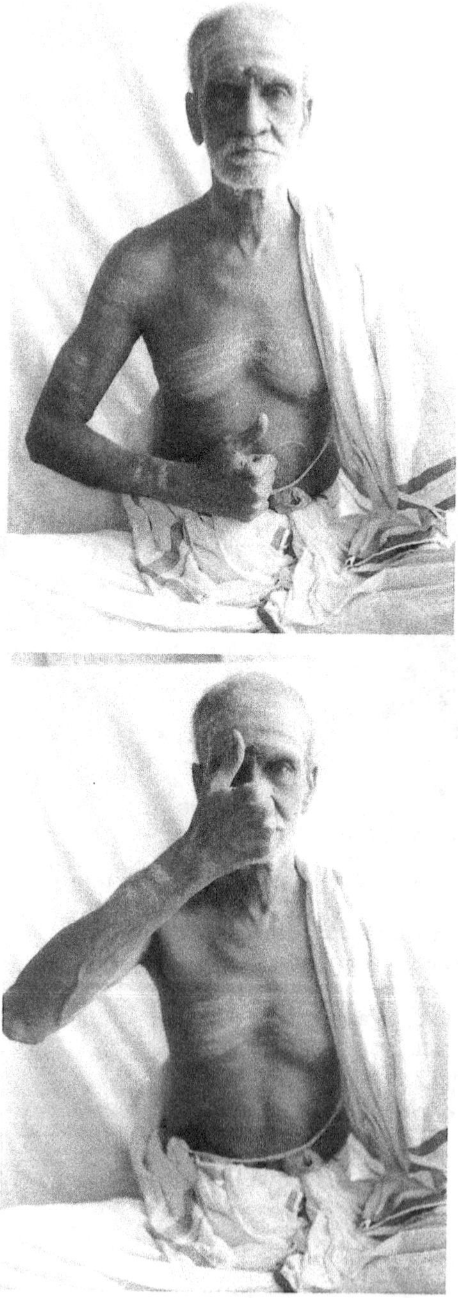

Plates 4a and b. Ejection of the attributes, following the order of reabsorption

Plate 5. Imposition of *brahmamantras* onto the liṅga

a. Imposition of ĪŚĀNA

b. Imposition of SADYOJĀTA

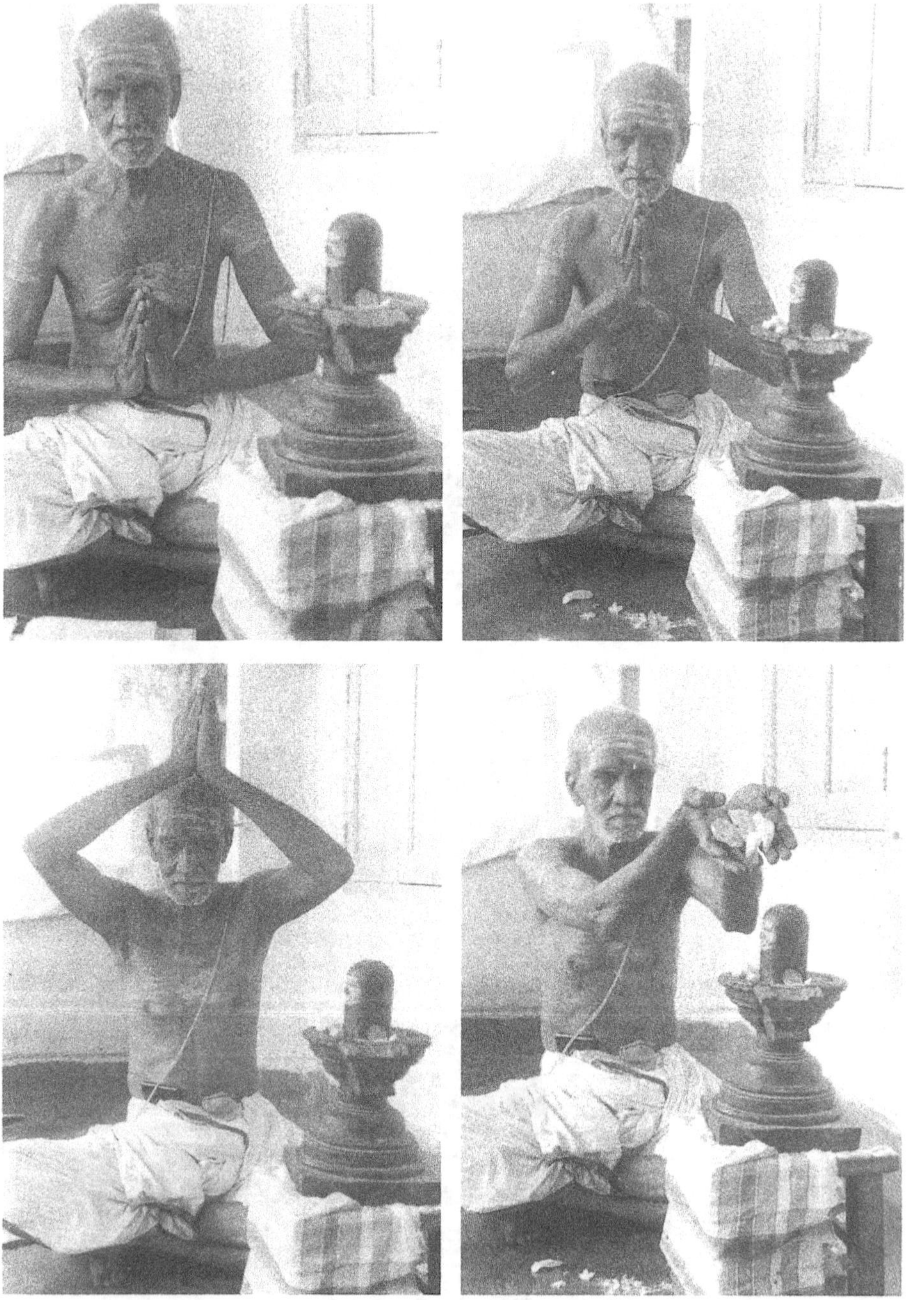

Plate 6. Ascending pronunciation (*uccāraṇa*) and invocation
6a–c. Ascending pronunciation of MŪLA
6d. Śiva descends into the liṅga

CHAPTER THREE

Becoming a Śiva

THE FUNDAMENTAL GOAL for the Śaivite, as for adherents of many other Hindu systems of thought, is to attain *mokṣa* ("final liberation"), the highest state of being that can be achieved by the human soul. For Śaiva philosophy, the central drama of the cosmos is that of the human soul, immersed in a state of bondage, moving gradually toward *mokṣa* through Śiva's grace. All else revolves around this. The entire oscillating universe, say the texts, is emitted and reabsorbed just to facilitate the soul's progress toward liberation. All of Śiva's five fundamental activities are oriented to enabling the soul to attain liberation. As *Mṛgendrāgama* asserts, "the soul is the reason for everything" (*MṛĀ vidyā* 6.7).

The Śaivas define *mokṣa* precisely as the process or event by which the soul is released from its bondage and becomes a Śiva. When one attains liberation, they say, the soul becomes completely equal to Śiva. It acquires a form identical to that of Śiva. A liberated soul does not merge into the divinity or become united with him, as some other systems of Hindu philosophy assert. Nor does it enter again into the manifest cosmos. Rather, it remains as an autonomous theomorphic entity, separate from Śiva but with all his powers and qualities. In this sense, the end point of the soul's "career," its final and most desirable destination, is to become a Śiva.

In the preceding chapter, I described how the worshiper "becomes a Śiva" within the ritual setting. The transformation that the ritualist performs on his own body, reconstituting it as a "divine body" by means of *ātmaśuddhi*, is a crucial part of daily worship. This "purification" is necessary to render the worshiper fit for performing services to Śiva, since "only a Śiva can worship Śiva." In this chapter I relocate the bodily transformation that the ritualist performs daily in his worship in a broader soteriological framework, that of the soul's ultimate attainment of *mokṣa*.

This chapter is an account of the human soul's religious passage from its beginning condition of bondage to the attainment of liberation, and of the crucial role ritual action plays in this passage. Rituals such as initiation and daily worship have significant effects on the person who performs them, effects that contribute critically to the liberation of his soul. In fact, the performance of these rituals, according to Śaiva soteriology, is the most direct means for the soul to gain liberation. At the same time, I will argue, the worshiper enacts the movement to *mokṣa* within these rituals. Becoming a Śiva temporarily in daily worship is identical in form to becoming a Śiva permanently through final liberation.

The Career of a Soul

The normal human condition is not, in the view of the Śaivas, a happy one. While Śiva is teaching them the *Kāmikāgama*, the sages interrupt his discourse to state their opinion of worldly life: "'O Lord, in this world living creatures have weak natures and short lives; they are filled with greed, delusion, conceit, passion, and hostility'" (*KĀ* 3.12–13). This pessimistic observation provides a starting place for an inquiry into the ultimate source of and cure for the predicament in which most humans find themselves. If these most eminent sages complain of their lot, how much more so should the rest of us, living our lives outside Śiva's grace.

Bondage and Liberation

Śaiva texts describe the normal human condition as a state of bondage (*bandhatva*). A human being is categorized as a *paśu*, a term used to designate the transmigrating soul (*ātman*) in the condition of bondage.

It is important to remember that the subject of bondage here is the soul, not the empirical human "person." Śaiva philosophy maintains a sharp ontological distinction between the soul and the other constituents that combine with the soul to make up the person. The soul is the nonmaterial locus of a person; it possesses consciousness (*cit*), which is the animating spirit of every living entity. The material body, the organs of perception and action, the ego, and the faculties of cognition and decision are considered inanimate substances (*jaḍa*), requiring some animating force to act upon them. The animate soul inhabits an inanimate body and with its powers of consciousness directs all bodily activities. The soul is bound; all other constituents of the person are forms of bondage acting upon the soul.

This state of bondage, though it is the only human situation most of us know, is not inevitable. To speak of bondage implies at least the possibility of freedom. In fact, say the texts, the inherent condition of the soul is far different from the plight in which we normally see it. The soul in its innate form (*svarūpa*) is like Śiva himself; it is characterized by *śivatva* ("Śiva-ness"). Like Śiva, each individual soul is endowed with consciousness, the animating energy that distinguishes it from all that is inanimate. By virtue of its consciousness the soul has vast powers of knowing and acting, amounting to omniscience and omnipotence (*sarvajñānakriyāśakti*). The soul is inherently pervading (*vyāpaka*), eternal (*nitya*), and autonomous (*svatāntrya*). These characteristics make the soul fully equal to Śiva—or would make it so, that is, if not for the interference of the fetters. From its very beginning, the human soul has been tethered by the snares of bondage, which overcome its inherent powers.

Because the condition of bondage is not intrinsic to the human soul, but is imposed on it by extrinsic fetters, it is possible for the soul to gain liberation from its predicament. The soul itself cannot be altered, since it is immutable. Nor would one wish to change it, since it is inherently like Śiva. Liberating the soul is a matter of transforming its condition or situation, not its essence. To do so, one must uncover the soul's immanent Śiva-ness by eliminating all the fetters that cover it.[1]

Accordingly, Śaivas portray the passage from bondage to liberation in terms of removal and emergence: removal of that which suppresses the soul, and emergence of its immanent but concealed qualities. The fetters must first be removed (*apanīta*) or eliminated (*nivṛtta*); their hold over the soul must be loosened (*viśliṣṭa*) or severed (*chinna*). Fetters are tenacious, but ultimately they can be eliminated. When the soul has been extricated from its fetters, its own inherent qualities are able to emerge (*vyakti*). "As soon as the bondage caused by fetters such as ignorance ceases," comments Nārāyaṇakaṇṭha, "the *śivatva* of the soul becomes manifest" (*MṛĀV vidyā* 6.7). The two events are linked: removing the fetters enables the soul's intrinsic powers to emerge, just as the elimination of a disease allows the body to recover its normal capabilities.

The category of *mokṣa* as an end point to the religious striving of the human soul is of course common to most schools of Indian philosophy. But, as Nārāyaṇakaṇṭha avers, the Śaiva conception of *mokṣa* as attainment of Śiva-ness differs conspicuously from the "so-called liberations" of other schools, which may consist of a reabsorption of the soul into Brahman, as Advaita Vedāntins claim, or the discrimination of *prakṛti* and *puruṣa*, as the Sāmkhya school contends (*MṛĀV vidyā* 2.29). Even among the Śaiva schools that accept equality with Śiva as the highest goal, the Śaiva siddhānta position is distinct from others in postulating an inherent Śiva-ness that is recovered at the moment of liberation. Śivāgrayogin terms this model of attaining liberation "equality through manifestation" (*vyakti*). Among other Śaiva schools, he tells us, the Mahāvratins hold that the soul's equality with Śiva comes about through an origination (*utpatti*) at the time of liberation, the Pāśupatas view this equality as arising through a transfer (*samkrānti*) from Śiva, and the Kāpālikas argue that it occurs through possession (*samāveśa*) of the soul by Śiva (*ŚPbh* pp. 341–43).

For Śaiva siddhānta, the long-term career of a soul consists in its gradual movement from a state of bondage, enmeshed in a multitude of fetters, to one of liberation. A movement in the opposite direction, deeper into bondage, is of course possible, but is not much discussed by Śaiva texts. They assume that no right-thinking person would consciously pursue such a course. In liberation a double transformation of the soul's condition takes place: the fetters that constrain it are completely eliminated, and its inherent "Śiva-ness" fully emerges. This alteration constitutes "becoming a Śiva" in the broadest sense. Achieving final liberation means, precisely, that the soul leaves behind its previous bondage and attains a permanent state parallel to that of Śiva.

Fetters and Their Ripening

Clearly fetters and their removal are the crux of the matter of liberation. Any progress on the path to *mokṣa* must involve elimination of these binding forces.

According to Śaiva siddhānta, the human soul is bound by three primary categories of fetters: *mala*, *karman*, and *māyā*.[2] The Śaivas understand these three as distinct realities, each with its own individual effects on the soul and its own characteristic pattern of evolution or "transformation" (*pariṇāma*).[3]

Of the three fetters, the most ubiquitous and tenacious is *mala*, primordial stain. *Mala*, identified with constraint and obscuration, is the fetter most responsible for suppressing the soul's capacities. Synonyms for *mala* include "darkness," "stupor," "covering," "debility," and "night"—indicating its general quality as a dark, oppressive fetter (*MṛĀ vidyā* 7.7). Arising concurrently with the soul, *mala* is the first fetter to adhere to it and the last to leave. In Bhojadeva's analogy, *mala* sticks to the soul from the soul's inception as a husk develops simultaneously with a grain of rice, and as tarnish with a copper pot. However, comments Aghoraśiva, just as the husk is broken off when the grain within has matured, and the tarnish may be wiped off a pot using chemicals, so *mala* can be removed from the soul through ripening and initiation (*TPV* 18).

Mala evolves through a process of "ripening" (*pāka*). The term *pāka* in common usage signifies processes in which the qualities of substances are modified due to some "heating" agency external to that which is modified: cooking, digesting of food, baking of bricks, ripening of fruits. Most often this results in a softening or loosening of the substance heated, as with boiled rice or ripened bananas. The texts do not specify exactly what is meant by the ripening of *mala*, but *pāka* does denote a process by which *mala's* grasp on the soul is gradually loosened or weakened (*kṣīṇa*).[4]

> Among worldly beings, conditions of superiority and inferiority are recognized as [indexes of] their *mala*. Just like rice that is first raw then cooked, so too *mala* may be either raw or cooked, depending on the action of *samsāra*. When *mala* is raw, a man is inferior; when it is cooked, he is to that degree superior. (*ŚPur* 1.31.71–72)

As *mala* ripens, its suppression of the soul's powers softens.

The term used for the second fetter, *karman*, means "action," though in philosophical usage it covers a still broader field. Along with many other schools of Indian thought, the Śaivas accept an extended concept of causality. Every action undertaken by a person engenders a consequence. The causal relationship between act and result is not simply physical, but moral as well. A meritorious act gives rise to some beneficial result that sooner or later accrues to the person; conversely, a wicked act produces subsequent pain. The consequence may ensue immediately or only after several lifetimes of lying dormant, but it is certain to occur eventually. Action and consequence are linked together in a beginningless "stream" (*pravāha*), as seed and shoot successively and inevitably engender one another.

For Śaivas, each action is connected to its results by a substantive "residue" of the action, which adheres to the actor until it produces its consequence. These residues, called *bhogyakarman* ("actions whose consequences are still to be experienced"), are responsible for binding the soul. In Śaiva philosophy, the term *karman* denotes these residues as well as the actions that produce them. The unfulfilled residues of past actions, whether good or evil, constitute a fetter for the soul precisely because their results have not yet been experienced.

Karman is transformed only when one experiences or "consumes" (*bhoga*) the "fruits" (*phala*) of past acts. The term *bhoga*, used generally for eating food or enjoying pleasurable things, here refers to consuming the fruit that is *bhogyakarman*. When the soul experiences the consequences of a past action, the residue is eliminated. Without that experience, however, the inert residue remains attached to the soul indefinitely. Unconsumed *karman* transmigrates from one body to the next along with the soul, awaiting fruition. "*Karman* that is not consumed," says Aghoraśiva, "does not diminish even in a hundred crore of eons" (*TPV* 36).

The Śaivas (as do other schools of thought) further distinguish three basic types of *karman*, according to the time of its genesis and its consumption.[5] Most immediate in its effects is *prārabdhakarman*,"active *karman*." *Prārabdhakarman* designates that portion of a soul's previously acquired *karman* that has brought about its present embodiment and is destined to be consumed during its present lifetime. The *karman* of this lifetime is already activated, literally "*karman* whose effects have already begun." Less immediate is *sañcitakarman*, "accumulated *karman*." This denotes the soul's entire collection of *karman* whose effects have not yet begun to manifest themselves. For most souls, *sañcitakarman* constitutes an enormous stockpile that will furnish the *prārabdhakarman* for many lifetimes to come. The third category of *karman* is termed *āgamin*, "future *karman*." *Āgamin* designates *karman* that has not yet formed, and that is not yet a fetter, because the action causing it has not yet taken place. The soul will acquire *āgamin* in the future due to its future actions. Śaivas employ this threefold classification of *karman* extensively in discussing the efficacy of rituals that contribute to liberation.

Śaiva siddhānta defines *māyā*, the third fetter, as the source-substance or "seed" (*bīja*) of the entire manifest cosmos. Nārāyaṇakaṇṭha defines *māyā* on the basis of its putative morphemes: "Since the entire world is contained (*māti*) there during reabsorption through powers, and it proceeds (*yāti*) into manifestation from there during emission, it is called *mā-yā*" (*MṛĀV vidyā* 2.7). *Māyā*, according to the Śaivas, is real and substantive (*vastutā*), not illusory or ephemeral as some other schools contend. The recurring emissions from and reabsorptions into *māyā* produce the oscillating universe, as we saw in the previous chapter. Properly speaking, undifferentiated *māyā* does not itself act as a fetter; rather, it is the thirty-one *tattvas* derived from *māyā* that truly bind the soul. When these derivative *tattvas* are emitted and enter into combination with each other, they bring about the bodies that souls inhabit and the worlds in which they live. These *māyā*-constructed bodies and worlds, in turn, provide the structures within which human *paśus* experience their bondage.

Caught up in the complicated fabric of creation, souls are easily led away from their own best interests. Even though real, *māyā* is nevertheless "deluding" (*mohika*) because it (or rather, its derivatives) leads the soul to false ideas, such as considering something impermanent to be permanent, or mistakenly identifying something separate from the soul as integral to the soul (*TPV* 39). These erroneous beliefs provide the basis for further misguided actions, causing the soul to accumulate still more *karman*. *Māyā* itself is transformed through the cyclical process of emission, preservation, and reabsorption. The delusion generated by *māyā* must be dispelled by correct knowledge, specifically the *śivajñāna* contained in the *āgamas*.

The transformative processes of the three fetters are closely linked to one another. The existence of *karman* is a precondition for the emission and reabsorption of *māyā*. If *karman* does not exist, no evolution of *māyā* will occur. The transformation of *karman* through consumption, in turn, depends on the emission of *māyā*. In order for the soul to consume its *karman*, some means of experience must be present. Emission of the *tattvas* derived from *māyā* facilitates the consumption of *karman* by producing the bodies and worlds through which experience takes place. The entire manifest cosmos, says Nārāyaṇakaṇṭha, is emitted just in order that souls can complete the consumption of their *karman* (*MṛĀV vidyā* 6.1).

Similarly, the existence of *mala* is the precondition for *karman*. Without *mala* there can be no *karman*. The ripening of *mala*, in turn, depends on the consumption of *karman*. Although the Śaivite texts do not spell out the dynamics of this relationship, they clearly suggest that the soul's consumption of *karman* induces a ripening of its *mala*. "During the time of preservation," says Aghoraśiva, "Śiva causes the consumption of some ripened *karman*, in order to ripen *mala*" (*TTNV* 19). The transformation of *karman*, that is, brings about a change in *mala* as well.

In this way, the three fetters develop in a connected series. Through the recurring emissions and reabsorptions of the manifest cosmos out of and back into *māyā*, the soul is able to consume its *karman*. The consumption of its *karman* causes the soul's *mala* to ripen. This linked process of evolution does not itself eliminate the fetters. However, it does cause a gradual softening or loosening of the fetters' grip, which prepares the soul for subsequent steps in the movement toward liberation.

The ultimate agent in this process of fetter transformation is Śiva himself. The two most important of Śiva's five fundamental activities, concealment (*tirobhāva*) and grace (*anugrāha*), are precisely directed toward the relationship between the human soul and its fetters. Śiva sets the fetters in motion using his power of concealment. His instigation of the fetters, causing each to perform its proper role in the scheme of things, acts as a suppressing power (*rodhaśakti*) on the souls. Through their actions, the fetters conceal from the soul its own intrinsic qualities.

At first glance this might seem a remarkably pernicious act for a god the Śaivas characterize as "giver of all grace." Yet in the long run Śiva's concealment is a form of grace to the soul, since it brings about the evolution of the fetters. Without evolving, fetters could never be removed. Thus, what might initially appear as an activity detrimental to the soul's welfare turns out to be highly beneficial, in fact necessary to liberation. In *Mṛgendrāgama*, Śiva's use of concealment is compared to the doctor's use of unpalatable medicine: "A doctor, even though he causes the patient much pain by administering bitter medicines and the like, is not considered to be the cause of pain because, in the end, he brings about the desired result" (*MṛĀ vidyā* 7.18). So Śiva's animation of the fetters, which initially causes the soul to suffer through many births and deaths, ultimately paves the way toward liberation.

Liberation through Initiation

The soul need not be simply passive in this process of evolving fetters. It may act to alleviate its own state of bondage. Attending temple services, listening to the teachings of one's preceptor, and observing proper everyday conduct are signs that one's fetters have ripened, and they also contribute significantly to further ripening. As fetters ripen, too, the soul becomes capable of exercising increasing agency in extricating itself from its predicament, performing and undergoing increasingly efficacious ritual actions. Finally the process of ripening may lead to the most important moment in the career of a soul: initiation.

Śaivas consider the ritual known as "liberating initiation" (*nirvāṇadīkṣā*) to be the pivotal event in the soul's movement toward liberation, the ritual through which the most far-reaching alterations in its condition take place. Through initiation, the religious aspirant is placed on the only direct route to achieving liberation during this lifetime. Without initiation, liberation cannot be reached. "Initiation alone liberates one from the extensive bondage impeding the highest goal and leads one upward to Śiva's abode" (*SvāĀ* quoted in *ŚRS* 69). Initiation is Śiva's most direct conferring of grace on the human soul. In fact, so closely are the ritual of liberation and Śiva's grace associated with one another that Śaiva texts use the two terms *dīkṣā* and *anugrāha* as synonyms.

The Fall of Śakti

Initiation cannot be conferred on all persons. For initiation to accomplish its far-reaching effects, the subject of the ritual must be ready for it. If his fetters have not evolved sufficiently and their hold on him therefore remains too tenacious, then even this most powerful ritual act will be to no avail. Only when the ripening of fetters has reached its fruition should a person be given initiation. "When Śiva sees that the soul's *mala* is ripened and ready for removal," Aghoraśiva states, "he prepares the instrument called initiation, whose form is his own Śakti, in order to liberate that soul" (*TTNV* 21). For this reason, preparations and observation are necessary before undertaking the ritual.

Śaiva texts often speak of the mysterious process by which a person becomes ready for initiation as the "falling of Śakti" (*śaktinipāta*).[6] Śiva's own transforming power (*śakti*) of grace falls upon the novice, gradually or abruptly as the case may be, altering his condition irrevocably. In order to judge the readiness of a novice for initiation, the preceptor must watch carefully for indications that Śiva's Śakti has indeed fallen upon him.

Śivāgrayogin sets out in detail the sequence of steps by which the fall of Śakti works its gradual metamorphosis. The process gets underway when the fetters have sufficiently ripened:

> When a *brahman*, *kṣatriya*, *vaiśya*, pure *śūdra*, or one of the *anuloma* castes such as *suvarṇa* reaches a state where his *karman* is equable (*sāmya*) and his *mala* ripened, then the highest Śakti first falls on him. A great faith in the highest knowledge is then born in him, and he becomes detached (*vairāgya*) by realizing the faults inherent in attachment to sensory objects and the like. When such detachment arises, he should approach the house of a teacher in order to learn the highest knowledge. (*ŚPbh* p. 287)

Ripening leads to an initial falling of Śakti, which in turn brings about some symptoms of a religious vocation. The pilgrim is well advised to place himself under the charge of an initiated Śaiva guru, who will be best able to evaluate his spiritual condition and capacities. "And from the teacher, who judges his competence (*adhikāra*) on the basis of his devotion, etc., the aspirant should receive *samayadīkṣā*" (*ŚPbh* p. 287). If the pupil shows the proper signs, the guru enables him to take the first ritual step on the path to Śiva-hood by conferring on him *samayadīkṣā*, "common initiation."

Samayadīkṣā is the general initiation by which one becomes a member of the Śaiva community. In the central rite of *samayadīkṣā*, the preceptor conducts the blindfolded novice into a specially prepared sacrificial pavilion and dramatically removes the blindfold so that the initiate is suddenly able to see Śiva's presence. The guru then gives the Śaiva initiate a new name.[7] Such rites point clearly to the primary effects wrought by *samayadīkṣā*: entry into the world of Śiva, awakening to the knowledge and vision of Śiva's presence, and a new identity in the community of Śaiva devotees. It is in no way comparable in transformative power to *nirvāṇadīkṣā*, and the *āgamas* do not generally discuss the effects of *samayadīkṣā* on fetters. But it does confer on the recipient the capacity to begin participating actively in Śaiva religious activities.

> When he has received *samayadīkṣā*, he follows the codes of conduct of a common member (*samayin*) of the Śaiva community: watching after Śiva's garden, sweeping Śiva's house, gathering flowers and other articles suitable for worshiping Śiva, honoring Śiva's devotees, smearing the body with ashes, placing the three horizontal marks on the forehead, wearing *rudrākṣa*, and the like. (*ŚPbh* p. 287)

Many texts would also prescribe that a common Śaiva's duties may also include performing worship on his own behalf (*ātmārthapūjā*), but Śivāgrayogin reserves that for a later stage of initiation.[8]

Through the initiate's performance of duties around the temple, the fall of Śakti gradually gathers force.

> As he follows the common duties in this way, the fall of Śakti which was initially very weak becomes less so, and an ardent desire to worship Śiva, study the *āgamas*, and so on, arises in him. When the preceptor recognizes the ripening indicated by such an ardent desire, he should immediately confer upon him *viśeṣadīkṣā*, which enables the pupil to study the *āgamas*, worship Śiva, and so on. (*ŚPbh* p. 288)

If *samayadīkṣā* is predominantly a rite of entry, *viśeṣadīkṣā* ("special initiation") is in essence a rite of rebirth. The initiating guru ritually removes the initiate's soul from his body, places it in the womb of Vāgīśvarī, a form of Śakti, installed in a sacrificial fire, and there subjects it to a series of life-cycle rites (*samskāras*) replicating birth. When the soul is then returned to the novice's body, he has been reborn as a "son of Śiva" (*putraka*).[9]

After completion of this initiation, the newborn son is able to worship Śiva on his own behalf, he is fit to conduct fire rites (*homa*), and he is eligible to study the Śaiva texts. For most Śaivas, this is as far along the path of ritual transformation as they wish to proceed. Those seekers of worldly benefits (*bubhukṣus*) who intend to remain householders generally have no reason to go beyond this stage. But some others, further along perhaps in the ripeness of their fetters, do show signs that they are ready for more.

As such a person conducts his regular duties of worship and study, says Śivāgrayogin, "the fall of Śakti, which was previously mild, becomes intense" (*ŚPbh* p. 288). New symptoms begin to appear:

> An ardent aversion toward *samsāra*, that ocean of suffering, arises; a strong desire to see Śiva's lotus feet also is born. New thoughts arise: "When will I see the Lord of Gods? When will I be released from my bonds? Who will show me Śiva?" (*PĀ* 4.39–41 in *ŚRS* 51)

Such signs serve as an observable index of the inner state of the soul, of the degree to which Śakti has indeed fallen. There is a shift, as Śakti falls, from worldly concerns to a longing for liberation.

> Śakti falls without fail on the bodies of those who show these signs: yearning for liberation and repugnance toward remaining in this world, devotion toward the devotees of Śiva, and faith in the teacher and in the rule of conduct taught by Śiva. (*MṛĀ vidyā* 5.4)

According to Aghoraśiva, a novice should stay with the preceptor for at least one year, time enough for the guru to examine carefully the condition of the prospective initiate. Only after such preparation and observation can the teacher be sure that *nirvānadīkṣā* will achieve its desired effect.

> Now, when the teacher recognizes that the pupil's *mala* has ripened and that Śakti has fallen on him, and when he has been consecrated through the common and special initiations and has remained with him for one year, then only the eligible guru should perform *nirvāṇadīkṣā*. (*KKD* p. 264)

The Efficacy of Initiation

Nirvānadīkṣā is a very powerful ritual. *Rauravāgama* compares the effects of initiation on the soul to those of a flame on cotton: "As a heap of cotton placed on a blazing fire is consumed completely, and never again is cotton, so that best of men, the initiate who approaches the *maṇḍala* and receives the mantra of initiation, is never again born" (*RĀ vidyā* 8.9–10). Initiation annihilates fetters like a blazing fire and in so doing also allows the soul's powers to emerge. Somaśambhu, for instance, defines initiation as "that by which the fetters such as *mala* and *māyā* are dissolved, and by which knowledge is born in the pupil" (*SP* 3.1.2). Anantaśambhu relates this twofold function of initiation to the morphemes supposed to comprise the word *dīkṣā*. "The word '*dīkṣā*' has a double meaning. The morpheme *dī* denotes 'giving' (*dāna*); *kṣā* denotes 'removal' (*kṣaya*). 'Giving' is used because initiation grants *śivatva*; 'removal' is used because it causes the destruction of the three fetters" (*SSV* 57–58). The results accomplished by initiation, then, are exactly the two alterations in the soul's condition that constitute liberation: eliminating fetters and manifesting innate powers.

Potent though it is, *nirvāṇadīkṣā* does not bring about immediate liberation. In *Kiraṇāgama*, Garuḍa asks the Lord about this. "If, through initiation, the god completely removes the fetters, why should the body remain upon completion of the ritual?" As Garuḍa knows full well, a soul without fetters would have no further need of a body. Yet it is apparent that a new initiate, unlike the incinerated cotton heap, does continue corporeal life after completing the initiatory ceremony. Śiva answers this conundrum first with an analogy. "This body remains after the consecration is accomplished, as a potter's wheel continues to spin even when the pot has been completed." Then he goes on to summarize tersely the effects of *nirvāṇadīkṣā* on the different types of *karman*: "The many [accumulated] *karman* are burned up like seeds by the 'atoms' [i.e., the mantras used in initiation], future *karman* are suppressed, and the *karman* by which this [present body] exists [are removed only] through consumption" (*KirĀ vidyā* 6.17–19). In other words, Śiva answers that the soul remains embodied after initiation because the ritual does not remove all fetters. If it completely destroyed them, the novice, no longer requiring a body, would pass directly from the ritual to liberation.

Initiation acts directly and completely only on *sañcitakarman*, the repository of *karman* that otherwise would cause the soul to be reborn many times. This constitutes by far the largest part of one's *karman*. By destroying this stockpile destined to be consumed in future lives, initiation enables the soul to forgo further rebirth. However, initiation does not fundamentally affect the other two categories of *karman*. It does not eliminate *prārabdhakarman*; this can be removed only by living out one's current life, consuming the active *karman* "by which this present body exists" along the way. Nor does initiation remove *āgamin*. Since this *karman* does not yet exist, initiation can at best prevent its occurrence. It must be dealt with later, as it comes into being. These latter two categories are the ones that keep the potter's wheel spinning, maintaining the initiate in his present body until his death.

Although the main action of *nirvāṇadīkṣā* is the destruction of fetters, initiation rites are also devoted to the emergence of the soul's inherent Śiva-ness. These rites are necessary, says Nirmalamaṇi, because *śivatva* does not automatically manifest itself when the fetters are removed. It is not like simply taking away a cloth so that a previously covered pot becomes visible. A better analogy, he suggests, is Aghoraśiva's eye doctor curing a case of cataracts. Here, "the eyes do not regain their power of perception just through the removal of the cataracts that have covered them." Rather, the doctor must use some ointment as well, to aid the eyes in recuperating. The initiation rites for the manifestation of *śivatva* are analogous to the doctor's ointment: they assist the soul's powers, which have been "debilitated by their beginningless bondage."

The ritual efficacy of initiation in removing fetters and unleashing Śiva-like powers results from Śiva's own action. Śiva makes his most direct intervention in the career of the soul during initiation, bestowing his "grace" (*anugrāha*) powerfully and irrevocably on the initiate. "As the sun illuminates the worlds with its rays," says *Rauravāgama*, "so Śiva shines through his powers (*śakti*) during the 'sacrifice of mantras'" (*RĀ vidyā* 8.4). Śiva acts in *nirvāṇadīkṣā* by entering into the guru performing the ritual, who thereby becomes Śiva's "support" or embodiment during the course of the ritual. All ritual actions performed by the guru are, in fact, the actions of Śiva; the initiating priest is simply Śiva's appointed agent (*adhikārin*) in carrying out this act of grace. The guru acts throughout with the "hand of Śiva." Thus the event most crucial to the soul's eventual liberation is also the highest expression of Śiva's grace.

Rites of Removal and Emergence

Initiation acts as an instrument through which the soul is brought toward liberation, by removing fetters and assisting its inherent powers to emerge. In a performance of *nirvāṇadīkṣā*, the rites specifically directed to accomplish these two tasks are the central, operative actions of the ritual. The pupil's fetters are removed through the construction and subsequent destruction of the *pāśasūtra*, the "cord of fetters," which serves as a "substitute body" (*pratikāya*) for the initiate within the ritual. After his fetters have been removed, the initiate's soul is united (*yojanikā*) with Śiva and his divine qualities are brought forth (*guṇāpādana*) through the offering of a series of oblations.

Nirvāṇadīkṣā requires two days for its complete performance.[10] The first day is devoted to preparations. The most important object prepared is the *pāśasūtra*, a cotton cord equal in length to the pupil's body. It is purified with water and mantras and suspended from the pupil's topknot down to his big toe. The initiating priest, the guru, then transfers out of the pupil's body all its constituents and imposes them onto the cord.

Here, as throughout the ritual, it is the priest who accomplishes the rite. The novice remains passive. The priest has already invoked Śiva into himself, and hence it is Śiva who acts through him. As for the initiate, his intrinsic powers of knowledge and action are still suppressed by fetters, and so he is not able to act for himself during the ritual. Only one who possesses unfettered powers can accomplish the great changes of initiation.

The method used by the guru to transport each of these realities is complex.[11] First the guru strikes the initiate with a flower, and with his own soul he enters into the pupil's body along one of its subtle channels. Inside, he gathers up the thing he wishes to transport, removes it from its place in the novice's body, and carries it to his own heart. Then he transports it upward and out of his own body and unites it with the cord. Once the constituent is joined with the cord, the guru worships it, constrains it there, performs a protective encirclement, and offers it three fire oblations. Each of these ritual actions is carried out with an appropriate mantra, and many require a specific *mudrā* as well. The guru repeats these steps each time he conveys something from the body of the initiate onto the cord.

The guru first transports the goddess Śakti, then (according to Somaśambhu) the three subtle channels of the body and the six "paths" (*adhvan*). Next he transports the pupil's soul and the fetters. Finally he transports the five *kalās*.

Of all the constituents imposed onto the cord, the five *kalās* figure most prominently in this ritual.[12] Like the thirty-six *tattvas*, the five *kalās* ("portions" of the cosmos) are cosmological entities. According to the *Śivapurāṇa*, Śiva brings about the emission of the five *kalās* at the time of creation.

> *Śāntyatīta* emanated from Śakti, then *śānti* was emitted in due order, then *vidyā*, and from that *pratiṣṭhā* arose. *Nivṛtti* came forth in due order from *pratiṣṭhā*. Thus is described fully the emission directed by Śiva. These five *kalās* are emitted in normal order (*anulomya*); reabsorption proceeds in the inverse direction (*pratilomya*). The highest creator animates the world from the five aforesaid entities, and so the five *kalās* permeate this entire world. (*ŚPur* 1.9.4–7)

So too in *nirvāṇadīkṣā* the *kalās* provide an ontological framework within which the entire manifest world is encompassed, differentiated, and ranked. All realities are contained or "enwombed" (*garbhita*) within them. The *Kāmikāgama* points to their all-inclusive character:

> Mantras, words, phonemes, *tattvas*, and worlds are encompassed (*vyāpya*); the bonds of *karman*, *mala*, and the derivatives of *māyā* are encompassing (*vyāpaka*). But the bonds such as *mala* are also encompassed, and the *kalās* are encompassing [in relation to them]. Therefore, when one grasps these *kalās*, one appropriates (*svīkaraṇa*) all the others. Similarly, through their placements and their purifications, everything is placed and purified. (*UKĀ* 23.31–34)

Before transporting each *kalā*, the guru must first visualize all that is included within it: *tattvas*, mantras, words, phonemes, worlds, seed-syllables, subtle channels, bodily winds, sense objects, qualities, and governing lords—in short, all constituents of the manifest cosmos. By gathering up and transporting these *kalās*, the guru also transports all the realities contained in them.

While the set of *kalās* contains all manifest realities, they also divide up and rank the encompassed realities among themselves. In order of relative purity or subtlety the *kalās* are: *śāntyatīta*, *śānti*, *vidyā*, *pratiṣṭhā*, and *nivṛtti*. Accordingly, the two purest, most subtle *tattvas* are included within *śāntyatīta*, the next three most subtle in *śānti*, and so on down to the least subtle, Earth, included in *nivṛtti*. Similarly, the most subtle worlds are found in the *śāntyatīta*, and the least subtle in *nivṛtti*. All other realities encompassed within the *kalās* are also ranked according to the same scheme. Thus, the *kalās* present five hierarchical planes or dimensions of being that, between them, encompass all that there is.[13]

There is one important exception to the all-inclusive character of the *kalās*. The *kalās* contain all the initiate's *karman* except *prārabdhakarman* and the *karman* arising as a consequence of that. This exception is necessary since, if initiation were to remove his active *karman*, he would have no need to remain embodied after completion of the ritual.

When he transports the five *kalās*, the guru begins with *śāntyatīta* and proceeds according to the order of emission. This order is appropriate here because the guru is ritually constructing the *pāśasūtra*. Each *kalā* occupies a portion of the pupil's body, with the most subtle *kalā* located in the highest place, as one would expect. (See Figure 7.) The *kalās* are correspondingly placed onto the suspended *pāśasūtra*. *Śāntyatīta* is joined onto the highest segment of the cord, then *śānti*, and so on down to *nivṛtti*, located on the lowest portion. After all *kalās* have been joined onto the cord, the guru marks it to indicate the location of each one, using colored powders to dye each segment and tying knots at each boundary.

Through this process of transferring constituents from body to cord, the *pāśasūtra* is impregnated with the pupil's complete makeup. It becomes a virtual reembodiment of the initiate, body and soul. The guru removes the cord, worships it, and places it near the Śiva-pot, asking Śiva to protect it overnight.

The following day the guru uses the *pāśasūtra* to perform a "purification of the *kalās*" (*kalāśuddhi*). During this rite the soul of the initiate is separated from the *kalās*, and the *kalās* are then destroyed together with the fetters contained in them. As on the first day, each *kalā* is treated separately, in sequence. This time, however, the guru follows the order of reabsorption, beginning with *nivṛtti* and ending with *śāntyatīta*, as is appropriate for a rite of purification. In this description, I use *nivṛttikalā* as a model; each subsequent *kalā* follows the same procedure.

The guru begins by once again visualizing *nivṛttikalā* and all the realities included within it. As part of the visualization, the guru also imagines wombs within the *kalā*. The *kalās* contain all possible wombs into which a soul might—as a result of previously acquired *karman*—be born. Like other encompassed realities, the wombs are differentiated and ranked according to the *kalās* in which they are found. In *nivṛtti*, for instance, are found the wombs of the fourteen lowest states of existence: wild animals, cattle, birds, snakes, plants, humans, demons, titans, demigods, Gandharvas, Indra, Soma, Prajeśvara, and Brahman. Wombs in purer *kalās* are of higher orders of beings.

Once the guru has fully visualized *nivṛttikalā*, he detaches it from the cord

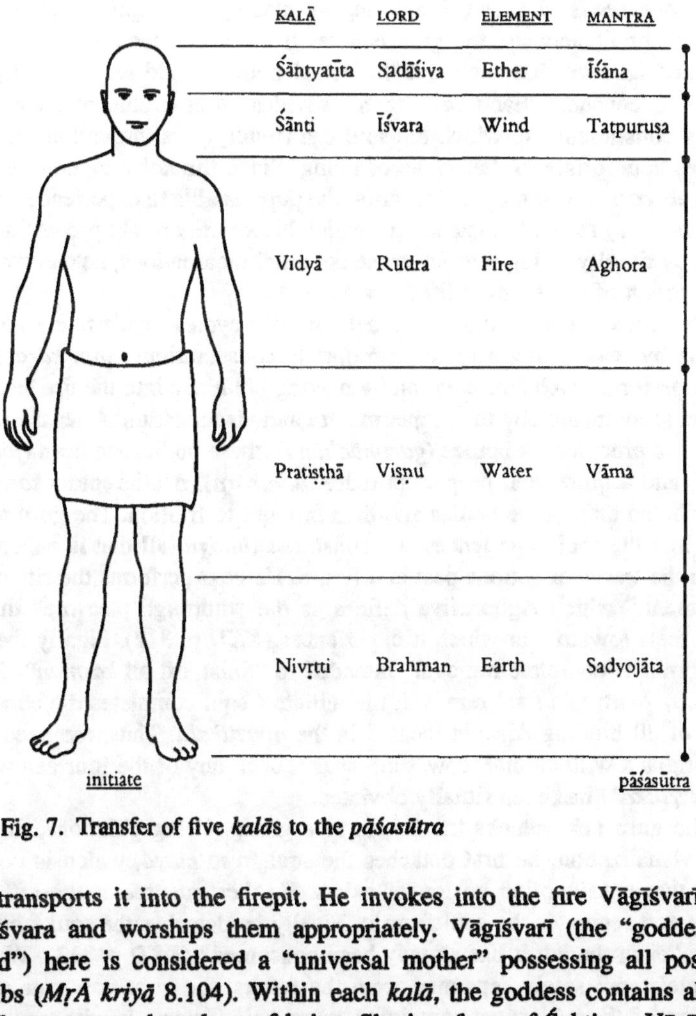

Fig. 7. Transfer of five *kalās* to the *pāśasūtra*

and transports it into the firepit. He invokes into the fire Vāgīśvarī and Vāgīśvara and worships them appropriately. Vāgīśvarī (the "goddess of sound") here is considered a "universal mother" possessing all possible wombs (*MṛĀ kriyā* 8.104). Within each *kalā*, the goddess contains all the wombs proper to that plane of being. She is a form of Śakti, as Vāgīśvara is of Śiva. The guru now gathers up the pupil's soul. He transports it to his own heart first and then, while conveying it toward the fire, he visualizes Śakti and Śiva copulating. He places the soul in all Śakti's wombs at once. In each womb the soul is joined with an embryo resulting from the sexual union of Śakti and Śiva.

The purpose in subjecting the initiate's soul to this multiple conception is to accelerate the process of consuming *karman*. Only consumption can remove *karman*, and consumption takes place during the soul's embodiment. Even ritual tactics cannot circumvent this principle of the cosmos, so instead one seeks to speed things up. By placing the pupil's soul in many bodies simultaneously, the guru enables it to experience rapidly the accumulated *karman* that—without this ritual help—would require many lifetimes to consume. Each *kalā*, then, provides an environment made up of many constituents, in which the soul can ritually pass through all the existences appropriate to that plane of being. Since the *kalā*s together encompass all possible wombs, in initiation the pupil is able to experience conception in every state of existence for which his *karman* might predestine him. And by ritually living through these potential incarnations, he can consume all *karman* of these future lifetimes as well.

The novice next summarily enacts the life cycles of his many embodiments by undergoing a set of appropriate consecrations (*saṃskāras*). The guru performs each consecration by making oblations into the fire, each oblation accompanied by the proper mantra and visualization. After the pupil's soul has procured its bodies (*garbhādhāna*), these bodies are born (*jātakarman*) and acquire their proper aptitudes (*adhikāra*). All the soul's *karman* is distributed among the bodies and then brought to fruition. The guru visualizes that the soul experiences and consumes (*bhoga*) all that is engendered from the traces of actions past and future. He next performs the rite of "attachment," which Aghoraśiva defines as the "thorough pleasure" that the soul feels toward that which it experiences (*KKD* p. 312). Finally the guru performs a "complete removal" intended to "finish off all *karman*" (*KKDP* p. 320). With this final removal, the initiate's soul completes the consumption of all binding *karman* located in the *nivṛttikalā*. Thus, the need to be reborn as a wild animal, cow, bird, snake, or in any of the fourteen wombs of *nivṛttikalā* has been ritually obviated.

The guru next attacks the fetters as a group. Using oblations, mantras, and visualization, he first detaches the soul from *māyā*, which is possible now that consumption no longer exists. He then suppresses the effects of *mala* and separates the soul from it. Finally he detaches the soul from *karman*, "even though it has already been consumed" (*KKD* p. 313). With the initiate's soul safely separated from the fetters, the guru now cuts off the section of the *pāśasūtra* containing *nivṛttikalā*, smears it with cow dung, rolls it into a ball, places it in the sacrificial ladle and mixes it with ghee, and burns it completely in the fire. As the segment of cord is annihilated, so are the fetters it contains. Much as the "heap of cotton" in the *Rauravāgama*'s analogy, the cotton cord is consumed completely in fire, allowing the initiate's body to shed its fetters but remain alive. The *pāśasūtra* is the necessary stand-in for his body, which could not be subjected to the same treatment as the cord without it resulting in physical death.

The pupil's soul has at this point experienced birth in every state of existence possible within *nivṛttikalā* and consumed all *karman* pertaining to it. It has been carefully detached from all three fetters. Those fetters have been destroyed in the fire along with the segment of cord on which they were situated. The purification of *nivṛttikalā* is complete. The guru visualizes the initiate's soul, "liberated from the net of *nivṛttikalā*, and resembling a pure crystal gem" (*KKD* p. 313). Once again he grasps the soul and transports it to the next-higher segment of the cord, where it awaits the purification of the next-purer *kalā*.

Through the sequential purifications of all five *kalā*s, containing all possible wombs and encompassing all fetters, the pupil's soul is liberated completely from its bondage and from the need for subsequent rebirth. Somaśambhu compares it, as it is freed step by step, to the moon slowly emerging from the grasp of the eclipse, in the end appearing like "the autumn moon fully arisen" (*SP* 3.3.215).

When the initiate's fetters have been removed, the inherent powers of his soul are free to manifest themselves. Unlike the autumn moon, however, the soul's powers do not immediately shine of their own accord. Here again rites are necessary. The soul's divine qualities (*guṇa*) are immanent, but they have been debilitated by their bondage. As the eye doctor uses an ointment to assist a patient in recovering his sight, in initiation the guru must unite his pupil's soul with Paramaśiva and offer oblations to "produce" (*āpādana*) or "animate" (*uttejana*) the attributes that make up its *śivatva*. The *Svacchandatantra* compares the production of these qualities to the royal *abhiṣeka*. "When the king attains sovereignty, a priest anoints him with pots, and bards proclaim his royal virtues throughout the land. In the same way, when the initiate attains *śivatva*, the wise priest will produce his divine qualities" (*SvaT* 4.443–44). In both cases, immanent capacities are made fully manifest through the efficacy of ritual action.

The guru first asks for Śiva's permission to unite the soul with Śiva. He does several preparatory purifications and again requests of Śiva, "Please cause this soul's *śivatva* to become manifest." Offering oblations into the fire, he performs the five life-cycle consecrations used previously, this time in the *śivatattva*. At this point, of course, there is no more *karman* to be consumed. These consecrations instead stimulate five qualities constituting the soul's *śivatva*: entry into the *śivatattva*, emergence of the powers of knowledge and action, complete sovereignty, self-arising joy, and the ability to identify with Śiva. This manifestation of Śiva-ness, however, is only a preparation for the more fundamental one to follow.

The guru prepares himself mentally by meditating on his identification with Śiva. He once again enters into the initiate's body, collects his soul, removes it from that body, and returns with it to his own heart. There the pupil's soul is united with his own. Then, reciting the PRĀSĀDA mantra, Śiva's own mantra, in an ascending order, the guru together with the pupil's soul rises along his *suṣumnā* to the *dvādaśānta*, where Śiva resides in his most complete form. (I will discuss PRĀSĀDA and the method of ascending pronunciation in the following chapter.)

The guru unites the initiate's soul with Paramaśiva, "of whom highest joy is the intrinsic form, who surpasses the mind's reach, who is empty of qualities and yet the eternal source of qualities." Then he animates the six divine qualities of the soul: omniscience, contentment, eternal enlightenment, independence, indestructible power, and infinite power. For each of these attributes, the guru offers three oblations into the fire and recites a mantra (using the seed-syllable of an *aṅgamantra*) that invokes the quality. Liberated from the fetters that had long suppressed it, and now animated by oblations and mantras, the soul's inherent *śivatva* is able to emerge. The guru, with a divine glance, sees the soul of the novice "ornamented by its own emanating energies (*tejas*), like the disk of the sun" (*KKD* p. 359). The initiate has fully become a Śiva while temporarily united with Paramaśiva.

To close the performance of *nirvāṇadīkṣā*, the guru returns the pupil's soul to his body so that it may consume its remaining *prārabdhakarman*. As indicated above, this category of *karman* was expressly omitted from inclusion within the *kalā*s, and consequently the initiation has not affected it. The initiate's condition has been fundamentally altered by the ritual. All *karman* that would otherwise engender future rebirths has been annihilated. Yet he must remain living in his present body in order to complete gradually the consumption of his residual *karman* and thereby gain final liberation. The guru, with the initiated pupil beside him, prays to Śiva: "'Taking on my form, you have granted grace to this initiate. Therefore, O Lord, make his devotion toward god, fire, and guru grow. By your favor, may he remain firm in unbroken ritual. Let him not be guilty of any fault that would again bind him'" (*KKD* pp. 360–61).

In summary, initiation is the decisive event in the soul's passage from bondage to liberation. The effects achieved by *nirvāṇadīkṣā* are precisely those two transformations in the soul's condition that characterize *mokṣa* itself: the removal of fetters that bind the soul, and the emergence of the soul's inherent powers. The initiate's fetters are removed through ritual actions centering on the *pāśasūtra*. This cord becomes, by a series of transfers, a reembodiment of the initiate. Using the cord as medium, the soul is able first to consume its accumulated *karman* and then to be separated from all its fetters. The fetters are destroyed in the sacrificial fire. Rites devoted to the emergence of the soul's *śivatva* follow. The soul is transported to the realm of the highest Śiva and united with him there, where the divine qualities it shares with Śiva are animated by oblations and mantras. With its powers thus manifested, it is returned to the novice's body so that it may consume its remaining *karman*.[14]

Completing the Passage

The daily worship of Śiva, says the *Kāmikāgama*, yields the fruits of both worldly enjoyments and liberation (*KĀ* 4.1). Now that we have looked at the philosophical model by which Śaivas understand the soul's passage from bondage to liberation, and followed the career of a soul through the ripening of its fetters and the performance of initiation, we are in a much better position to understand the role of daily worship in granting liberation.

In daily worship, the primary rite directed toward liberation is that of *ātmaśuddhi*. This rite, in which the ritualist "becomes a Śiva" as a preparation for worshiping Śiva, was described in the preceding chapter as a transformation of the ritualist's body. More fundamentally, however, it should be seen as a liberation of the soul. The body is an objectification of the soul's bondage. By transforming his body, the worshiper alters the condition of his soul. He frees the soul from its most intimate fetters and replaces them with a body made of mantras.

Ātmaśuddhi is a quotidian enactment in reduced form of the ritualist's liberation. Like *nirvāṇadīkṣā*, the "purification of the soul" in daily worship puts into practice the double alteration in the soul's condition that constitutes liberation: removal of the fetters and manifestation of the soul's powers. This operation produces effects beyond the limits of the ritual itself. The performance of worship gradually diminishes the soul's remaining fetters so that, at death, none remain to prevent it from attaining final liberation. During *ātmaśuddhi*, the initiated "son of Śiva" (*putraka*) daily exercises his own capacities of self-transformation, both rehearsing his final liberation and at the same time gradually bringing it about. Daily ritual is the best means available to the soul to complete its passage to *mokṣa*.

Body and Soul

Initiation, we have seen, brings about a radical alteration in the spiritual condition of the initiate, but it does not engender immediate liberation. According to Śaivism, the "fruit of initiation" that is ultimate liberation is obtained only upon bodily death, when the soul's remaining *prārabdhakarman* has also been fully consumed. This raises the issue of just what the initiated Śaiva should do in the meantime. How should he act for the rest of his life to facilitate his own final *mokṣa*?

At the completion of initiation, the novice is like a potter's wheel, according to Śiva's analogy in the *Kiraṇāgama*. Though the pot itself is finished, the wheel continues to revolve due to its own momentum. The initiate has removed his accumulated *karman* in initiation, and thereby eliminated his need to be reborn, but he must return to his present body under the impulsion of *karman* whose effects are already in motion.

The potter's-wheel analogy is useful, but it oversimplifies the situation. The wheel is inanimate (*jaḍa*), therefore inert, and its rotation will automatically cease due to friction unless the potter again sets it in motion. The *putraka*, on the other hand, is an animate soul, with powers of knowledge and action. He is not able to wait passively until his body ceases its spinning. He must continue to act in the world after his initiation, and these actions are liable to engender new fetters, which could prevent his final liberation. In the language of *karman*, he must be sure not to contract any *āgamin*, while at the same time consuming his remaining *prārabdhakarman*.

The best course of action for the potential Śiva, according to Aghoraśiva, is to behave in accord with *samayācāra*, the rules of conduct incumbent on all initiated Śaivites. All human activities pose the risk of creating *karman*. Actions based on this code, however, do not give rise to new *karman* in the way that others do. One who has undergone initiation must faithfully follow *samayācāra*, preventing *karman*, if he is to reach final liberation when his *prārabdhakarman* is completed and his body passes away.

One invariable rule of *samayācāra* is that the initiated Śaiva must regularly perform daily worship. "You should offer worship to Śiva, to the fire, and to your guru until the end of your life," the priest instructs his pupil at the completion of initiation (*SP* 3.2.23). Failure to worship Śiva entails a fault, leading to more residues of *karman*. However, it is not simply to avoid a transgression that the initiate should offer *pūjā*. Daily worship—and more specifically *ātmaśuddhi*—plays a continuing role in resisting and removing fetters.

Daily worship serves as a prophylactic, claims the *Mataṅgapārameśvarāgama*, counteracting the acquisition of any new fetters.

> Thus sin does not arise in the one who daily worships the Prime Cause with devotion, as darkness is not born after the rising of the sun. When his body ends, he does not reenter the world on account of his stock of *karman*. Therefore this daily ordinary worship brings good results [(or) conveys the sunrise]. (*MPĀ kriyā* 3.100–101)

Initiation is the sunrise that removes the earth's darkness, while daily worship is the continuation of sunshine during the day, preventing its return. In day-to-day life, the initiate is bound to make small transgressions of the rules. Daily worship, acting like a recurring initiation, removes the effects of these misdeeds as they arise.

Going beyond this counteractive view of *Mataṅga*, Aghoraśiva sees daily worship as a ritual method of gradual removal, affecting existing fetters as well as newly arisen ones: "During the period after initiation, one may accomplish a removal of the fetters whose effects have already begun, such that they diminish daily, by following the common rules of conduct, beginning with bathing and worship" (*TST* 39). Both regard daily worship as a necessary, efficacious action instrumental in the attainment of *mokṣa*. It takes up where initiation left off, removing any remnants of fetters not destroyed during *nirvāṇadīkṣā*, and brings to completion the process initiated by that ritual.[15]

The rite within daily worship that causes this removal is *ātmaśuddhi*. Through this rite, we have seen, the worshiper becomes a Śiva in order to worship Śiva. "In this way the worshiper attains the form of Śiva (*śivarūpatā*), albeit separate from it, by first purifying his soul and his body and then imposing a mantra-body onto his own form, and thereby he becomes fit to offer worship to Śiva" (*ŚAC* p. 29). At the same time as it fulfills this function within the context of ritual, it also contributes to the larger project of liberating the soul through the removal of fetters.

In the preceding chapter, I described the rite of *ātmaśuddhi* as a transformation of the worshiper's body. There are good reasons to view it in this light, not least of which are the terms used for its component procedures: "purification of the subtle body," "purification of the gross body," and "imposition of the mantra-body." *Ātmaśuddhi* does indeed ritually transform the body. But more fundamentally it is a "purification of the soul," an enactment of the soul's liberation. In fact, *ātmaśuddhi* purifies the soul precisely through the metamorphosis of the worshiper's body. The body is treated as the locus of the soul's bondage, and a ritual transformation of the body brings about the soul's temporary liberation.

The soul, as we have seen, is itself immutable. It cannot be altered; only its condition or situation may be changed. The entire passage of the soul toward liberation is regarded by the Śaivites as a sequence of processes—ripening, initiation, proper conduct, and so on—that gradually alter its condition by loosening and removing the fetters that bind it.

The soul inhabits a body only because it has fetters. For the soul, the body is a necessary means of experience. It allows the soul to consume *karman* and thus instigates the ripening of the fetters. However, the body is also the most intimate projection of the soul's state of bondage. The body is brought into being solely because of *karman*, and it is composed of the derivative *tattvas* of *māyā*. As an objectification of the soul's fetters, it also acts as an instrument of this bondage. The body is a receptacle for the soul, which, once contained, is also constrained by it. For this reason, the body is the object that instantiates most concretely and most closely the soul's bound condition.

This essential relationship between the soul's fetters and the body it inhabits provides the underlying motive of *ātmaśuddhi*. In *ātmaśuddhi*, the worshiper's body is treated as a limited and highly concentrated manifestation of fetters. All the constituents of the body in its normal state are regarded as "impurities" that stain the soul. Consequently, the means of purifying the soul—that is, of removing it from its condition of bondage—must involve a transformation of the body. The impure constituents must be somehow removed. In the process the ritualist's body is transformed from an objectification of the soul's fetters into an instrument of the soul's intrinsic powers. No longer posing an obstacle to worship, the worshiper's body empowers the soul to act in the ritual. This "body of powers"—parallel to Śiva's own body—is the means by which the worshiper is able to carry out all subsequent ritual actions of worship.

Rehearsals of Liberation

As an enactment of the soul's liberation, *ātmaśuddhi* has many elements in common with *nirvāṇadīkṣā*. Both act on the soul through the medium of the body. Both achieve their effects by an equivalent two-phase process: first a removal of fetters, then a manifestation of Śiva-like powers. The purification of the elements (of the gross body) in *ātmaśuddhi* is particularly similar to the purification of the *kalās* in initiation. The construction of the divine body in *ātmaśuddhi* also suggests parallels with the production of divine qualities in *nirvāṇadīkṣā*. *Kāmikāgama* supports this linking of the two rituals, stating that a worshiper should employ the same method of purification in daily worship as was used in his initiation (*KĀ* 4.60–61).

In the following description I will emphasize the parallelism between the worshiper's daily self-purification and the ceremony of initiation. However, there are also some significant differences between the two. *Ātmaśuddhi* is a regular, repeated action undertaken daily by the initiated Śaivite; initiation is a singular event in the career of a religious aspirant. *Ātmaśuddhi* is a rite embedded within the larger ritual of daily worship, whereas liberating initiation is itself an extensive, independent ritual unity. Most important, *ātmaśuddhi* is a rite performed by the worshiper himself, while initiation is accomplished on the initiate by Śiva acting through the guru. *Ātmaśuddhi* does recapitulate many of the important features of *nirvāṇadīkṣā*, but I do not wish to suggest that it is simply a repetition in miniature.

The performance of *ātmaśuddhi*, we have seen, takes place in two converse sequences of actions. First comes a phase of removals, of purification, intended to bring about the destruction of impure or binding constituents. This phase may be further divided into two series, correlated to a differentiation of the subtle body and the gross body. Second is performed a phase of impositions, of construction, meant to build a new body of divine powers. Before the purifying phase of *ātmaśuddhi*, which is highly destructive, it is necessary to protect the soul and its remaining *karman* from annihilation. The soul is gathered up from throughout the body and moved to a safe place, twelve inches above the head, where it is temporarily absorbed into Śiva. After purification is completed, the soul is returned through a descending movement, placing it on a lotus throne in the worshiper's heart. Thus, *ātmaśuddhi* may be sequentially outlined as follows:

1. protection of the soul, removal from the body
2. purification of the body
   a. purification of the subtle body
   b. purification of the gross body
3. return of the soul to the body
4. construction of a divine body

The purpose of protecting the soul is succinctly stated by *Kāmikāgama*: "This joining [of the soul with Śiva] is done by priests to protect their *karman* remaining to be consumed. . . . This *karman* is not destroyed [during this rite] due to the Lord's command" (*KĀ* 4.54–55). The ritual method employed to purify the body is a harsh one and poses a threat to the soul's *prārabdhakarman*. This *karman* should not be destroyed prematurely, and so it must be removed from the body to a safer asylum. Accordingly, the worshiper collects the consciousness pervading his body into the seed-syllable HŪṂ, which he visualizes as a flame in the middle of his *suṣumnā*. With an ascending breath, he transports this syllable upward, bursting open as it proceeds all the nodes (*granthi*) that might otherwise obstruct its path. He returns his consciousness and absorbs it into his soul. Placing his soul now in the syllable HĀṂ, he expels his breath upward to the *dvādaśānta*, where he unites his soul with Śiva.

With the soul safely placed in the *dvādaśānta*, the worshiper may now purify his body. The overall purpose is to neutralize and destroy all impure constituents of the body and to remove them as fetters from the soul. Nirmalamaṇi defines the purification of the body with the soul's liberation in mind:

> Purification of the *tattvas* located in the gross and subtle bodies by visualizing their reabsorption is done in order to stop their binding nature (*bandhakatvanivṛtti*), as [a tantric healer] visualizes himself as Garuḍa in order to stop the effects of poison. (*KKDP* p. 68)

The constituents of the body are fetters to the soul, and their "binding nature" must be somehow terminated for the soul to be free of them.

Aghoraśiva divides the procedures of purification into two parts, one directed at purifying the subtle body, the other at purifying the gross body. As described in the preceding chapter, the purification of the subtle body consists in a reabsorption of all thirty-six *tattvas* constituting the subtle body into their two source-substances *māyā* and *mahāmāyā*. The worshiper visualizes each *tattva* going within its source, according to the order of reabsorption, until only the two undifferentiated substances remain. Undifferentiated *māyā* does not itself constitute a fetter. Rather, the thirty-one *tattvas* of the impure domain emitted from *māyā*—referred to as *māyeya*—are what actually bind the soul. By causing all these derivative *tattvas* to be reabsorbed into undifferentiated *māyā*, the worshiper is able to remove the binding character of *māyā*. Purifying the subtle body effectively neutralizes *māyā* as a fetter.

The second purification is directed against the impurities of the gross body. In one sense, the gross body is easily understood as that composed of the five material elements.

> The "gross body" denotes the body made of elements (*bhūtaśarīra*), born in a certain world, whose form is both general and particular (*sādhāraṇāsādhāraṇa*): [general in that it is] the locus that causes notions such as "birth-community," "family," and so on, [particular in that it is] an aggregation of the elements Earth, Water, Fire, Wind, and Ether. (*KKDP* p. 67)

The five elements indicated here are the five least subtle of the thirty-six *tattvas* that constitute the cosmos. Together they form the substratum for the five perceptible qualities, which inhere in them. Being gross elements, they are of course considered impure, and the worshiper's body must be purified of them in *ātmaśuddhi*.

In another sense, however, the five elements appear as more than mere elements. They are termed "cosmic supports" (*dhāraṇā*) and are linked closely with the five all-inclusive *kalās*. Each element serves as the support for a *kalā*. At the beginning of its description of purification, *Kāmikāgama* refers to this second sense of the elements as cosmic supports.

> When its faults have been entirely annihilated, the soul remains, without *mala*, like gold whose impurities have been cleansed by fire. Similarly, a person destroys many sins and becomes pure by means of [this purification of] the cosmic supports, and then returns to his bodily state to fulfill his assigned role (*adhikāra*). (*KĀ* 4.57–58)

This connection of the elements with the *kalās* is reinforced by several similarities between this portion of *ātmaśuddhi* and the rite of *kalāśuddhi*. When the five elements of the gross body are viewed in this sense, as the supports of the entire cosmos, then the purification of the gross body takes on a wider dimension. Not simply a purification of bodily elements, it becomes also a purification of the cosmos itself as a source of fetters. The worshiper's body in its composition of five elements is at the same time a concentrated embodiment of fetters. Its purification, like that of the *kalās* in initiation, liberates the soul from fetters.

The rite used to purify the gross body operates on both levels. (This double level of reference is reinforced by the vacillation in terms used by the texts; sometimes they refer to "gross body," sometimes to "elements," to "cosmic supports," or to "*kalā*s" as the object of purification.) First the worshiper visualizes the domain of each element. Each element is specifically "endowed with" or "connected to" a *kalā* (*KālĀ* 8.6–7).

bhūta	*kalā*
Ether	*śāntyatīta*
Wind	*śānti*
Fire	*vidyā*
Water	*pratiṣṭhā*
Earth	*nivṛtti*

Their positions on the scale of emission are equivalent; most subtle element is paired with most subtle *kalā*. The domains are located in specified parts of the body, just as the *kalā*s are in initiation. (Compare Figures 3 and 7.) Furthermore, the domains that the ritualist visualizes are in almost every respect parallel to those of the *kalā*s visualized in initiation. Thus, as the *kalā*s encompass all manifest realities in initiation, so here the domains of the elements include all realities among them.

If the visualization of domains suggests the cosmic level of reference, the next procedure switches to the material. Each domain has a number of attributes, which are the perceptible qualities inherent in each element.[16] Earth contains all five perceptible qualities, Water contains four, and so on. The relationships here between material elements and perceptible qualities are clearly those of the *tattvas*. The worshiper expels these qualities, one by one, using ascending expulsions of breath. After the attributes are ejected, the worshiper absorbs each element into its "opponent," so that each comes to resemble the other. In effect, he neutralizes the binding power of his bodily elements.

With the elements fully visualized and neutralized, the worshiper visualizes his own form in a liberated state. "He should imagine that he has liberated his own form from impermanence, limitation, impurity, and so on, and that it is now endowed with permanence, pervasiveness, purity, and such qualities" (*KKD* p. 58). Next he destroys all bodily elements. "Then, with the fire arising from his right big toe and with ASTRA, he burns the impurities of the elements located in the body resulting from *karman* whose consequences have begun (*prārabdha*), and then inundates it" (*KKD* p. 58). Here both levels of reference appear. Aghoraśiva speaks first of visualizing the Śiva-like qualities of the liberated soul, then of a physical destruction by fire of the body's five material elements. The gross body is purified at two levels: as an aggregate of five material elements, and as the "support" for the *kalā*s.

Like *kalāśuddhi* in initiation, this purification of the gross body begins with visualizations of each individual element. There is no transporting of these elements—as in *kalāśuddhi*—to a substitute body. In both purifications, a procedure is used to neutralize the elements, though *kalāśuddhi*, with its complicated sequence aimed at consuming accumulated *karman*, is by far the more complex. Destruction by fire is the culminating operation in each rite. Here the fire is an internal one, arising from the worshiper's toe; in initiation it is an external fire into which Śiva has been invoked. Here the fire acts directly on the ritualist's actual body; in initiation it destroys the stand-in body, the *pāśasūtra*. In both, there is a complete removal of fetters except for the soul's *prārabdhakarman*, whose consumption cannot be circumvented by ritual means. The two rites are closely linked, though not exactly identical.

The ritualist's body is now empty. Without impurities or fetters, it poses no danger to the soul, which may safely be returned to its normal location in the body. To do this, the worshiper first mentally constructs in his heart a throne in the form of a lotus. Following the order of emission, he leads the soul downward from the *dvādaśānta*, where it has been united with Śiva, and places it on that throne. He unites the soul in the *puryaṣṭaka*, the conditioned form of the body, establishes the soul there, and finally bathes it with a stream of nectar.

This procedure parallels that of invocation, by which Śiva or any divinity is brought into a prepared form. This is suitable since, as Aghoraśiva tells us, the soul is "located in the *dvādaśānta* in the form of *bīja*, and is made of Śiva" (*śivamaya*)" (*KKD* p. 59). By its separation from fetters it has become a Śiva, and it must be treated as such. The soul is reinvoked into its body much as Śiva will be later invoked into the liṅga.

The imposition of mantras onto the worshiper's purified body reconstitutes it as a body of powers, a divine body appropriate to the soul that has become a Śiva. As indicated in the previous chapter, this successive imposition of mantras invokes the form and powers of Śiva onto the body: most important among these, the five *brahmamantras* invoke the five faces of Sadāśiva, identified with Śiva's five fundamental activities, and the six *aṅgamantras* impose Śiva's powers. At one level this rite constructs for the worshiper a body like that of Śiva, saturated with the same mantra powers, capable of carrying out the ritual actions to follow. At a second level, these mantra powers may be seen as external forms of the soul's own intrinsic powers, the realization of the soul's Śiva-ness as a divine body.

During initiation, six perfections—aspects of the soul's *śivatva*—are produced or animated while the novice's soul is united with Paramaśiva. Here the divine powers are imposed after the soul has been returned to its body. In initiation the qualities appear to arise from the soul, animated by fire oblations; here the powers are imposed from the outside onto the body, invoked through mantras.

Yet beneath these differences, the powers themselves appear to be the same. At the least, there is a parallel between Śiva's six divine powers represented by the *aṅgamantras* and the six perfections of the soul. The *aṅgamantras* are often described as embodying specific divine qualities of Śiva, as in this passage from *Kāmikāgama*.

> HṚD is his existence, and ŚIRAS is his lofty preeminence. ŚIKHĀ is his independence. KAVACA would be his protective powers. ASTRA is the power by which he annihilates. NETRA is his power of omniscience, which illuminates everything. Thus the six perfections of the creator of the world, Śiva, are stated here. (*KĀ* 4.363–65)

The imposition of *aṅgamantras* in *ātmaśuddhi* invokes Śiva's powers onto the worshiper. These powers are the same in character as the inherent powers of his soul, the divine qualities animated during initiation. Īśānaśiva points to this connection when he speaks of the soul's perfections produced in initiation as "limbs" (*aṅga*) that "belong to Śiva" as well. "Meditating that the pupil has become a Śiva, the guru should produce the six perfections, which are limbs, and which belong to Śiva" (*ĪP* 3 p. 185). The divine qualities of the soul, animated in initiation, are parallel to the powers of Śiva imposed onto the worshiper's body in *ātmaśuddhi*.[17] Both make manifest the soul's inherent *śivatva*, which is able to emerge when the fetters suppressing it have been removed.

Last Rites

The soul's passage to final liberation, to becoming a Śiva permanently, is brought about by removing its fetters and enabling its inherent powers to manifest themselves. It is a long process. A gradual evolution of the fetters eventually brings the soul to a state where it is ready to undergo *nirvāṇadīkṣā*. Initiation effects an enormous alteration in the soul's condition, destroying completely *karman* that otherwise would condemn the soul to many future rebirths. Yet even after initiation the passage is still not complete. Due to the remaining *prārabdhakarman*, the soul must remain in its body until all *karman* already in motion has been consumed. During this period, the daily performance of *pūjā* and particularly of *ātmaśuddhi* removes or resists any fetters that might arise from day-to-day living. This regular rehearsing of the soul's liberation, performed every day from initiation to death, gradually prepares the initiated Śaiva to become a Śiva permanently.

Even this is not enough. One final ritual remains to insure that the aspirant attains final liberation: the cremation of the body upon death (*antyeṣṭi*).[18]

Śaivas identify death as the moment when a person completes the consumption of *prārabdhakarman*, the *karman* conditioning the present lifetime. For the seeker of *mokṣa* who has undergone *nirvāṇadīkṣā* and who has diligently observed proper conduct thereafter, this completion should signal the final extinction of all *karman*, and hence of all fetters. "And so, for one on whom Śiva's Śakti falls strongly due to the complete ripening of his *mala*, and who has no deficiency in his initiation, and who does not transgress the common rule of conduct—for him, *mokṣa* occurs immediately upon bodily death" (*TST* 39). But it is difficult to be sure. There is a danger that omissions or ritual oversights may have occurred.

Śaivas regard the ritual of cremation primarily as an "expiation" (*prāyaścitta*). It expiates any *karman* the subject may have contracted through ritual errors, such as "deficiencies" in one's initiation or "transgressions" of proper conduct thereafter. And by removing any lingering fetters the deceased may have unintentionally or unknowingly gained, cremation becomes the final door to liberation. As the *Rauravāgama* defines it, cremation is the "sacrifice" (*iṣṭi*) that leads to the "final" (*antya*) state, the supreme state of Śiva-hood (*RĀ* 46.1–2).

Cremation necessarily involves, first of all, the incineration of the corpse (*śavadāha*) in a sacrificial fire. After suitable purifications and preparations, the body of the deceased is placed on a funeral pyre. The sacrificial fire Agni, identified as a form of Śiva's power of reabsorption, then consumes the body. In the conflagration, all the *māyā*-derived elements that previously constituted the body are reabsorbed into their sources. The soul becomes free of its embodiment, which has acted as a force of bondage upon it throughout its lifetime.

More important, from the Śaiva point of view, the ceremony of cremation also provides an opportunity to reenact the *nirvāṇadīkṣā* of the deceased. Since cremation is an expiation that removes finally any remaining fetters, what better way to accomplish this than by repeating the most powerful liberating ritual in the Śaiva system right in the middle of the funeral rites. This embedded initiation involves a condensed repetition of the most essential ritual actions of the *nirvāṇadīkṣā* previously performed on the living initiate, this time administered to his corpse.

Just before the body is placed atop the funeral pyre, the officiating priest begins the rites of crematory initiation by capturing the errant soul with the "Great Net" mantra and restoring it to the corpse. Then, just as in *nirvāṇadīkṣā*, he transfers all constituents from the body of the deceased and imposes them onto a cord of fetters. He follows exactly the same set of purificatory actions as in *kalāśuddhi*, consuming and destroying one by one all the fetters in the Śiva-Agni fire, until they are completely annihilated. This time, the *prārabdhakarman* has also been extinguished. Then the guru transports the soul of the deceased upward and unites it with Paramaśiva, where its divine qualities may fully emerge. In crematory initiation, however, unlike in *nirvāṇadīkṣā*, there is no subsequent need to remove the soul from the presence of Śiva and return it to the body. Rather, the guru simply leaves the soul where it is, in the state of Śiva, and burns the corpse like a heap of cotton.

Through this final ritual recapitulation of initiation, all obstacles to liberation are overcome. Every bit of the soul's *karman* has now been consumed; the potter's wheel finally stops spinning. The soul is released, fully liberated from all bondage, and attains permanently what it has repeatedly experienced temporarily through ritual practice, the highest ontological state of being a Śiva.

CHAPTER FOUR

Summoning the Lord

THE LORD ŚIVA is not limited the way we humans are. Theological descriptions of Śiva emphasize that the many limitations we experience as embodied human beings in a state of bondage do not in any way affect Śiva. Human beings are limited in time; Śiva is eternal, without beginning, middle, or end. Our human bodies are confined in space; Śiva is pervasive, omnipresent. As *paśus*, we are constrained by fetters; Śiva is eternally without *mala*, liberated without beginning. Humans are characteristically agitated by psychic disturbances, alternately attracted and repulsed by the things of the world; Śiva is completely calm. We humans are always dependent on and subordinate to other beings; Śiva is the one completely independent, autonomous being. Humans possess finite capacities; Śiva's powers of knowledge and action are infinite. Ultimately, Śiva is not bounded even by our capacity to conceptualize him. Śiva is the one "whose domain surpasses our speech and mind."

Such a transcendent god cannot, according to Śaiva siddhānta, be worshiped directly. He cannot be said to have a particular form, and it is not possible for humans to meditate upon or offer worship to a completely formless being. According to a text quoted by Aghoraśiva, "It is only to the extent that You possess a visible form that one is able to approach You. The intellect cannot approach something lacking any visible form."[1] Yet for Śaiva worship to take place, it is absolutely necessary that Śiva enter into the ritual domain. He must be present to receive the offerings of his worshiper.

This is the problem at the heart of invocation (*āvāhana*): how does one summon a divinity that is by definition limitless into a limited sphere of ritual, so that a bound human of limited powers may offer him worship? The problem is both theological and procedural, a concern for both knowledge and action. And the solution Śaiva siddhānta texts offer, likewise, provides both a way of knowing Śiva and of invoking his presence.

THE THEOLOGY OF ŚIVA'S PRESENCE

In its description of Śiva's "inherent form," the *Ajitāgama* pointedly proclaims that he is "not bound by space, time, or the like" and that "his domain surpasses speech and mind" (*AĀ* 2.26–27). Similarly, the *Svāyambhuvāgama* describes Śiva's "essence" (*tattva*) as "unfathomable, indescribable, incomparable, without defect, subtle, pervasive, eternal, firm, imperishable, and lordly."[2] As Śivāgrayogin elaborates,

> Śiva is unfathomable because he is without end; indescribable because he is not to be characterized (*alakṣya*); incomparable because there is nothing like him; without defect because he has no *mala*; subtle because he is not perceivable (*anupalabhya*); pervasive because ubiquitous; eternal because he is devoid of cause; firm because unmoving; imperishable because he is complete; lordly because he is master of the world. (*ŚPbh* p. 62)

The emphasis that Śaiva theology places on the unlimited qualities of Śiva raises a difficult question concerning human access to Śiva. Characterizations of Śiva place him in a domain far beyond human powers of knowing and acting. If Śiva is unfathomable, indescribable, incomparable, and imperceivable, what means do we have to know him? How can we offer worship to a god who is imperceivable, pervasive, unmoving, and complete? How do humans of limited powers gain access to one who surpasses all limits?

Two Levels of Śiva

The only ultimate resolution of this enigma lies in the liberation of the soul. When the soul attains *mokṣa*, the limitations that normally inhibit its powers are removed, and the soul is able to approach Śiva fully, just as he is. (Yet in liberation, the *āgamas* remind us, one "does nothing" because "there is nothing to be done."[3] Offering *pūjā*, for instance, is an act appropriate to bound souls, not to liberated ones.) Since we are not liberated, however, it is necessary to address the quandary posed by Śiva's unlimited nature and our limited powers from the perspective of bondage. Human knowledge and action presuppose limitation, yet it is nevertheless crucial for us to approximate the infinite as best we can.

Śaiva philosophers deal with the epistemological problem by first distinguishing two levels of Śiva. The first level, said to be true in the highest sense (*paramārthika*), is the limitless, transcendent Paramaśiva ("Highest Śiva") described in the passages above: a formless, undifferentiated Paramaśiva "without parts" (*niṣkala*). Positive knowledge of Śiva at this level is beyond human reach. Śiva is said to be "unfathomable," the *Vātulāgama* tells us, "because he surpasses every human means of knowledge."[4] The *Acintyāgama* elaborates, "Śiva's highest nature cannot be known through observation (*adhyakṣa*), nor from its marks (*liṅga*), nor through verbal authority (*śabda*)."[5] Descriptions of Paramaśiva are therefore essentially negative ones, pointing to the absence of any limiting qualities.

Similarly, worship of Śiva at this level is impossible. "It is not possible," says Aghoraśiva, "to meditate on or give worship and the like to an entity without form" (*TPV* 6). Considered in his highest state, Paramaśiva surpasses the capacities of bound *paśus*.

The second level of Śiva, true only as a partial approximation or synecdoche (*upacāra*), is Śiva as he is understood to manifest himself and act in multiple ways upon the world: a differentiated Śiva "with parts" (*sakala*). The *āgamas* stress the completeness of Śiva's activities affecting the world and everything in it. He is the "unique seed of the world," that is, the instrumental cause of all creation (*TP* 1), and the one who grants all grace. He performs the five fundamental activities that set in motion the most essential processes of the cosmos and of souls.

It is through this active presence in the world that Śiva becomes accessible to humans. Embodied souls do not generally perceive Śiva's activities directly, but we are able to observe the many effects resulting from his activities and to relate these effects to particularized aspects of his character. Śiva's effects on the world are pervasive and multifarious, and we posit a differentiated Śiva composed of many parts to account for these. Hypostatizing his activities, we may speak of the "powers" he uses to act and to know, the "faces" with which he carries out the five fundamental activities, the "limbs" whereby he acts upon the world.

We know Śiva, then, through synecdoche and through partial approximation. Bhojadeva summarizes the two levels of Śiva in this way: "In an ultimate sense, the entity we call Śiva is one, inlaid with hundreds of various powers. We postulate his divisions due to the diverse actions of his powers" (*TP* 33). Commenting on this passage, Aghoraśiva elaborates: "Due to the diverse activities of Śiva's powers, we postulate his divisions such as Sadāśiva and so on as a synecdoche, but this postulation (*kālpanika*) is not true in the highest sense (*paramārtha*)" (*TPV* 33). Humans are able to know and act toward this secondary, particularized Śiva precisely because names and forms are applied to partial facets of a single integrated divinity. In this way Śiva is given a metaphorical "body" that we are able to meditate upon and worship.

This epistemological division in our conceptualization of Śiva's character has no ultimate effect on Śiva himself, of course. Śiva's ontology encompasses both levels. The texts point out that Śiva is not only both "without parts" and "with parts," but also "both with and without parts" (*sakalaniṣkala*). With Śiva, there can be no contradiction between transcendence and activity, nor between states of integration and differentiation. The distinction we make between two levels is only an apparent one (*upādhi*); it is not fundamental. Śiva surpasses these conceptual categories as well.

Śiva's Multiple Forms

Philosophical texts may caution us that the secondary Śiva "with parts" is not the highest aspect of Śiva. Nevertheless, since it is through this aspect that humans are able to comprehend Śiva and act toward him, this secondary level is of intense interest. The *āgamas*, in fact, speak of several different forms by which we are able to approach Śiva.

The most comprehensive differentiated form of Śiva is known as Sadāśiva, the "Eternal Śiva." Sadāśiva is virtually identical with Śiva's five fundamental activities. Śiva accomplishes his most far-reaching effects on the cosmos, we have seen, through five activities: emission, protection, reabsorption, concealment, and grace. Yet it is not possible to act without a "body" of some sort. Accordingly, even Śiva must employ an instrument (*kāraṇa*) to accomplish his purposes. For each fundamental activity, Śiva uses a corresponding mantra power: for emission the mantra is SADYOJĀTA, for preservation it is VĀMA, and so on. The five mantras through which Śiva carries out his most profound operations in the world, collectively known as the five *brahmamantras*, constitute the five "faces" of Sadāśiva. Thus, Sadāśiva represents Śiva's most fundamental presence in the world, the "body of mantras" with which Śiva acts. "As the soul comes and goes by means of the body, so one must acknowledge that Śiva comes and goes through his body of mantras" (*KĀ* 4.356). Or as Rāmakaṇṭha succinctly puts it, "Śiva does everything using Sadāśiva as his body" (*KālĀV* 22.2–4).

The Sadāśiva body is emphatically not a body like those of humans. It is made of mantras or of powers, and it is completely without bondage, which is the determining feature of human bodies. In *Sarvadarśanasaṃgraha*, Mādhava admirably summarizes the conception of Sadāśiva in his discussion of Śaiva siddhānta philosophy:

> The body of Parameśvara is not a common (*prākṛta*) one, since the net of fetters—*mala*, *karman*, and the others—is absent from it. Rather, it is a body of powers (*śākta*), since its heads and other parts are composed of the five mantras beginning with ĪŚĀNA, which have the forms of Śaktis. As is generally known, Śiva has ĪŚĀNA as his heads, TATPURUṢA for faces, AGHORA as heart, VĀMA for genitals, and SADYOJĀTA as feet. And his body, which is not like our bodies, is the instrument fashioned by his own will with which he performs the five fundamental activities: grace, veiling, reabsorption, maintenance, and emission, in that order. (*SDS* 7.57–63)[6]

As Mādhava's description implies, it is not strictly accurate (though for us it will be linguistically convenient) to refer to this body of powers as "Sadāśiva's body," as if Sadāśiva were a distinct being possessing a body. Rather, the mantra-constituted body is Sadāśiva, and it is an instrumental part of the larger, encompassing Śiva that Mādhava refers to as the "Highest Lord" Parameśvara.

Uncommon though it may be, this Sadāśiva body is nevertheless accessible to humans; it can be visualized and worshiped. We can give specific visual form to Sadāśiva in meditation, impose this form onto some physical support, and present offerings to it. As we will see, Sadāśiva's body of mantras, imposed onto the liṅga, serves as the embodiment that the highest, inaccessible Śiva comes to inhabit during daily worship. Sadāśiva thereby stands at the meeting point between Paramaśiva and his human worshipers in Śaiva ritual.

While material representations of Sadāśiva are comparatively rare in Śaiva temples, he does have a form (or forms) that humans may perceive through a process of visualization (*bhāvanā*).[7] Sadāśiva is most often portrayed as a single divinity with five-faces and ten arms.

> One should meditate that Sadāśiva has five faces, ten arms, and three eyes [in each face]. Crystal in color and calm, he has a crescent moon as his crest, and his hair is fastened with a snake. His seat is a lion-throne made of mantras, and he sits atop a white lotus. Ornamented with bracelets, earrings, necklaces, the auspicious thread, waistbands, upper-arm bracelets, golden bracelets, and chest-bands, he is a lovely, tranquil, smiling sixteen-year-old. In his right hands he holds trident, axe, sword, thunderbolt, and fire; the *mudrā* of security and the noose, along with the bell, snake, and hook, are in his five left hands. (*KĀ* 4.329–34)

Each of the five faces can be visualized individually, either as separate visages of a single body or as independent figures. In addition, each mantra is associated with a portion of the body, arranged hierarchically: IŚĀNA is located at the head, TATPURUṢA at the mouth, and so on, as Mādhava outlined.

Śiva's capacities for action in the world are also instantiated in his six "limbs" (*aṅga*), corresponding to the six *aṅgamantras*. These limbs, like the rays of the sun, are intrinsic extensions of Śiva's being by which he accomplishes his aims.[8]

> Just as fire and the sun are powerful because of their rays, Śiva is likewise invincible and all-performing because of his limbs, which arise from his inherent nature (*svabhāva*). The heart (HṚD) is existence, and his head (ŚIRAS) is his lofty preeminence. His topknot (ŚIKHĀ) is his autonomy. His armor (KAVACA) would be his protective powers. His weapon (ASTRA) is the power by which he annihilates. The eye (NETRA) is his power of omniscience, which illuminates everything. Thus the six divine qualities of the creator of the world, Śiva, are stated here. (*KĀ* 4.362–65)

When the body of Sadāśiva is visualized and constructed in ritual, these limbs are superimposed onto it as additional enhancements of his being.

Sadāśiva's powers are also specified by the panoply of "weapons" (*āyudha*) he carries. According to one typical list, Sadāśiva holds in his five right hands the trident, axe, sword, thunderbolt, and fire, and in his left hands he holds the snake, noose, bell, *mudrā* of security, and hook (*KĀ* 4.332–33). However, Nirmalamaṇi warns us, we should not imagine these to be everyday weapons of violence. Rather, these are weapons of grace; Śiva uses them to destroy the bonds that ensnare the soul (*KKDP* pp. 100–101). When visualizing Sadāśiva, the worshiper meditates on them not simply as physical weapons, but in their inherent form of being (*bhūtasvarūpa*), as aspects of Śiva's power.[9]

> His three-pronged trident is called the three qualities, and the axe is said to be existence. The sword would be the radiance of his lordship. The thunderbolt is his indivisibility. The fire is the power of reabsorption, which reduces fetters to ashes and illuminates the *tattvas* which lie above *mahāmāyā*. Holding the snake indicates his power to accomplish everything. His noose is the three fetters, known as *māyā*, *karman*, and *mala*. The bell represents undifferentiated sound (*nāda*), denoting his mantra-body. The *mudrā* of security is his power to protect all creatures. His hook represents the rule by which the soul obtains the consequences resulting from previous actions. (*KĀ* 4.335–39)

Sadāśiva is the form that, for Śaiva theologians, most closely approximates the totality of Śiva's active presence in the world. His several superimposed layers of mantras and powers successively manifest portions of Śiva's presence: the five faces accomplish the five fundamental activities, the six limbs extend his capacities, and the ten weapons enable him to grant grace. Ultimately, even Sadāśiva is a synecdoche for Śiva's complete nature, but it is the most comprehensive such form accessible to human powers.

Sadāśiva is not the only form in which humans may perceive Śiva. As Maheśvara (the "Great Lord"), Śiva takes on many aspects or embodiments that are also manifest to humans. These aspects are distinct, individual forms of Śiva related to particular aspects of his being or to his specific exploits in the world, and they are familiar to us through the iconic statuary of Indian images and through the narrative descriptions of the *purāṇas*.[10] The *Rauravāgama*, for instance, lists and describes thirteen typical forms of Maheśvara: Sukhāsana, Someśa, Somāskanda, Vṛṣārūḍha, Tripurāri, Candraśekhara, Kālahāri, Kalyāṇasundara, Nṛttamūrti, Bhikṣātana, Kaṅkāla, Ardhanāri, and Dakṣiṇāmūrti.[11]

Where Sadāśiva is a comprehensive body of Śiva, the forms of Maheśvara are partial embodiments or aspects of Śiva's character. Of Maheśvara's multiple forms, some specialize in emission, others in preservation, and still others in reabsorption. "First Somāskanda, then Sukhāsana, and Kalyāṇasundara, Candraśekhara, Gaṅgādhāra—these five are called the 'emitting embodiments' (*sṛṣṭimūrti*). Vṛṣabhavāhana, Ardhanāri, Kirāṭa, Vīreśa, and finally Bhikṣātana are the five forms called 'preserving embodiments.'"[12] Forms in which Śiva carries out his more destructive activities, such as Tripurāri and Kālahāri, represent his "reabsorptive embodiment." Partial is always inferior to whole, so these individualized forms are distinctly ancillary to Sadāśiva. Forms of Maheśvara are not generally central liturgical objects, but they do serve as iconic representations of Śiva within the scheme of any large Śaiva temple. A collectivity of these partial aspects of Śiva's totality, situated at appropriate places within the temple complex, further specifies his comprehensive character and makes it accessible to his devotee.

In addition to these particularized bodily forms by which Śiva acts, he also employs an energy or "instrument" (*kāraṇa*) to accomplish his ends. This instrument of unlimited efficacy is known as Śakti: "By means of that instrument which is Śakti, Śiva becomes powerful (*śākta*), that is, capable of accomplishing the five fundamental activities so that the souls may achieve worldly pleasures and liberation" (*TPV* 3). Arising intrinsically from Śiva as heat arises from fire, Śakti is essentially one, undifferentiated and without form. Like Śiva, however, Śakti must perform many tasks in a variegated creation, and to do so she assumes a plethora of appropriate forms. When things are to be known (*jñeya*), Śiva's energy adopts the form of Jñānaśakti; when actions are to be undertaken (*kārya*), it appears as Kriyāśakti. According to one common classification, Śakti has five principal, hierarchically ranked forms: Parāśakti, Ādiśakti, Icchāśakti, Jñānaśakti, and Kriyāśakti. In accomplishing the five fundamental activities, the five *brahmamantras* are said to have the "form of Śaktis." Another group of eight Śaktis act as the governors of the Vidyeśvaras, divine agents of Śiva. The thirty-eight *kalās*, or "portions" of Sadāśiva, are Śaktis that differentiate and constitute the active body of Śiva's highest manifest form. These forms of Śakti and other, still more differentiated Śaktis are particularized aspects of a unitary Energy that adapts itself with infinite flexibility to the many circumstances of its activities.

This portrait of Śiva's bodies and his powers still does not depict completely his active presence in the world, since Śiva does not always carry out his activities himself. He often acts through agents (*adhikārin*), whom he instigates (*preraṇa*) to act on his behalf, as an imperial king assigns lesser kings to perform the functions of sovereignty in smaller, encompassed portions of the kingdom. These subordinate lords enact Śiva's universal lordship in specific domains or parts of the world.

Śiva's agents are separate beings, not aspects of Śiva. They are distinct souls whose fetters are almost completely removed, and whose powers of knowledge and action have been activated or enhanced by their proximity to liberation, enabling them to carry out the assignment (*adhikāra*) given them by Śiva. Most powerful among them are the eight Vidyeśvaras. These "lords of lords of kings of kings," as *Mṛgendrāgama* calls them, and particularly their leader, Ananta, act as Śiva's agents over the entire impure domain. "In the pure domain, Śiva is called creator; in the impure, Ananta is the Lord" (*KirĀ vidyā* 3.27). Each Vidyeśvara is presided over or governed (*adhiṣṭhita*) by one of Śiva's eight Śaktis. The Vidyeśvaras in turn rule over a variety of subordinate lords—Maṇḍaleśvaras, Mantreśvaras, Bhuvaneśvaras, World Guardians, and so on—who exercise sovereignty in more restricted domains. One group of Maṇḍaleśvaras particularly important in ritual is the group of five Kāraṇeśvaras: Brahman, Viṣṇu, Rudra, Maheśvara, and Sadāśiva. These lords govern the domains of the five *kalās* and appear wherever the *kalās* are. Śiva's lordship is thus differentiated as it extends into particularized parts of the world.

Śiva's Special Presence

The specific purpose of invocation is to summon Śiva to enter into a particular form for the duration of the ritual so that the worshiper may offer his services. The analogy used most frequently in the *āgamas* to conceptualize this process is that of a soul entering a human body. Śiva, like the soul, is essentially consciousness (*cit*), while the liṅga, like the body, is composed of inanimate substance (*jaḍa*). When properly invoked, Śiva enters into the transformed liṅga as a soul penetrates a newly born human body.

Yet this very notion of entrance, implying that Śiva might have previously been absent, raises a philosophical objection. It seems to contradict Śiva's pervasiveness. As the sages ask Śiva in *Kāmikāgama*, "How is it, O Lord, that one can invoke Śiva who is omnipresent? If one acknowledges invocation, this would contradict his omnipresence" (*KĀ* 4.354). Is Śiva not already in the object into which he is summoned? If not, then he would not be pervasive. But if he is already present, what is the point of invoking him? How can Śiva enter into an object when he is already there?

To solve this apparent dilemma, the *āgamas* distinguish two degrees of Śiva's presence. Śiva is indeed present everywhere, but in some places he is more present than in others. Invocation is a rite that enhances or manifests (*abhivyakti*) Śiva's presence in some particular location. It establishes a special or "marked" presence (*viśiṣṭa saṃnidhāna*) of Śiva, or makes him "evident" (*āvirbhāva*) in a liṅga (*MPĀV kriyā* 3.26–29, *AĀ* 20.179). It persuades Śiva to "face toward" or to "be favorable toward" (*abhimukha, sammukha*) the worshiper. Though Śiva is already in the object, invocation in some sense alters the scope or intensity of his presence.

To describe this alteration, many Śaiva siddhānta texts cite an analogy comparing invocation to kindling fire in wood.

> As fire, though present in a tree from its root to its tip, may become manifest in one place, just so the manifestation of consciousness in one place does not contradict its pervasiveness. Just as fire is made to arise in wood by rubbing it and so on, Śiva is manifested through the power of mantras and through devotion. (*KĀ* 4.355, 352)

Fire pervades wood in a latent or potential form. Kindling a flame through friction alters the character of the fire already present from latent to active, from immanent to manifest. Invocation likewise activates or manifests Śiva, who is already present in the liṅga as he is present everywhere.

A second analogy, given by the monist author Appayadīksita, concerns embers whose glow is obscured by a covering of ash. "One may manifest a heap of burning embers covered with ashes, even though the embers glow by themselves" (*ŚAC* p. 65). Similarly, invocation brings about a change in the palpability of Śiva's presence. Blowing away ashes to reveal the burning embers does not alter the character of the fire itself. Rather, it makes the embers evident. It discloses the presence of a fire that was previously hidden. Invocation likewise reveals to the worshiper the presence of Śiva where before he had been inaccessible to the worshiper's perception.

Invocation, then, is understood as a rite that makes Śiva's presence within the ritual domain "manifest" in two senses of that word. It alters the character of his presence from latent to active, and it changes the worshiper's awareness of Śiva's presence, disclosing what was previously concealed.

Supports for Śiva

Considering Śiva's all-pervading presence and unlimited potentiality, it is not surprising that he can manifest his special presence in many different material forms: not just in icons, but also in pots, flowers, human bodies, chalk diagrams, fire, and still other objects as well. *Kāmikāgama* provides one list of possible supports for Śiva in *pūjā*. In addition to various types of liṅga, it advises,

> A circular diagram, a painting on cloth, a sketch on a wall, a pedestal-shaped stone consecrated by mantras, fire, water, guru, tree, and so on, a book on its stand, in particular a naturally occurring liṅga-shaped stone or gem, a liṅga formed from sand or some such material, and other objects also are said to be suitable for use as liṅgas. According to circumstances, one may prepare any of these individually in order to worship Śiva. (*KĀ* 4.270–72)

Similarly, in initiation Śiva becomes present in five different supports. He is simultaneously in the diagram on the central altar, in a full water-pot, in the sacrificial fire, in the initiating guru, and finally he comes also to be present in the initiate.[13]

Yet not all supports are equal. Some texts, for instance, distinguish between "subtle" (*sūkṣma*) liṅgas, which are internal, mentally constructed forms, and tangible, "gross" (*sthūla*) ones, which are external and substantive, evincing a clear preference for the more subtle.

> They say there are two types of liṅgas, exterior and interior. The exterior liṅga is tangible, O excellent sages, while the interior one is subtle. Persons devoted to external rituals and sacrifices, and those gratified by worshiping a tangible liṅga,

are themselves gross. The tangible form is only for those unable to visualize. The inner liṅga is not perceptible to the dull-minded person who considers that exterior reality is everything and that nothing else exists. The unstained, unchanging subtle liṅga is just as evident to persons of knowledge, however, as a gross liṅga made of some material like mud or wood is to those who are not practiced in yoga. (*LPur* 75.19–22)

Subtle is always best in the Śaiva siddhānta scheme of things. However, such dismissive characterizations of gross worshipers, as we will see, fail to take into account the careful yogic visualization and knowledge of Śaiva theology necessary to transform even the most tangible liṅga into a ritually suitable embodiment of Śiva. Gross may become subtle, Śiva-like, through proper ritual action.[14]

The texts generally employ a threefold classification of the physical icons most suitable for Śiva's manifestation: undifferentiated (*niṣkala*), differentiated (*sakala*), and mixed (*sakalaniṣkala*). "That which is undifferentiated is called the 'liṅga.' That which is differentiated is termed 'image' (*bera*). The liṅga with faces (*mukhaliṅga*) is a mixture of the two and resembles the liṅga in height and form" (*MM* 33.1–2). An austere upright cylinder, the liṅga is physically nonpartite.[15] An image, by contrast, is an anthropomorphic form with all the characteristic parts and marks of a body. Intermediate between these two forms, the liṅga with faces is in its basic shape and dimensions a liṅga, but with one or, more often, five faces partially emerging from the central shaft in the four cardinal directions. The fifth, upward face is not discernible to humans of limited visual acuity. The three categories of supports are ranked according to the now-familiar criteria of emission and reabsorption, whereby the undifferentiated liṅga is considered superior and the fully partite image is inferior.

Moreover, the texts assert that these different types of icons parallel the three levels or aspects of Śiva's totality.[16] The undifferentiated liṅga, appropriately, corresponds to Śiva in his most encompassing, transcendent, and undifferentiated aspect, Paramaśiva. At the other end, the various human-like images of Śiva, depicting him iconographically as he has acted in the world and appeared to his devotees, correspond to the level of embodiment called Maheśvara. In between, where Śiva is seen halfway between transcendence and manifestation as it were, with five faces appearing from the once-undifferentiated liṅga, the *mukhaliṅga* clearly parallels five-faced Sadāśiva.

Yet the question of accessibility once again arises. While the *āgama*s certainly prefer the undifferentiated liṅga as the support for Śiva par excellence, and a Śaiva temple almost always contains a liṅga as its liturgical center, Śaiva theology tells us that the Paramaśiva represented by the liṅga is beyond human powers of knowing and acting. Conversely, while Śaiva *pūjā* appears to be particularly directed toward Sadāśiva as the fullest form of Śiva

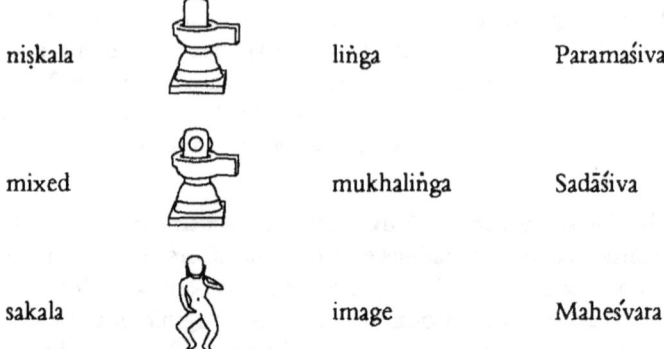

niṣkala	liṅga	Paramaśiva
mixed	mukhaliṅga	Sadāśiva
sakala	image	Maheśvara

Fig. 8. Śiva's supports

accessible to humans, it is quite rare to encounter a *mukhaliṅga* as a central object of worship in a Śaiva temple.

This seeming disjuncture between theology and practice points us to a central fact of *pūjā* as Śaiva siddhānta formulates it. The Śaiva worshiper does not worship the object itself as Śiva or as representing Śiva; he directs his worship toward it as the physical support for Śiva's special presence. And before any object can serve as proper support for Śiva, it must be transformed into a suitably divine, Śiva-like state.

Accordingly, the ritual work of summoning Śiva into the liṅga requires two main actions, the first constructive and the second more strictly invocatory. First the worshiper must impose a series of mantras onto the liṅga and its pedestal, reconstituting them in the process as a divine body seated atop a divine throne. The undifferentiated liṅga is remade into Sadāśiva, in effect. Then and only then, the worshiper may approach Śiva in his highest Paramaśiva state, residing in the *dvādaśānta* twelve inches above the worshiper's crown, and summon him to enter into that ritually prepared embodiment. Śiva in his grace descends, infusing the accessible form of Sadāśiva with the animating energy of Paramaśiva, which normally lies beyond our limited powers.

Invocation of Śiva

After he has purified himself, the place of ritual, the substances to be offered, and the mantras, the worshiper shifts his attention from the suitability of the overall ritual environment to that of the liṅga, the receptacle of Śiva's presence during daily worship. He has now reached the point where he must make ready to summon the Lord to the ritual domain.

Invoking Śiva into the liṅga depends on considerable preparation. Prior to its use in any Śaiva ritual, the liṅga must have been subjected to a detailed ritual "establishment" (*pratiṣṭhā*) that activates it as a fit support for the divinity.[17] A proper stone is located and carefully examined, worked into the appropriate form, and ritually infused with the being of Śiva. A sequence of eighteen distinct rites is required for the complete establishment of a liṅga. This elaborate procedure transmutes the physical, fabricated object into an icon worthy of receiving Śiva's presence, much as initiation enables the initiate to offer worship directly to Śiva. Only after this establishment has been performed may the liṅga be used in worship. It must thereafter be physically purified during each ritual performance, to remove any impurities that may have infected it since the preceding ritual.

Yet establishment and purification of a liṅga are not sufficient in themselves. Before Śiva may be summoned, both the liṅga and its pedestal must be ritually transformed. During each performance of daily worship, the worshiper superimposes a "construction" (*kalpana*) of visualizations and mantras onto the stone icon. Over the pedestal is imposed a "divine throne" (*divyāsana*), and the liṅga is infused with a "divine body" (*divyadeha*) composed of mantras. These superimposed constructions enhance and perfect the physical forms of pedestal and liṅga, transfiguring them into divine ones.

In fashioning these divine forms, the worshiper articulates through his actions a highly concentrated, differentiated, organized theophany of Śiva. Together the divine throne and the body of mantras embody the entire manifest cosmos and the multiple aspects through which Śiva pervades and animates it, compressed as it were onto the physical substratum of pedestal and liṅga.

A ritually constructed body encompassing within its parts the entire differentiated cosmos, of course, hearkens back in India to the Vedic Puruṣa, the cosmic Being whose primordial dismemberment in sacrifice emanated all the multifarious phenomena of the world. Śaiva *purāṇa*s repeatedly assert that Śiva is that Puruṣa, that he has usurped—or rather, has always held—the totalizing role that the Vedic texts claim variously for Puruṣa, Prajāpati, and Brahman. It is no accident, therefore, that this Puruṣa is ritually put back together again, daily, in Śaiva *pūjā*.[18] Only such a comprehensive, divine form can serve as the appropriate support of Śiva's special presence during daily worship.

The Divine Throne

Śiva's divine throne is composed of five individual stages. To construct the throne, the worshiper begins by visualizing, in ascending order, each of these stages. Distributed hierarchically among the throne stages are the thirty-one *tattva*s of the impure domain (*aśuddhādhvan*), from Earth up to *māyā*, as well as *śuddhavidyā*, the lowest constituent of the pure domain.[19] The throne also includes within it other divisions of being: the five *kalā*s, the multiple worlds (*bhuvanas*), the letters of the alphabet, and so on.[20] The divine throne, much like the ritualist's body in the rites of initiation and *ātmaśuddhi*, is a condensed ritual instantiation of the manifest cosmos and all its constituents.

Each stage of the throne has one or more inhabiting powers who act as presiding lords of that stage and all the constituent realities arrayed there. The worshiper visualizes the form of each divinity and then imposes it onto the pedestal, using that lord's proper mantra. Through this sequence of visualizations and impositions of mantras, the pedestal is systematically transformed into a much more comprehensive divine throne fit for the Lord of All Creation.

The worshiper himself ascends toward Śiva as he prepares the divine throne. Before he can honor Śiva directly, he must first worship the differentiated aspects of Śiva's power, the forms through which Śiva acts upon our cosmos. Following the order of reabsorption, which is always the route to approach Śiva, the ritualist passes through all levels of manifest reality and does homage along the way to all manifestations of Śiva's sovereignty. As each upward stage of the divine throne is constructed, the worshiper reaches closer to the place where the highest Lord can be summoned.

The worshiper begins the construction of the divine throne at the floor stone that supports the pedestal. The throne rests on a "tortoise stone" base, and Ādhāraśakti (the "Supporting Śakti") is visualized there, "spotless as a moonbeam, gentle, with four faces and four arms, resembling the milk-ocean" (*KĀ* 4.292).[21] Atop the tortoise stone sits the throne of Ananta (*anantāsana*), the first stage of the divine throne. The worshiper should here imagine the Vidyeśvara Ananta: "indigo-colored, crowned with many hoods, with one face and four arms, hands respectfully folded at his chest, like a lotus arising from the milk-ocean" (*KĀ* 4.293–94).[22]

The next stage is the square lion throne (*siṃhāsana*), with handsome leonine forms stationed at each of its four corners. These lions embody the four lordly powers of Ananta: *dharma*, *jñāna*, *vairāgya* (equanimity), and *aiśvarya* (dominion). The worshiper invokes each royal power onto the corresponding corner of the throne with its mantra. Also located on the lion throne in the cardinal directions are four more lions, which represent the contraries of these powers, *adharma*, *ajñāna*, *avairāgya*, and *anaiśvarya*.

The yoga throne (*yogāsana*) surrounds the lion throne. This stage is frequently omitted, however, and instead two coverings (*chadana*) are placed atop the lion throne, at the boundary between pedestal and liṅga. Not coincidentally, the coverings also serve to separate the impure and pure domains. According to *Kāmikāgama*, these coverings are themselves Śaktis, whose purpose is to bind, liberate, and so on.

Above the two coverings at the very base of the liṅga, the worshiper constructs the lotus throne (*padmāsana*), imagined as a horizontally unfolded lotus of eight petals. The petals, Aghoraśiva tells us, are the eight Vidyeśvaras, and the eight Śaktis that govern the Vidyeśvaras are situated atop the petals in circumambulatory order.[23] "They are brilliant as the rising sun, with three eyes, four arms, and crowns of twisted locks adorned with the crescent moon. With their lotus-hands they hold yak-tail fans, display the *mudrās* of granting boons and security, and cling to Śiva" (*KKD* p. 89). The Śakti Vāmā presides over Ananta on the eastern petal, the Śakti Jyeṣṭhā presides over Sūksma in the southeast, and so on. Various other constituent realities may also be imposed onto the petals: the eight yogic powers, the five elements and three qualities. In the center of the lotus sits Manonmanī, the undifferentiated Śakti of Sadāśiva.

The fifth stage, the stainless throne (*vimalāsana*), is superimposed atop the lotus throne. The worshiper visualizes three concentric *maṇḍalas*: the sun *maṇḍala* on the tips of the petals, the moon *maṇḍala* on the stamen tips, and the fire *maṇḍala* on the perimeter of the pericarp. These *maṇḍalas* are identified with the three categories of impure *tattvas*: *ātman*, *vidyā*, and *śiva*.[24] He invokes onto these *maṇḍalas* their respective presiding deities, the Kāraṇeśvaras Brahman, Viṣṇu, and Rudra. Again, the worshiper may also impose onto the three *maṇḍalas* other groups of three, such as the three qualities, the three sacrificial fires, and the three Śaktis Jñāna, Kriyā, and Icchā. Finally, the worshiper imposes Śakti in her highest form in the middle of the stainless throne, completing the construction of the divine throne. "Thus," says *Kāmikāgama*, "Paramaśiva's throne begins with Śakti and ends with Śakti" (4.313).

throne stage	*inhabiting powers*
stainless throne	Brahman, Viṣṇu, Rudra, Parāśakti
lotus throne	Manonmanī, eight Śaktis, eight Vidyeśvaras
two coverings	unnamed Śaktis
lion throne	four lordly powers, four contrary powers
Ananta's throne	Ananta
tortoise stone	Ādhāraśakti

The divine throne, encompassing all constituents of the impure cosmos, becomes in this way suffused with the powers and agents through which Śiva exercises his sovereignty. The throne that supports him in ritual is imbued with all the energies that support and enact his presence in the world.[25]

Body of Mantras

Only when the divine throne has been fashioned may a divine form sit upon it. As he has transformed the pedestal, the worshiper now superimposes onto the liṅga a divine body, the body of mantras that is in fact Sadāśiva, the most complete form of Śiva humans are able to comprehend and worship.

This body occupies the *tattvas* of the pure domain (*śuddhādhvan*), just as Śiva carries out his activities directly in that portion of the cosmos.

The divine body is composed of mantras, unlike the impure, fettered bodies of humans. It does, however, mirror the divine body that the worshiper has already imposed onto himself in *ātmaśuddhi*. Exactly the same mantras transform the ritualist's body as enhance the liṅga. "He should impose mantras on the deity just as he has imposed them onto his own body," directs *Kāmikāgama* (4.349). The resulting bodily parallelism of ritualist and Śiva reinforces the state of relative equality that the two come to share during worship.

The worshiper begins by visualizing Sadāśiva.[26] "When he has thus constructed Śiva's throne, the priest with firm mind and restrained faculties should fill his cupped hands with flowers, and visualize an embodiment" (*AĀ* 20.158). Following meditation verses like the ones I quoted earlier to describe Sadāśiva, the worshiper imaginatively puts together, portion by portion, a complete portrait of Sadāśiva. He visualizes in order each of the five faces, ten weapons, and so on, then consolidates these parts into a unified image. He next transports the visualization into the liṅga. "When he has visualized the embodiment, the worshiper should then invoke it onto that previously described throne of Śiva, using the flowers in his cupped hands and the MŪRTI mantra" (*AĀ* 20.164–65). The visualization is first transferred into the flowers, which are then scattered atop the liṅga. The constructed embodiment flows from the flowers downward into the liṅga. Simultaneously reciting the mantra of embodiment, MŪRTI, the worshiper invokes into the liṅga the full form that he has mentally constructed. The visualization infuses the liṅga, supplanting it in the mind of the worshiper. "He removes [the physical form of] the liṅga from his imagination, since the shape of the liṅga interferes [with his visualization of Sadāśiva]" (*KKD* p. 99). The physical liṅga has been transformed into the visualized form of Sadāśiva.

The worshiper now imposes the five mantras of Sadāśiva onto their proper locations. On each section of the liṅga, now viewed as the body of Sadāśiva, he places one of the *brahmamantras*: IŚĀNA on the head, TATPURUṢA on the face, and so on in descending order. (See the photographs of *brahmamantranyāsa* onto the liṅga, Plate 5.) He next places the thirty-eight *kalāmantras*, which further articulate the body of Sadāśiva. According to some texts, he then imposes still more mantras: the *aṅgamantras*, the mantras of the alphabet, VYOMAVYĀPIN, and so on. Whatever mantras have been placed on the ritualist's body in *ātmaśuddhi* should also be used here. Finally, the body of Sadāśiva is fully imbued with the powers of mantras, and the worshiper imposes the VIDYĀDEHA mantra, the mantra that unifies and completes this variegated construct.[27]

The body of Sadāśiva, according to *Kāmikāgama* and *Kriyākramadyotikā*, is made up of two aspects, much as a human body is composed of both a subtle and a gross body. These two must be invoked separately into the liṅga. First the worshiper visualizes the "subtle embodiment" (*sūkṣmamūrti*): "an embodiment shaped like a staff of emanating energy (*tejas*), not divided into parts, pervading the highest *bindu* which is identical with the *śiva-tattva*" (*KKD* p. 95). Next the worshiper visualizes and invokes the body of mantras known as *vidyādeha* (literally, "knowledge-body"), the super-anthropomorphic body of Sadāśiva with five faces and ten arms. "In the middle of this embodiment, at the top of the Śiva-liṅga, the priest should impose the *vidyādeha* that is Sadāśiva. This Lord made of pure knowledge is endowed with the thirty-eight *kalā*s, and has a body formed from the *brahmamantra*s and the *aṅgamantras*" (*KĀ* 4.326–27). These two aspects of Sadāśiva's embodiment represent two dimensions of Śiva's active presence. The subtle embodiment corresponds to Śiva's undirected potentiality, the *vidyādeha* to his active engagement in the world.

Throughout the construction of Śiva's divine body, the worshiper follows the order of emission. He invokes first the undifferentiated subtle embodiment, then the differentiated *vidyādeha*. In constructing the *vidyādeha*, he begins with ĪŚĀNA and ends with SADYOJĀTA, following a descending path. After placing the five *brahmamantras*, he imposes the still more differentiated *kalāmantras*, again proceeding from the head down. As indicated earlier, emission is the general order for rites of construction, since ritual construction is a form of emission.

The preparation of liṅga and pedestal for Śiva's presence reconstitutes them as divine forms, which together substantiate an entire cosmos, concentrated within their physical support. Figure 9 summarizes the complex set of impositions that brings this about. First, all *tattva*s that make up the manifest world are distributed between the body and the throne. Second, the forms are imbued with the mantras and powers that preside over these two

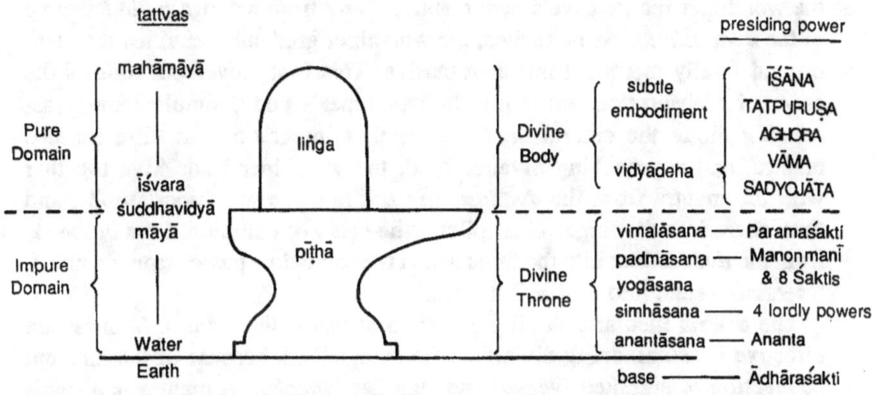

Fig. 9. Divine throne and divine body

domains. Onto the divine throne, composed of the impure *tattvas*, the worshiper invokes the multiple Śaktis and agents that govern the lower domain. The divine body is that of Sadāśiva, the body of mantras with which Śiva acts directly in the pure domain.

Ascent of the Mantra

Complete as they are, the divine body and throne remain inanimate until Śiva himself enters. The central ritual act of invocation remains: to lead Śiva into form. Śiva in his highest aspect as animating consciousness must be summoned to inhabit and enliven his divine body.

The divine body is a highly differentiated embodiment of Śiva's active powers. Yet in his highest state, Śiva is undifferentiated. To enter into this constructed form, Śiva must be led from his undifferentiated realm into a particularized body.

> When he has constructed this body of powers, the worshiper should make undifferentiated Śiva—the highest cause of this world, constant, eternal, consisting in knowledge, joy, and pleasure, pervading every *tattva*, immeasurable and incomparable, free from signifier and signified, whose domain surpasses our powers of speech and cognition—specially manifest in a differentiated form, compelling him there with the ŚIVA mantra accompanied by the *mudrās* of invocation and so on. (*KĀ* 4.349–51)

Śiva descends from his formless state in the *dvādaśānta* into the differentiated body superimposed onto the liṅga. It is a passage by which unknowable, unworshipable Paramaśiva unites with and infuses the more accessible Sadāśiva.

To effect this passage requires two converse ritual movements: an ascent by the worshiper to approach Śiva, and a descent of Śiva into the liṅga. First, the worshiper recites Śiva's own mantra, rising from his own *mūlādhāra* up to the *dvādaśānta*. As he recites, the worshiper gradually reunifies the mantra and finally merges it into Paramaśiva. This first movement follows the order of reabsorption traversing the worshiper's body: simultaneously ascending along the central breath channel, reintegrating the differentiated mantra, and approaching Śiva. Second, the worshiper leads Śiva together with the mantra from the *dvādaśānta* back into the worshiper's body, and from there into the liṅga. This follows the order of emission. Śiva descends from the *dvādaśānta* into the liṅga and at the same time passes from an undifferentiated state into a manifest form.

The central mediator in all Śaiva invocations is the mantra. Mantras are effective for summoning divinities, the texts tell us, because of the inherent connection of signified (*vācya*) and signifier (*vācaka*). A mantra is a signifier, and the divinity to which it refers is its signified. The two are part of the same reality; the mantra is often called the "form" or the sonant aspect of the divinity that it signifies. Thus, reciting the mantra of a divinity can automatically render that divinity present.

When invoking Śiva, the worshiper recites the MŪLA ("root") mantra, "Oṃ hauṃ, I bow to Śiva." Also referred to as ŚIVA and PRĀSĀDA ("lofty"), this mantra signifies Śiva in his totality.[28] For that reason it is the most important and most powerful of all mantras.

The worshiper employs the technique called "ascending pronunciation" (*uccāraṇa*) when reciting the MŪLA mantra. The term *uccāraṇa* generally means "to raise up" and "to pronounce"; its specialized usage here combines both meanings. This method of pronouncing mantras is used at various points throughout this and other Śaiva rituals, always to reintegrate differentiated unities or to transport things to a higher level of being. In previous chapters we have seen ascending pronunciation utilized to protect the soul during *ātmaśuddhi* by transporting it upward to the *dvādaśānta*, and to merge temporarily the soul of the initiate with Paramaśiva at the conclusion of *nirvānadīkṣā*. It is used also to purify the mantras and to invoke Śiva onto the hands and body during self-purification. According to Appayadīkṣita, the worshiper employs it as well with each offering he makes in daily worship, as will be discussed in the next chapter. In invocation, ascending pronunciation enables the ritualist to reunify the mantra within his own body and finally to merge the reintegrated mantra into the deity that it signifies, Paramaśiva.

Initially the MŪLA mantra is spread out in twelve or sixteen "portions" (*kalā*s again) throughout the worshiper's body, distributed along the vertical axis formed by the central breath channel, and divided by its nodes. Each mantra portion has a name and a physical form or mark. Each extends a particular length in the body, has a characteristic color for purposes of visualization, and is presided over by one of the Kāraṇeśvaras.[29] The first mantra portion, *medhā*, for instance, extends in the worshiper's body a distance of twelve fingers between his navel and his heart. It consists in the sound A or AU of the syllable HAUM (which is the seed-syllable of MŪLA) and is the color of a flaming fire. It is ruled by the lord Brahman. The next mantra portion, *rasa*, situated between the heart and the throat, eight fingers in extent, consists in the sound U and is governed by Viṣṇu. The portions of the mantra reach all the way up to the *dvādaśānta*, twelve fingers above the worshiper's head, where Paramaśiva resides. Figure 10 summarizes the twelve-*kalā* arrangement of the mantra.

Once again, all constituent *tattva*s of the manifest cosmos are contained within this differentiated unity, distributed among the mantra portions. As usual, they are vertically arranged in hierarchical order. All *tattva*s of the impure domain are situated in the three lowest portions, corresponding to the audible portions of the mantra. The five higher *tattva*s of the pure do-

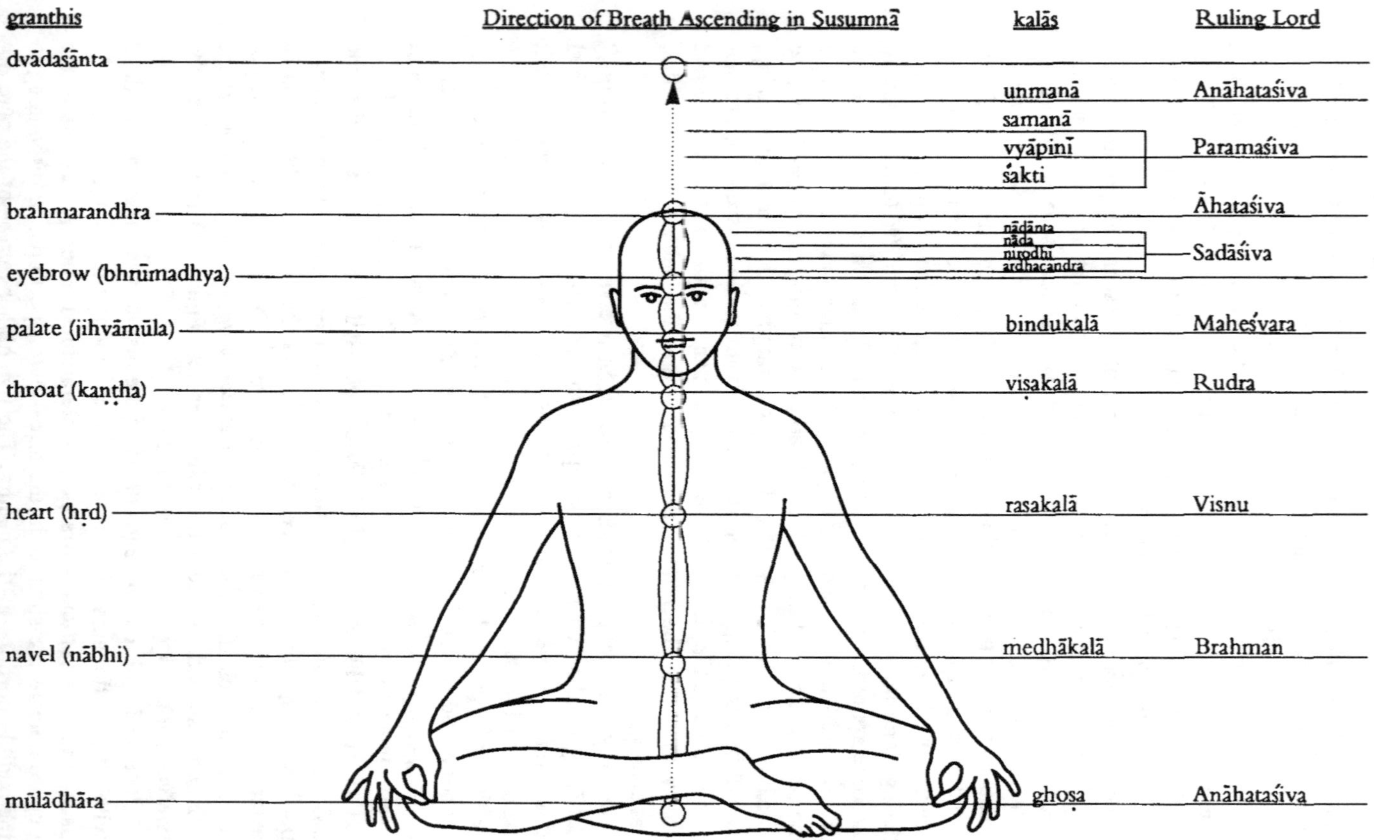

Fig. 11. Locations of the twelve *kalās*

main are located in subtler, inaudible mantra portions. According to Anantaśambhu, the five *kalās* are also contained within the parts of the mantra.

To perform the ascending pronunciation, the worshiper prepares himself physically and mentally.

> He first makes his body firmly upright and restrains his mind and senses, requesting, "I wish to honor with mantras the Lord Īśvara, who is immeasurable, undefinable, without equal, without pain, subtle, ubiquitous, eternal, unchangeable, and imperishable." He fills his body with wind via the *iḍā* and retains it. He places his flower-filled hands in *añjali* at the level of his heart, firmly forming the *mudrā* of invocation. (*ŚAC* p. 61)

Then he begins to recite the seed-syllable of the mantra. He draws out the initial H sound of HAUM from his *mūlādhāra* and begins very gradually to enunciate the portions of the mantra. At the navel, the sound H is united with the sound A of the *medhā* portion. At the heart, this HA is united into the U of *rasa*. At the throat, the sound M is added. Thus all the audible sound components of the HAUM seed-syllable are reunited. As the mantra continues upward, still other subtler, inaudible portions of the mantra are reintegrated. Stage by stage, the portions of the differentiated mantra are reabsorbed into their more fundamental unity.

This ascending movement of reabsorption occurs simultaneously in several dimensions. As the worshiper pronounces the mantra, he directs his breath upward along the *suṣumnā*, dismissing in order the Kāraṇeśvaras along the way. He moves his hands filled with flowers upward, an outward correlate to the inward motion of the breath. He visualizes each mantra portion as well: *medhā* is the color of a flame of fire, *rasa* is like the sun and moon, and so on. While joining together the portions of the mantra, then, the worshiper must also unify his actions. Voice, breath, hand gesture, and mental visualization ascend together. If worship overall requires "the activities of mind, speech, and body," as Sūryabhaṭṭa tells us (*ŚSPbh* p. 37), invocation is a rite in which the ritualist must direct all these activities concurrently in a single direction and toward a single end. (See photograph sequence on *āvāhana*, Plate 6.)[30]

The target of these ascending movements is the *dvādaśānta*, the point of reabsorption (*laya*). Paramaśiva resides there, twelve inches above the ritualist's body as he is also beyond all limitations of form. When the ascending pronunciation reaches the *dvādaśānta*, the fully reintegrated mantra is absorbed into Paramaśiva. The worshiper visualizes Paramaśiva becoming united with the mantra that signifies him. Just as the differentiated portions of the mantra have been reabsorbed into a unity through ascending pronunciation, here the mantra itself is reunited with its referent. The fundamental unity of signifier and signified, mantra and divinity, is restored.

With the union of mantra and Śiva, the ascending phase of invocation is completed. The worshiper has used the MŪLA mantra to approach Śiva at the highest level. Pronouncing the mantra upward, he has reunified the differentiated portions of the mantra and then merged it into Paramaśiva. At the same time he has fused all his own activities—of mind, speech, and body—and directed them along the same path of reabsorption. The whole process, requiring just a single long breath to perform, is itself a compressed metaphor of reintegration.

Śiva's Descent into Form

When Śiva and his mantra are reunited, the worshiper next leads Śiva into the form that has been constructed for him. As Nārāyaṇakaṇṭha puts it, "One should convey Śiva from the *dvādaśānta*, the place where the sound arising from the ascending pronunciation of the mantra ceases, into the embodiment according to the order of emission" (*MṛĀV kriyā* 3.12). The worshiper escorts Śiva by means of the mantra.

Śiva's descent begins with the worshiper meditating on Paramaśiva. "He imagines Paramaśiva: all-accomplishing, undifferentiated, omnipresent, composed of knowledge and joy, intrinsically radiant" (*KKD* p. 101). Visual imaging of the deity is not possible at this level since Paramaśiva transcends form; rather, the ritualist can only call to mind the unlimited qualities of Śiva in his highest state.

Identifying the mantra and Śiva, the worshiper leads Śiva downward from the *dvādaśānta* to the forehead, reversing direction along the same path that the mantra has just ascended. Once again he meditates on Śiva, but now in a more visual form, that of an exceedingly radiant orb. Aghoraśiva tells us that "Śiva there resembles a crore of suns, whitening every direction with pieces of nectar that issue forth" (*KKD* p. 102). Appayadīkṣita describes him at this point as "a thousand flowing moons" (*ŚAC* p. 62). Midway between the *dvādaśānta* and the liṅga, Śiva is neither fully *niṣkala* nor fully *sakala*. He has a visual form that contrasts him with the formless Paramaśiva. Yet the form is a single, undifferentiated glowing circle, not the highly differentiated bodily form of Sadāśiva.

The worshiper next lowers his hands to the level of his heart and exhales. Śiva passes from the forehead along the breath channel and out of the worshiper's body through the right nostril. He enters into the flowers held in the worshiper's hands. Reciting the HṚD mantra, the worshiper places the flowers atop the liṅga, and Śiva enters into the divine body constructed for him, descending from the *brahmarandhra* of the embodiment to its heart. Śiva is now embodied as Sadāśiva, in a differentiated divine body comprised of mantras, yet infused too with the presence of Paramaśiva.

Once Śiva is fully present in the liṅga, the worshiper immediately acts to keep him there. "He establishes him with the *mudrā* of establishment, makes him present with the *mudrā* of presence, and restrains him with the *mudrā* of restraint. He declares, 'Welcome to you, O Great God.' And he imagines the reply of the lord, 'Greetings, my child'" (*KKD* pp. 103–4). The worshiper then humbly requests that Śiva stay: "'O Lord, protector of all the worlds, please remain present in this liṅga until worship is completed, out of your love (*samprīti*)'" (*KKD* p. 104). Even after the elaborate invocatory work he has performed, the Śaiva worshiper still regards Śiva's presence in the liṅga not as a matter of ritual compulsion, but as a manifestation of benevolent disposition, of Śiva's "love." He then offers Śiva the ritually prepared *arghya* water of hospitality, the first of many services he will perform for the manifest Lord before him.

Śiva's Two Levels Reunited

The particular task of invocation, we have seen, is to bring Śiva, who is described theologically as formless and without limit, into a limited form through which the ritualist may worship him. This descent of Śiva is possible because Śiva has more than one level of being. In his highest state, Śiva is inaccessible to human powers. But Śiva has a secondary level, through which he engages in activities and by which he comes within the range of our knowledge and action. Sadāśiva, Śiva's body of mantras, is the most comprehensive form of Śiva at this secondary level.

The rite of invocation treats these two aspects of Śiva's being as ontologically separate entities, then reunifies them within the liṅga. The first set of ritual actions transforms the liṅga and pedestal, the physical supports of Śiva's presence, into divine forms appropriate to Śiva. The worshiper superimposes onto the liṅga a differentiated body of mantras, the precise form of Sadāśiva. This complete embodiment of Śiva's secondary level serves as the form or body that Śiva will inhabit during worship. The second set of rites summons Śiva to enter into this form. The worshiper uses the MŪLA mantra, reintegrated and finally merged into Paramaśiva, to lead Śiva from his highest, undifferentiated state into the limited, particularized body of mantras. Like a soul entering a body, Śiva inhabits and animates the divine body of mantras that the ritualist has constructed for him.

From Śiva's point of view, this entry into form entails an apparent diminishment. Śiva descends from his undifferentiated, all-pervading, formless Paramaśiva state into a differentiated, limited embodiment as Sadāśiva. The diminishment is only apparent, however, since any subtraction from infinity leaves infinity as its remainder. And from the perspective of the human worshiper, Śiva's descent enhances his presence. From an immanent but unknowable and unworshipable divinity, Śiva becomes accessible to the worshiper's powers of knowing and acting. It is this special presence of Śiva in the liṅga that makes possible all subsequent acts of worship. Śiva is made fully manifest, and the worshiper may now begin to offer his services of devotion.

Common Ground

Śaiva daily worship consists, at its core, in a series of transactions between a human worshiper and the god Śiva. Yet in the normal course of things, such transactions appear nearly impossible. The distance between human and god seems insuperable. The human worshiper is a soul encrusted with fetters that seriously impede his power of knowing and acting, and the soul is bound within an impure body that is a kind of congealment of its fetters. Śiva, by contrast, is in his highest state utterly transcendent. Formless, not constrained by any of the limitations that affect humans, Śiva is beyond all human capacities of knowledge and action.

Fortunately, there exist ritual means to bridge this gap. In the two preceding chapters, I have discussed the procedures through which Śaiva daily worship reduces the difference in status between the worshiper and Śiva, thereby enabling them to engage in direct relations with one another. These processes are, strictly speaking, merely necessary preparations for the rites of homage that follow. Yet in another sense they are central to the ritual. They articulate and enact fundamental metaphysical propositions of Śaiva siddhānta, which organize the world of ritual as well as the world itself.

In daily worship, two converging processes of transformation bring the worshiper and Śiva from their very divergent initial states to meet on an equivalent plane of being. The worshiper first transfigures his own body, through the rite of *ātmaśuddhi*, into a body of mantras like that of Sadāśiva. In the process, he enacts the passage by which his soul "becomes a Śiva" in liberation. After transforming himself, the ritualist summons Śiva to enter the liṅga prepared for him. He first superimposes onto the liṅga a body of mantras mirroring his own, and then he uses the MŪLA mantra to lead Śiva from his highest, transcendent state into this body. The formless, inaccessible Paramaśiva becomes embodied as Sadāśiva, a form of Śiva that can be meditated on and worshiped.

These converging paths of transformation, as Figure 11 illustrates, correspond to the orders of reabsorption and emission, respectively. The ritualist moves from outside the temple into the central sanctum. As he does so, he gradually attains a higher state of purity. In the rite of self-purification he systematically reabsorbs all the impure constituents of his body into their pure sources, a process that parallels the long-range passage of his soul toward liberation through the gradual removal of fetters. While invoking

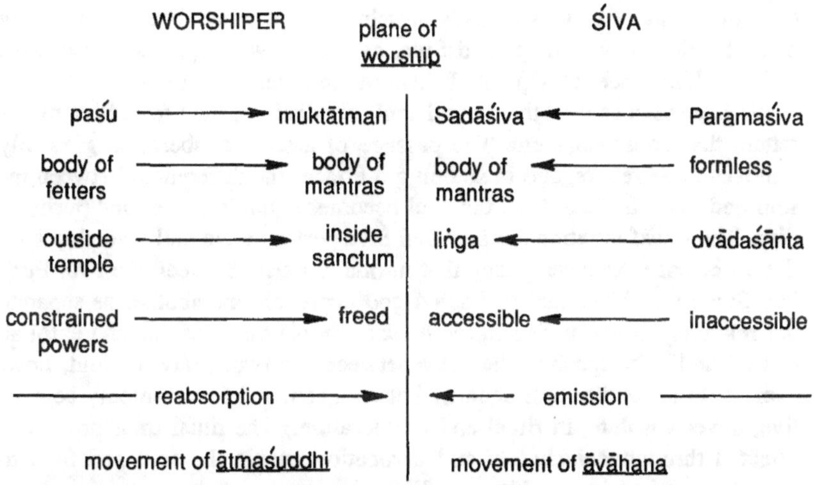

Fig. 11. The meeting of worshiper and Śiva

Śiva, the worshiper again follows the path of reabsorption to approach Śiva, first in constructing the divine throne and then in the ascending pronunciation of the MŪLA mantra. Śiva, on the other hand, descends from the *dvādaśānta* into the liṅga according to the order of emission. In this descent, Śiva passes from the undifferentiated *niṣkala* state to a particularized *sakala* one, from formlessness to embodiment, from completely subtle to relatively gross.

Through these two procedures, the worshiper and Śiva are able to encounter one another on common ground, in a temporary condition of relative equality. No mediator—animal, human, or divine—is necessary, since the distance between the two parties has been ritually negated. In temple worship performed on behalf of others, the priest capable of such self-transformation acts as mediator for those who wish to make offerings to the Lord but who are not able (because not initiated) to engage in direct transactions with Śiva. The worshiper who performs *pūjā* on his own behalf meets with and makes his offerings directly to Śiva.

This pattern of daily worship, by which the worshiper and Śiva follow converging paths to meet on a common ritual plane, parallels the modified dualistic metaphysics of Śaiva siddhānta and contrasts with both monist schools such as Advaita Vedānta and more *bhakti*-oriented dualist schools. Ritual procedures do not negate the fundamental separateness of the worshiper and Śiva but do diminish the adventitious differences between them.

As we have seen, Śaivas presume an ontological separation between souls and Śiva, both before and after liberation. Even when the soul becomes an autonomous Śiva through *mokṣa*, it remains distinct from Śiva. Similarly, the ritual transformations of daily worship do not bring about any merging or unification of worshiper and Śiva, as monist worshipers suppose. Śiva and worshiper meet as separate beings in the domain of ritual.

We have seen as well that bound souls are distinguished from Śiva by the fetters that constrain them. The passage of a soul to liberation gradually removes these fetters, and in so doing it effaces the differences between the soul and Śiva. In liberation, the soul becomes equal in power and purity to Śiva. The transformations of soul and Śiva performed in daily worship similarly decrease the discrepancy that normally exists between the two. Purified Śaiva worshiper and embodied god approach one another as separate but relatively equal, unlike in the *bhakti* schools that presume and extol an eternal and unbridgeable hierarchy between the two. (Śaivas admit, however, that the condition of equality between soul and Śiva can only be relative, never absolute, in ritual and in liberation.) The ritual transformations effected through *ātmaśuddhi* and invocation enable the soul and Śiva to meet face to face in worship as in liberation.

CHAPTER FIVE

Relations of Worship

"THE WORSHIP of Śiva consists in delivering over to a Śiva-liṅga or the like purified substances according to one's own volition, with faith, and accompanied by activities of mind, speech, and body, such as particularly meditations, mantra recitations, and *mudrās*, and accompanied also by the various auxiliaries of worship preceding and following it" (*ŚSPbh* p. 37). As in many Hindu schools of ritual, the Śaiva author Sūryabhaṭṭa defines *pūjā* by its core action: the "delivering over" (*samarpaṇa*) or "presentation" (*dāna*) of substances to the god. He regards other ritual actions such as self-purification and invocation, which have occupied our attention in previous chapters, as "auxiliaries" that establish the setting in which the transactions between human and god may take place. The central and irreducible act of worship occurs only when the worshiper presents his "services" (*upacāra*) or tokens of homage to Śiva.

As with any gift, there are three main participants in the presentation of *pūjā*: the giver, that which is given, and the recipient. The worshiper, as donor, gives substances and services to Śiva, the recipient. For Śaiva siddhānta philosophy, the three parties in the transaction here are, at the same time, the three fundamental categories of the universe. The worshiper who makes the gifts is an embodied soul (*paśu*), the substances given to Śiva are objects of the material cosmos (*pāśa*), and the recipient is the Lord Śiva (*pati*), taking up temporary residence in the liṅga. When the worshiper presents offerings to the liṅga, it is soul, substance, and Śiva that are brought into relation with one another.

The transactions between the worshiper, the offerings, and Śiva during daily worship reflect and express the basic relationships between the three categories of being. For Sūryabhaṭṭa, the essential character (*svabhāva*) of each participant determines the role it assumes during worship. Śiva is the highest Lord, and therefore he is always "to be served" by other conscious beings. So in *pūjā*, Śiva receives the prestations of those dependent beings. The worshiper is a bound soul, inferior and subservient to his Lord, and consequently he should always remain "fixed in service" toward Śiva. Even though the rites of *ātmaśuddhi* and invocation have reduced the difference between worshiper and god, their fundamental hierarchical relation persists. In daily worship the worshiper instantiates in a whole series of offerings and actions his attitude of respectful service. And the offerings themselves are the impure, inanimate derivatives of *māyā*, which "should be delivered over to Śiva's feet" (*ŚSPbh* p. 37).

In its simplest formulation, then, Śaiva siddhānta portrays the transactions of *nityapūjā* as an enactment of the most fundamental relations of the cosmos.

The Three Categories, Interrelated

While Sūryabhaṭṭa is basically correct in his summary, he oversimplifies both the ontological relationships between the three categories of being and also the transactions established between the three participants in worship. The material world, of which worship offerings are a part, cannot simply be "delivered over" to Śiva. Śiva is pure; the material world derived from *māyā* is impure. Śiva's essential nature is *cit*; the material world is made up of *jaḍa*. The relationship between Śiva and substance is too problematic to allow a simple, unmediated delivery of one to the other. Nor can the worshiper act solely and simply as a servant to Śiva. As a bound soul partaking of both consciousness and material fetters, his situation is too ambiguous to allow him the passivity and simplicity of service; his relation to Śiva is more complex than that. In both cases, there are complications in the relations between categories of Śaiva metaphysics that we must examine more closely, both as a theoretical concern of *jñāna* and as a practical matter for the *kriyā* of daily worship.

Śiva and the Material World

As I have described previously, Śaiva metaphysics posits a firm ontological separation between Śiva and the material world. Śiva, whose essential form is consciousness (*cit*), is an animate being whose powers of agency are not constrained by any obstruction. The material world, composed of inanimate substance (*jaḍa*), is inert stuff that acts only when acted upon by some force or agency outside itself. Śiva is essentially one, integral; the material world is a multifarious combination of mixed constituents. Śiva is eternal and tranquil; the material world restlessly oscillates between moments of emission and reabsorption, creation and destruction. The two categories might appear to have nothing in common. Yet they inhabit the same universe and necessarily become involved with one another.

Śaiva philosophy displays two seemingly opposite views concerning the relationship of Śiva with the material world. On the one hand, the texts frequently stress his aloofness from matter. Śiva is, and always has been, free from all blemishes. As the only being "liberated without beginning" (*anādimukta*), Śiva has never been contaminated by any of the fetters that condemn other souls to lifetimes of bondage. Śiva surpasses (*atīta*) or transcends the constituents of material being and thereby maintains his state of utter purity.

On the other hand, texts just as often point to Śiva's ubiquity and to his all-performing agency. Śiva pervades (*vyāpti*) the cosmos; he is omnipresent. If he is present everywhere, Śiva could hardly remain outside all material creation. Similarly, Śiva is the agent (*kartṛ*) of all creation. Through his activities of emission, preservation, and reabsorption, Śiva sets the elements of the material cosmos in motion. Not simply present in creation, Śiva appears to be its most essential controlling agent, the instrumental cause of the material world.

By turns Śiva is said to be aloof and pervasive, outside and within the cosmos. He seems to take a hands-off approach to the created universe, and yet also to involve himself intimately in its most basic processes. How can Śaiva siddhānta reconcile these two apparently contradictory depictions of Śiva's relation to the world of inanimate substance? Does he participate in it, or does he not?

The simplest answer to this apparent dilemma locates it as yet another example of Śiva's incomprehensibility to bound souls. Śiva, after all, "surpasses the purview of speech and mind." It is a measure of his greatness that he encompasses categories or attributes that we with our limited powers of knowledge regard as antithetical. As his exploits narrated in the *purāṇas* also attest, Śiva Maheśvara can be simultaneously auspicious (*śiva*) and fearsome (*raudra*), ascetic and erotic, male and female, and so on. Both purity and pervasion, separation and participation are true attributes of Śiva; the habits of thought by which we see these as incompatible with one another result from our bondage. The problem, to put it most simply, lies in our intellects, not in Śiva's character.

This answer does not fully satisfy the Śaiva siddhāntins, for they develop in greater detail two other theological solutions to the problem of Śiva's participation in matter. These two solutions focus not on the epistemic limitations of *paśus*, but rather on ontological differentiations within the two categories of *pati* and *pāśa*. In both cases, these differentiations play a mediating role; they introduce hierarchized gradations into otherwise distinct categories and thereby enable Śiva to participate and not participate in matter simultaneously.

The first solution has to do with the emanating nature of Śiva's lordship. As discussed in the preceding chapter, Śiva employs many instruments and agencies to carry out his multifarious activities in the world. He makes use to begin with of the seventy million mantras. To perform the five fundamental activities, for instance, he uses the five *brahmamantras* that together constitute the five faces of Sadāśiva. Śakti acts as his "instrument" (*kāraṇa*), taking on many differing forms according to what needs to be done. Śiva also engages the assistance of other powerful beings—Vidyeśvaras, Kāraṇeśvaras, World Guardians, and others of that ilk—to administer his commands in other domains. This theological portrait of Śiva's emanating lordship is best illustrated in the ritual spaces constructed by the worshiper in *nityapūjā*. Śiva sits at the center of these constructions, amidst concentric circles of increasingly active, differentiated entourages. Śiva is still; he acts through these other agencies, which are "drawn out" from him.

By postulating this heuristic distinction between Śiva and the instrumentalities that emanate from him, Śaiva siddhānta is able to describe Śiva as simultaneously "peaceful" (*śānta*) and "all-accomplishing" (*sarvakartṛ*). In himself Śiva remains absolutely aloof from material creation, a transcendent Paramaśiva. Yet to carry out his far-reaching actions in the world, he employs mediating powers and beings, through which he pervades and acts upon every part of the material cosmos, a fully engaged immanent divinity.

This first solution to the paradox of Śiva's presence in the world is important, as we have seen, in the rite of invocation, but it does not have major consequences for the offering of worship. It is the second solution that has greater bearing on the services.

The second solution has to do with gradations of purity and impurity within the material cosmos. Here we must begin with the principle of emission and reabsorption, as outlined in Chapter 2. Generally, we saw, the path of emission moves in a direction of greater differentiation, less subtlety, and greater impurity; the path of reabsorption leads toward integrity, subtlety, and purity. This can be seen clearly in the case of the constituents of the material cosmos, the *tattvas*. At one end of the scale, undifferentiated *māyā* is completely pure; at the other end, the five Elements (*bhūtas*) are extremely impure. The world is made up of a hierarchy of things of greater and lesser purity.

The notion of graduated purity reveals a possibility. If there are portions or states of being within the created cosmos that are completely pure, then Śiva could participate there directly without compromising his own immaculate nature. Śaiva siddhānta, in fact, does envision such domains. For instance, the *āgamas* speak of two separate paths along which the thirty-six *tattvas* are emitted: the "pure path" (*śuddhādhvan*) and the "impure path" (*aśuddhādhvan*). The pure domain is made up of the source-substance *mahāmāyā* and the five constituents emitted from that source; the impure domain, in which our world is located, consists of the source-substance *māyā* and the thirty-one emitted *tattvas*. (See Figure 1.) In the pure domain, say the texts, Śiva acts directly, without intermediary. In the impure domain, however, Śiva assigns the Vidyeśvara Ananta and other agents to carry out his lordly functions. Similarly, beings of greater powers and few fetters such as the Vijñānakevalas and Pralayakevalas, who generally occupy the pure domain, are said to receive initiation directly from the hand of Śiva, while we humans of many fetters and lowly powers, living in the impure domain, receive only a mediated initiation from Śiva. For the initiation of humans, Śiva uses the guru as his intermediary.

While worship remains the action of a human being offering substances and services derived from *māyā*, the principle of hierarchized purity is nonetheless crucial. If Śiva participates more directly in domains of greater purity, it follows that objects and services, when purified sufficiently, may be offered to and received by Śiva directly. Consequently, what appears initially as an insurmountable ontological separation of Śiva and matter may be recast in ritual as a practical problem. Śiva does not remain completely aloof from all matter, only matter that is too impure. The worshiper's concern, accordingly, is to make sure that all the material offerings he makes to Śiva are suitably pure. He must ritually transform them into *amṛta* ("nectar"), substances imbued with the quality of "Śiva-ness." Then Śiva may "enjoy" them directly.

Śiva and Bound Souls

At its most fundamental, the relationship between Śiva and bound souls is one of absolute hierarchy. Śiva is the One, the absolute Lord, without a second. Humans by contrast are beings of limited powers, veiled from a correct apprehension of the nature of things. Śiva is lord over all divinities; how much more so is he master over bound souls.

This hierarchical relationship determines a basic attitude of devotion and subservience toward Śiva on the part of humans. For Sūryabhaṭṭa, these attitudes are duties (*viniyoga*) deriving from the fundamental character of the two categories *pati* and *paśu*. One should fix one's attention on Śiva through yogic concentration because Śiva is "to be meditated upon" and the human being is "to be meditator." One should make one's offerings of worship because Śiva is by nature "to be served" and the bound soul "should be directed toward his service" (*ŚSPbh* p. 37). But our engagement with a figure so central to our destiny is necessarily more complex than Sūryabhaṭṭa's emphasis on difference in rank would suggest.

This becomes clear when one looks at *stotra*s addressed to Śiva. *Stotra*s are hymns of praise, originally the spontaneous poetry uttered by gods, sages, and seers when in the manifest presence of Śiva, and now employed as regular, repeated panegyric during *pūjā* and other Śaiva rituals. Because these *stotra*s exemplify the way humans should address Śiva, they serve as a good précis of the basic relationship between bound souls and Śiva, which underlies the services of daily worship.

Consider the paradigmatic case of the great sage Mataṅga.[1] Once his meditations were interrupted by the sweet hum of wind whistling across a hollow in a bamboo stalk, where a bee was making its home. Thinking that Śiva too might find the sound pleasing, he cut down the stalk and made it into a flute, which he then played with great feeling. Mataṅga's desire to please his lord does not appear motivated by any specific aim, at least not initially. Suddenly Śiva "displayed his own bodily form" to the amazed flautist, much as Śiva comes to inhabit a manifest form in *pūjā*. "Falling to the earth like a stick, Mataṅga worshiped his feet, and overcome with a feeling of devotion toward Śiva, he sprinkled those feet with the pure water of his own eyes. And then the sage began to praise Śiva" (*MPĀ vidyā* 1.13–14). Mataṅga's first response was a mixture of submissive homage, dutiful hospitality, and devotional joy. Just as one should offer guests "foot-water" (*pādya*) to refresh them after a journey, he washed Śiva's feet—but here with foot-water from the tears of his own effusive happiness.

Then Mataṅga expressed his praise to his lord in seven impromptu *stotra*s (*MPĀ vidyā* 1.15–21). He begins by declaring Śiva's superiority over all other divinities: "O Blessed One, Lord over what has been and what is to be! Ruler over Brahman, Viṣṇu, and Indra! The divinities in the sky, filled with the excellence they have received through your grace, sing your praise." This common trope of Śaiva panegyric relies on the human analogy of kingship: Śiva is to other gods as a human king is to his subjects. As their lord, Śiva receives their praises and dispenses grace to the gods, just as he does with us.

Mataṅga goes on to acknowledge Śiva's ubiquity: "You completely pervade the creatures of the world, both immobile and mobile." Though Śiva stands before him in a limited bodily form, Mataṅga does not forget the completeness of Śiva's presence in the world and the limitless extent of his agency. Similarly, the worshiper should look beyond Śiva's synecdochic presence in the liṅga to the full character of Śiva revealed in the actions of invocation.

Finally Mataṅga speaks of Śiva's penetrating benevolence.

> Merely by recalling the power of your lotus-feet, even sinners have all their sins destroyed and come to enjoy success; how much more so wise sages whose minds are fixed upon you, who have relinquished all sins, who are disciplined, whose desires are extinguished, who are free from passion and from sorrow, and who have passed beyond emotional agitations. And for that matter, men have also obtained what they desired as boons.

Śiva is, of course, the one who grants all grace, and he may even favor—as the commentator Rāmakaṇṭha here points out—sinful demons like Andhaka and Rāvaṇa (*MPĀV vidyā* 1.17). But often, as here, the praise is two-sided: it both acknowledges Śiva's generosity and seeks to persuade Śiva to extend that grace in the supplicant's direction. Mataṅga concludes by describing his previous sorry state and pointing to the ripening of fetters already brought about through Śiva's grace, and he makes an earnest request for Śiva's continued favor.

> I was one of small fortune, filled with sorrow and abandoned by happiness. My own sin was great and hard as diamond, O Lord. But your powers are strong in

> rescuing souls from *samsāra*; they have taken up my store of sin and made it soft and light. So therefore, Lord, may you grant my wish.

There was no compulsion in this request. But Śiva was pleased by Mataṅga's outpouring and allowed the sage to request a favor. Mataṅga requested *śivajñāna*, and Śiva proceeded to deliver the discourse that has been handed down by Śaivas as the *Mataṅgapārameśvarāgama*.

The worshiper should repeat these same seven verses, Aghoraśiva tells us, along with other *stotras*, near the end of daily *pūjā*, when he too wishes to praise Śiva's greatness (*KKD* p. 123). As the model sage Mataṅga did, the worshiper may, through his desire to please Śiva, his submission, his hospitality, his recognition of Śiva's full nature, and his praise, persuade Śiva to look favorably on him. Through daily worship, one may even hope to receive the boon of *śivajñāna*.

The Transformation of Substance

The worshiper and Śiva are not the only ones who must be prepared for the transactions of worship. All participants in the ritual domain undergo a process of purification and transformation. The *āgamas* speak of "five purifications" the worshiper must perform prior to offering worship: purification of himself, of the place, of the mantras, of the liṅga, and of the substances. He purifies and protects the place of worship by constructing fortifications with mantras to keep away intruders. He purifies the mantras by reciting them in an ascending manner (*uccāraṇa*), removing them from contact with impure substances and transporting them to the higher level of pure *tattvas*.

He must likewise prepare and purify the substances (*dravyaśuddhi*) to be offered as services before they may be received by Śiva. In their "natural" state, substances are considered highly impure and completely inappropriate for offering to Śiva. It is necessary, therefore, to employ ritual means to purify them, to remove them from their material origins and transform them into "nectar" (*amṛta*), the undying food of the gods. The worshiper carefully selects only excellent specimens of each substance and submits them to a complex ablution that metamorphoses them into nectar suitable for Śiva, imbued with the quality of Śiva-ness. (As will be shown in the discussion of pure remains, the substances are transmuted still again when Śiva consumes them.) To illustrate this transforming process, let us follow one category of substance, flowers, as they are readied for presentation to Śiva. The same scheme applies, with some variations, to most substances used as services.

Kāmikāgama provides detailed instructions for the initial selection and collection of flowers for worship (*KĀ* 5.40–65). To begin, only flowers from certain sources should be used. "One should worship with flowers grown in one's own garden, or grown in the forest, or with flowers purchased for money, and not otherwise" (*KĀ* 5.65). Even among these, only certain species are appropriate for ritual. The text lists thirty suitable types of white flowers, thirteen red, eight yellow, and one species of blue flower; it lists as well nine types to be avoided. The text also ranks the suitable flowers, with the blue lotus considered the finest. Some types are particularly appropriate for worship during the day, while others should be presented only at nighttime services.

Of the proper species, only perfect specimens at the peak of their bloom are acceptable.

> One should exclude all flowers that have been eaten by hair-lice, those which are broken or wilted, flowers that have fallen by themselves, and those that are damaged. One should not offer worship using unopened buds, nor should one present immature flowers to the god. (*KĀ* 5.60–61)

Fragrance is another important criterion, since flowers, consisting of Earth, must please Śiva's sense of smell. The worshiper should not select flowers that lack scent or have an unpleasant odor, and he should not use flowers that have been smelled previously. Finally, in gathering and carrying them, he must not allow the flowers to be polluted by the touch of an unbathed person or by an impure container.

Given these rather strict guidelines, it may be impossible for the worshiper to procure suitable flowers. He is then allowed to make substitutions.

> If flowers are unavailable, one may offer leaves. If leaves are also unavailable, one may present fruits. If fruits are also unavailable, then grass, shrubs, and herbs are acceptable. But if herbs as well are unavailable, the god may be worshiped with devotion (*bhakti*) alone. (*KĀ* 5.61–63)

Within the domain of *māyā*, one should select the best available objects for offering, but when only inferior substances are available, these are still preferable to none at all.

The ritualist has these most excellent flowers brought to the place of worship and placed with the other offerings. But no matter how "pure" substances may be in their natural state, they are not yet fit for offering to Śiva. Flowers, water, sandalwood paste, incense, and the rest are, after all, derivatives of the source-substance *māyā* and therefore inherently impure. Nirmalamaṇi puts it this way:

> Aren't substances like flowers, water, and the like pure in and of themselves? They are not. These substances are derivatives of *māyā* arising in the impure worlds, and they are not worthy for Śiva's consumption because they do not have Śiva-ness (*śivatva*). Nor may it be argued that they do have Śiva-ness because they are connected with all-pervading Śiva. Śiva does not blend with substances, as a drop of water does not merge with a lotus leaf. (*KKDP* p. 80)

To raise his offerings out of their impure origins in the realm of *māyā*, the worshiper must perform *dravyaśuddhi*, a purification of the ritual substances that transforms them into nectar. This, says *Mṛgendrāgama*, renders them suitable (*yogyatā*) for Śiva's consumption (*MṛĀ kriyā* 3.32–33).

To carry out the purification, the worshiper first prepares a special ritual concoction called *arghya* ("reception-water"). The term *arghya* literally means "valuable," that which is to be honored, and it refers most commonly to the water offered as a respectful reception to a guest. In Śaiva ritual, *arghya* is employed in a similar fashion: one presents reception-water as an offering of hospitality to Śiva and other divinities who come as "guests" to one's temple or shrine. But *arghya* also has for the Śaivas a special purifying capacity, and therefore they use it to prepare other substances as well that are to be presented to Śiva.[2]

The worshiper begins his preparation of *arghya* by first purifying the *arghya* vessel with the ASTRA mantra. As the substance to be contained in it will be highly pure, it is necessary that the container itself be without impurity. Aghoraśiva takes this concern one step further by directing that the vessel should be made of gold or some other excellent material (*KKD* p. 79). ("Made of gold, silver, copper, or clay, free of flaws, and round," Nirmalamaṇi pragmatically specifies.) The worshiper then fills the pot with pure water, reciting the HṚD mantra.

Water always has a certain capacity to cleanse, but here the addition of other substances and mantras enhances its purifying power. The worshiper first adds a set of substances, most often milk, tips of kuśa-grass, rice, flowers, sesame, barley, and white mustard.[3] Then he imposes onto the mixture a sequence of mantras that follow the paradigm of invocation: ĀSANA (throne), MŪRTI (embodiment), the five *brahmamantras*, VIDYĀDEHA (body of mantras), NETRA (eye), MŪLA, the six *aṅgamantras*, then again MŪLA, *brahmamantras*, and *aṅgamantras*. He recites here all the mantras that, elsewhere, bring about Śiva's presence in the liṅga or other support. The mantras infuse the water with Śiva's powers.

Like all highly pure things in the world, the *arghya* must be protected from the possibility of contamination. The worshiper protects it with ASTRA (weapon) and surrounds it with KAVACA (armor). Finally he "pleases" it with the cow *mudrā*, which finally transforms the *arghya* into the highest nectar.

With *arghya* ready at hand, the ritualist proceeds to purify the other substances. He first sprinkles a bit of *arghya* on his own head, restoring his own state of purity, and then sprays the offerings with *arghya*, reciting the protective mantras ASTRA and KAVACA. Next he recites HṚD, protects the offerings once again with KAVACA, and then forms with his hands the cow *mudrā* (*dhenumudrā*). The cow *mudrā*, consistently employed when transforming substances into nectar, imitates the udders of a cow; Nirmalamaṇi suggests it is like "nectar flowing from the forehead to the ten channels near the ten fingers" (*KKDP* p. 79).[4] At this moment, the worshiper has successfully transformed the flowers and other substances into nectar, suitable for offering to Śiva.

Food destined for Śiva's consumption undergoes a somewhat different purificatory procedure. Perhaps because Śiva will ingest it, food receives a more elaborate purification than materials meant for Śiva's exterior use. As with flowers, the worshiper must be careful in his choice and preparation of the foodstuffs. The *Kāmikāgama* gives strict guidelines not only for procuring the best possible ingredients, but also for the kinds of pots fit for cooking Śiva's meal and for mantras that should be recited during the cooking. When the cooking is completed, however, it is not enough simply to sprinkle the food with *arghya*; instead, the worshiper must perform upon it a "fourfold consecration" (*catussamskāra*).

As its name suggests, the fourfold consecration is a set of four purifying rites, always deployed in the same order: "divine glance" (*nirīkṣaṇa*), "sprinkling upward" (*prokṣaṇa*), "striking" (*tāḍana*), and "sprinkling downward" (*abhyukṣaṇa*). One uses this consecration for a variety of purposes in Śaiva ritual, such as purifying the pots that are to hold Śiva's bathwater, purifying the fire pit when preparing for a fire oblation, and purifying the ghee that is offered into the fire. Here the worshiper begins his consecration of the cooked food by touching the thumb and ring finger of his right hand to his eyes, pronouncing the MŪLA mantra, and gazing at the food with the resulting "divine glance."[5] He next sprinkles some *arghya* water upward, his palm raised, and recites ASTRA; then he strikes the food with his index finger, again reciting ASTRA; and finally he sprinkles *arghya* downward, his palm this time toward the ground, and recites the KAVACA mantra. Together, the four consecrating acts turn the food into *naivedya*, food worthy of offering to a divinity.

One text provides an explanation of the metamorphosis effected by the fourfold consecration in theological terms.

> One should know that the divine glance distinguishes between what is inert (*jaḍa*) and what is animate (*cit*) through Śiva's own power of vision. Sprinkling upward renders an object suitable [for offering to Śiva] by separating it from *jaḍa*. Striking brings about the manifestation of *cit* in that object, as the striking of stones [manifests sparks], and sprinkling downward nurtures these sparks still more.[6]

The transformation of normal food into *naivedya*, then, requires that the worshiper remove it from its normal status as inert matter and infuse into it the animating energy of consciousness. This process instills "Śiva-ness" into the substance, since Śiva's own nature is consciousness, and thereby makes it suitable for intimate contact with Śiva.

There is yet one final stage in this transfiguration of worldly substance. At the moment they are presented to Śiva, some offerings need to be raised up to a still higher level. Here the worshiper employs the method of "ascending pronunciation" (*uccāraṇa*), which he has used previously in invoking Śiva into the liṅga. Taking the flowers, food, or other object in his hand, he recites the MŪLA mantra in a gradually rising manner, reabsorbing the constituent parts of the mantra as he raises it. At the same time, he directs the breath along the *suṣumnā* in an upward direction and correspondingly raises the object in his hands. The movement follows the path of reabsorption, bringing the offering toward a reintegration with Śiva.

According to Appayadīkṣita, for instance, the first four offerings presented to Śiva must each be transported upward to its own appropriate level. Beginning from the *mūlādhāra*, the worshiper should raise foot-water (*pādya*) up to the level of the eyebrows (corresponding to the *īśvaratattva*), sipping-water (*ācamana*) to the level of the aperture at the top of his head (which corresponds to the *sadāśivatattva*), and *arghya* all the way to the *dvādaśānta*, twelve fingers above the crown (corresponding to the *śivatattva*). Finally, says Appayadīkṣita, he raises flowers up to Śiva, residing in the *dvādaśānta*, and imagines that this offering brings him into communion with Śiva (*ŚAC* p. 68). Just as the technique of ascending pronunciation enables the worshiper to approach Śiva and summon him into the liṅga during invocation, here it allows him to transport offerings to the point where Śiva may partake of them.

The route substance takes to become suitable for Śiva's enjoyment, then, is one of progressive purification and transfiguration. Starting with careful selection of the materials to be offered, the worshiper purifies them with *arghya* or the fourfold consecration, turning them into *amṛta*, and finally raises them up to Śiva with an ascending pronunciation of Śiva's own mantra. In the process, objects that are initially inert substance attain the quality of Śiva-ness and are therefore eligible for presentation. In daily *pūjā*, the worshiper ritually resolves the theological problem of Śiva's participation in matter by transforming matter into something akin to Śiva himself.

The Pattern of Services

In daily worship Śiva is a divine person, superior above all others, to whom the worshiper must express his respect and subservience. He is a guest, summoned to stay temporarily in the shrine, and must be treated to the finest hospitality that his host, the ritualist, is able to provide. Śiva is, moreover, a lord ruling over the entire cosmos and must be served in ritual as one would serve a human king. Śiva is the granter of all grace, a beneficent Lord, whom the worshiper may supplicate for favors. All these themes—respect, subservience, hospitality, royal service, and petition—play a part in the pattern of services that the worshiper now offers.[7]

It is essential to realize, however, that the services of worship do not simply imitate human prototypes, "playing at" or "reflecting" human hospitality or royal service. In the Śaiva view, Śiva *is* a person, a soul temporarily inhabiting a body; he *has* made a journey from the *dvādaśānta* to the liṅga; he *is* a lord, a king over all other kings; and he *is* the source of all grace to bound souls. The same principles of proper conduct that determine, for instance, the way a host should receive a respected guest or the way one should pay homage to a sovereign also govern the activities of the worshiper here. The ritualist expresses and enacts through his services the actual relationship existing between himself and Śiva.

Incarnated through invocation in a body of mantras, Śiva is refreshed, bathed, clothed, adorned, entertained, fed, and praised during worship just as any superior person might be. The *āgamas* present various lists of services that the worshiper must perform for Śiva, ranging from a minimal list of four *upacāras* up to sixteen or even more (*KĀ* 4.372–76).[8] Further, each service offered may vary quantitatively, according to the means of the worshiper. The *Kāmikāgama* (4.377–400) specifies nine ranked grades of worship, from "lowest of low" to "highest of high" forms, based on such criteria as the quantity of rice served, the number of lamps lit, and the musical instruments employed to serenade the Lord.

rank	*food (in quarts)*	*lamps*	*instruments*	*dancers*
1. highest of high	280	500	50	216
2. middle of high	208	200	34	50
3. lowest of high	56	108	24	10–34
4. highest of middle	28	70	all	—
5. middle of middle	14	24	—	—
6. lowest of middle	8	12	—	—
7. highest of low	6	8	—	—
8. middle of low	4	4	—	—
9. lowest of low	2	—	—	—

One should make offerings "insofar as one is able" (*yathāśakti*), with larger numbers of services and larger quantities of substances appropriate for wealthy sponsors and well-endowed temples. But whatever the number of services the worshiper employs and however munificent the substances offered, the relationship established between the worshiper and Śiva is in essence the same.

Receiving Śiva as Guest

When Śiva has arrived in the liṅga, the worshiper first presents him with refreshing waters, a suitable reception for one who has just completed a journey. He gives Śiva foot-water (*pādya*) to rinse off his feet, sipping-water (*ācamana*) to cleanse his mouths, and *arghya* to sprinkle atop his heads. Flowers and other soothing substances may also be showered upon his heads. Each offering is presented to the appropriate part of the liṅga, following the ascending order of reabsorption.

Next the worshiper bathes (*snāna*) Śiva, and he may also give him an anointment (*abhiṣeka*). In private worship, Śiva's bath may consist of only a single drop of special *arghya* accompanied by visualizations of the other parts of bathing. In public rituals, by contrast, bathing the Lord is an elaborate affair, involving repeated ablutions with various substances.

> [One bathes Śiva], using bowls of various colors, with diamonds and other jewels, with cow dung [and the other products of the cow], with nicely prepared powders, with black mustard seed and salt, with tepid water, sandal-water, and herb-water, with milk, curd, ghee, honey, and jaggery. . . . If money permits [one may also bathe Śiva] with coconut milk or the juice of other succulent fruits, with flowers and the like, with gold-water, with jewel-water, and with sandal-water. (*KĀ* 4.405–9)

After this bath of many colors, the ritualist anoints Śiva, using the pots that he has earlier prepared. While an ablution is appropriate for any person, anointment is particularly suitable for kings, preceptors, and others who have extensive powers and responsibilities. In a royal anointment, the ceremony constructs or constitutes the king's sovereignty by depositing manifold powers, instantiated in the bathing pots, onto a single man. In the anointment of a guru (*ācāryābhiṣeka*), similarly, Śiva's fundamental energies are infused into water-pots, and the contents of these pots are poured over the preceptor-to-be, thereby transmitting to him the ritual powers necessary to his new priestly status. Both these anointment rituals are substantive and accretive in character: they add "lordly" qualities or powers to the subject through an affusion with substances bearing or embodying those qualities.

The anointment of Śiva during daily worship likewise involves the instantiation of powers in pots and the pouring of their contents over a recipient. As described in Chapter 2, the priest sets up anointment pots numbering from 5 to 1,008 in a specified geometrical order, fills them with water and an array of substances, and then invokes into each pot an aspect of Śiva's kingship. He pours the contents of the pots over the liṅga, and with each drenching the divine power of that pot is reabsorbed within the liṅga. What distinguishes this *abhiṣeka* from those onto human subjects is that here the recipient of powers is also the ultimate source of them. The powers and divinities the worshiper infuses into the *abhiṣeka* pots are Śiva's inherent lordly powers and his delegated agents; by affusing the liṅga with them he simply returns them to their proper fount. With each successive pot the worshiper ritually reconstructs Śiva embodied in the liṅga as the Lord of the Universe, adding onto him all the powers and agencies through which he perpetually exercises his lordship over the cosmos.

After these watery affairs, Śiva must be newly dressed and ornamented.

(Parallel rites of investiture follow the inundations of the king and preceptor in their *abhiṣekas*.) In private performance, the worshiper may dress and decorate Śiva through visualization, imagining that Śiva puts on mentally constructed decorations. In the public worship of temples, however, the adornment of the liṅga should use the finest physical materials available.

> The priest should ornament the liṅga with golden diadems, with crowns and leaves made of gold, with golden shoots of durva-grass, with many golden Lakṣmī medallions, with a crescent moon, and with many golden flowers. He should ornament it suitably with a triple string of pearls, an upper cloth, a waistband, a golden skin and a golden garment, with other ornaments such as flowers, with a covering made of gold, and also with various kinds of gems. (*KĀ* 4.428–31)[9]

As throughout the services, one offers ornaments according to the principle stated by *Kāmikāgama*: "one should offer small or large services in accord with one's wealth" (*KĀ* 4.372). A greater quantity of offerings is of course considered superior, and should be given if possible, but greater or smaller amounts do not affect the fundamental relationships involved in worship.

Pleasing Śiva

When the worshiper has attended to Śiva's outer needs by bathing, clothing, and adorning him, he shows his hospitality with services meant to gratify Śiva's senses. He presents sweet-smelling flowers. He perfumes the sanctum with incense while ringing a "handsome, deep-voiced bell." He pleases Śiva's eyes with "perpetual lamps, circular gateway lamps, trident lamps, lamp garlands, and various other kinds of lamps" (*KĀ* 4.443). He decorates the sanctum with hanging flower garlands.

Further, the priest should present entertainments for the eye and ear. *Kāmikāgama* suggests a veritable variety show for Śiva, including songs made of mantras, recitations from other sacred texts, songs in several languages, instrumental music, and dances from different regions.

> He should have songs consisting of mantras sung, or else vina music may be played. After the offering of incense, there should be Vedic recitations or readings from other sacred texts, and after that songs in the Gauḍa and other languages. Afterward he should have performed songs composed in the Dravidian language, or in uncorrupt Sanskrit, joined with dance, or songs in the eighteen languages using many tones. (*KĀ* 4.436–39)

In the "highest of high" form of worship, 50 instruments supply the music and 216 temple dancers perform.

All these services aim to provide Śiva with pleasurable sensory experiences while he is embodied and present in the shrine. In fact, the worshiper strives to please all of Śiva's perceptual faculties (the five *jñānendriyas*) by offering him the finest representatives of each category of matter (the five *bhūtas*). According to one text, the worshiper honors Śiva

> with sandal-paste, flowers, etc., consisting of Earth; with drinking water, clothes, etc., consisting of Water; with jewels, lamps, ornaments, and the like made of Fire; with yak-tail fans, incense, and so on made of Wind; and with songs, music, and the like consisting of Ether. (*SP* 1 p. 199)

The goal of the worshiper here is to be complete in his offerings: the services he presents partake of all five material elements, they contain all five perceptible qualities, and they engage all five sense organs of Śiva's embodiment. As Sūryabhaṭṭa would have it, *all* matter is "to be delivered" to Śiva.

Every king has a court, and the Lord Śiva is no exception. His court is made up of the mantra powers and subordinate divinities who carry out his commands. As described in Chapter 2, these agents of Śiva's lordship are now drawn out from Śiva, in the order of emission, so that the ritualist may show his homage to them as well. The worshiper invokes from one to five entourages (*āvaraṇa*), concentric circles of Śiva's agency, onto thrones surrounding Śiva in a specified order, and offers to each divinity a set of eight consecrations. Later he feeds them and pleases them with other services. The arrangement of these subordinate lords around Śiva follows a prescribed order of priority. All particularized agencies are inferior to and encompassed within Śiva's sovereignty, just as feudatory rulers are subordinated to the dominion of their overlord. Yet the services offered the members of Śiva's court indicate a second hierarchical relationship. The worshiper expresses his homage not just to Śiva, but also to the powers and divinities who carry out Śiva's command. By participating in Śiva's sovereignty, albeit in an inferior station, each member of Śiva's entourages becomes worthy of the ritualist's respect.

Next it is time for Śiva's meal. The services of worship follow a pattern of increasing intimacy with respect to Śiva's body. First concerned with the outer surface of his lord's body, then gratifying his senses, the worshiper now presents a food offering that not only pleases Śiva's sense of taste, but will also be "consumed" and incorporated by him. Carefully prepared, purified food is brought and placed before the liṅga. As we have seen, this meal has been transformed through the fourfold consecration into a suitable state of Śiva-ness, so that Śiva himself may consume it. According to Īśānaśiva, one last round of purifications remains to be performed, for safety's sake: the worshiper "protects the food with ASTRA, encircles it with KAVACA, asperses it [with *arghya*] reciting 'BHŪR, BHUVAR, SVAR,' and sprinkles all around."[10] Then he offers the food to each of Sadāśiva's five faces and also to the limbs of his divine body.

The worshiper should express his hospitality to all attending divinities comprehensively, yet in proper order. He first serves his preeminent guest,

Śiva, and then proceeds outward, feeding all the members of Śiva's entourages, starting with the innermost circle. In temple worship, the priest must leave the sanctum and feed as well the surrounding divinities (*parivāradevatā*) who make up Śiva's outer entourages (*bahyāvaraṇa*) outside the sanctum, and he presents food to the lords guarding the doors (*dvārapāla*). Last, and least, he feeds—or gives "tribute" (*bali*) to—the lesser spirits (*bhūtas*) who have also managed to be present at the ceremony. The priest thus gives offerings of sustenance to all, in order of rank and (correspondingly) in order of their proximity to the centermost divinity, Śiva.

After the meal, naturally, come the after-dinner accompaniments. When Śiva has finished eating, the worshiper gratifies him by giving him sandal-powder for washing his hands, sipping-water to rinse his mouth, mouth-perfume for freshening the breath, and betel-leaf to aid his digestion. Then he delights Śiva with the sounds of a five-headed drum, with mirror, parasol, and yak-tail fan, and with more entertainment. At the completion of all this hospitality, the worshiper finally meditates "that Sadāśiva is happily seated together with the goddess" (*KĀ* 4.501), or that "Śiva is delighted by the praises of Ananta and the other Vidyeśvaras" (*KKD* p. 115). He has achieved his goal, to please Śiva through his generous offerings.

Requesting Śiva's Favor

There remains one more major service for the worshiper to perform: the recitations of mantras (*japa*). The focus shifts here from Śiva to the ritualist himself, for in offering recitations of mantras the worshiper seeks his own ends more than Śiva's pleasure. A new aspect of the relationship between Śiva and worshiper becomes apparent. Acting less the host than the supplicant, the worshiper requests Śiva's favor.

Mantra recitations gain results for those who perform them. In *Mṛgendrāgama*'s definition, mantra recitations "make the object of meditation favorable" to the reciter (*MṛĀ yoga* 8). For this reason, *japa* is frequently used for restitution, attainment of powers, and propitiation. When a Śaiva transgresses proper conduct, the most common expiation (*prāyaścitta*) consists in repeating the purifying mantra AGHORA a specified number of times. For instance, a Śaivite who voluntarily fails to perform his daily worship should perform one thousand recitations of AGHORA (*SP* 2.3.13–14); if one's personal Śiva-liṅga is lost or destroyed, one should recite AGHORA one hundred thousand times (*SP* 2.3.19–20); and so on. For an adept (*sādhaka*) who seeks particular powers, recitations of a "mantra to be attained" (*sādhyamantra*) form a major part of his discipline. An adept performing his mantra vow, for instance, might recite his mantra a million times, accompanied by one hundred thousand oblations (*KirĀ caryā* 20.8–15). In daily worship as well, one recites Śiva's mantras in order to make Śiva favorable.

For the Śaivas, the recitation of mantras is not merely an inward discipline or verbal meditation. Mantras are, as we have seen, real external powers, and in this rite the worshiper seeks to direct these powers outward, presenting them to Śiva as a service. To do so, it is not enough simply to recite the mantras for Śiva's audition. Rather, the worshiper must first substantiate the mantras in some material object before he can give them to Śiva. As in invocation, flowers serve here as the medium by which a subtle entity may be objectified and transported. Nirmalamaṇi explains that flowers are "the place where the mantra recitations become manifest" (*KKDP* p. 116).

The worshiper holds a flower and repeats the appropriate mantra a specified number of times. The mantra thereby becomes embodied in the flower. Once embodied, the mantra flower must be carefully protected with an enclosure (*sampuṭa*) of other mantra powers. As Aghoraśiva describes the method:

> Holding a flower in his hand, the worshiper should recite the MŪLA mantra one hundred and eight times, using a rosary which has been worshiped with HṚD. He emboxes [the flower] between ASTRA, KAVACA, and HṚD mantras, then HṚD, KAVACA, and ASTRA mantras. Protecting the flower with ASTRA and encircling it with KAVACA, he holds it in his right hand and, with his knee on the ground, offers the recitation [substantiated in the flower] to Śiva, accompanied by *arghya* and the *mudrā* of emission. (*KKD* p. 115)

When the worshiper places the flowers on the liṅga, Śiva receives the mantras that are manifested in them and looks favorably upon the one who has presented them.

The ritualist, however, gives more than just his recitations of mantras. Reciting three verses directed to Śiva, "the worshiper presents his mantra recitations, his *karman*, and his soul, in order, to the boon-granting hand of Śiva" (*KKD* p. 116). From offering substances apart from himself, he has now moved to giving his own inner constituents to Śiva, ending with his most essential part, the soul. In these offerings of an increasing intimacy, the worshiper betokens a complete humbling before his Lord, a prostration that is enacted physically a bit later when the worshiper "bows with all eight limbs, like a stick" (*KKD* p. 123), in front of Śiva.

Yet the verses contain a request as well.

> "O Protector of the secret and the very secret, accept this recitation I have made. [The recitation] remaining in you, may success come to me, by your favor.
>
> "O Lord, consume and destroy all my *karman*, good and bad. I am at your feet, O Beneficent One.
>
> "Śiva is the donor; Śiva is the one who consumes; Śiva is this entire world. A Śiva worships everywhere. I am indeed that Śiva." (*KĀ* 4.511–14)

As the prayers stress, Śiva is a protector, a beneficent lord, one who grants favor. Having pleased and honored Śiva to the best of his ability, the worshiper now makes his petition, asking that the undertaking be successful and that his *karman* be consumed. The undertaking, if successful, will "increase the longevity, health, victory, and prosperity of the ruler" and will "make the villagers and others thrive" (*KĀ* 4.5). Removal of *karman* brings about the liberation of the soul. Thus, the worshiper requests no less from Śiva than the two goals of human activity, worldly enjoyments (*bhoga*) and liberation (*mokṣa*). If these all-encompassing requests are not enough, he may also ask for more specific benefits by reciting optional (*kāmya*) mantras after the three verses.

Finally the worshiper gladdens Śiva with verses of praise (*stotra*). The verses proclaim in words Śiva's preeminent place in the universe, just as the worshiper has proclaimed it in action through his services.[11] Not coincidentally, they also seek to remind Śiva of his benevolent character, with the implicit hope that some of Śiva's favor may grace the worshiper.

Śiva is indeed "to be served" in the offerings of daily worship, and this service takes many forms. The relationship between Śiva and a human worshiper is a multifaceted one, and accordingly the worshiper enacts a complex relationship through his services to Śiva. The worshiper receives Śiva, bathes him, clothes and decorates him, entertains him, does homage to his court, feeds him, worships him with mantras, and praises him. He treats Śiva as a guest and a king, a superior and a benefactor; he seeks to please him by offering substances of every category, gratifying all of Śiva's senses; he even offers his own inner constitution.

The Problem of Pure Remains

We have seen how the worshiper collects and refines substances to a high state of purity so that they are suitable for Śiva's enjoyment, and how he presents these substances as expressions of his homage, meant to gratify his Lord. Yet the substances do not cease to exist when Śiva consumes them. Śiva eats only the most subtle part of his meal, the portion that shares in his *śivatva*. The material remains (*ucchiṣṭa*) of the meal are left on his plate after he has finished, as are the remains of all the flowers, unguents, and other offerings used in worshiping him.

It is a general principle of Hindu science that the use or enjoyment of substances alters their condition. Among humans, the leftovers from one person's meal become impure for most others, due to their contact with his inner fluids such as saliva. Such polluted remains are fit only for consumption by a social inferior.

The situation is somewhat different with the meals of the gods. The consumption of food by a god alters the leftovers not to a lower status, but to a higher one, as far as humans are concerned. Since the highest gods are so far superior to humans, even their remains—which may very well be impure in relation to other gods—are highly pure and imbued with good qualities with respect to humans. Contact with a god, even through his spittle, is beneficial.

For this reason many Hindu sects, including some Śaiva ones, distribute the material remains of the god's meal to worshipers and devotees for secondary consumption. The god eats the subtle portion; his human followers eat the remaining "gross" portions. The leftovers are *prasāda*, a form of divine "favor" returned to humans, and vast powers are ascribed to it. For instance, Appayadīkṣita extols Śiva's leftover bathwater:

> Water from Śiva's feet and his leftovers should be used zealously by his devotees; sins born of mind, voice, or body will not touch them. . . . The Pṛthūdaka, the Mahātīrtha, the rivers Gaṅgā, Yamunā, Narmadā, Sarayu, Kṣipra, as well as Godāvarī, are always present in Śiva's bathwater, O sages. One should use the water of Śiva's bath, since it is made of all *tīrtha*s. (*ŚAC* p. 119)

Eating the remains of a divine meal likewise confers many benefits: it purifies, destroys sin, cures cases of poisoning, and much more.

Śaiva siddhāntins agree that Śiva's enjoyment of substances alters them to a higher state. In fact, they argue, the contact of a substance with Śiva so transfigures it that it can no longer be used by humans at all. "Humans cannot bear it, and should avoid it diligently," as *Kāmikāgama* (4.527) succinctly puts the case. And consequently, there can be no distribution of Śiva's edible leftovers to human devotees in a Śaiva siddhānta temple.

When Śiva enjoys a substance, that substance becomes *nirmālya*.[12] According to Nirmalamaṇi's practical definition, the term refers particularly to flower garlands: "*Nirmālya* denotes garlands (*mālya*) that have been removed (*nirasta*) [from the liṅga]. . . . [Garlands] which first have mantras recited upon them, are consumed by Śiva, removed, and given to Lord Caṇḍa are said to be *nirmālya*" (*KKDP* p. 132). From garlands, *nirmālya* is extended to cover all substances that undergo the same process of preparation, consumption, and removal. *Kāmikāgama* gives a more philosophical definition to the term. "It is called *nirmālya* because it has reached a state of stainlessness (*nirmalatā*)" (*KĀ* 6.86). Without *mala*, *nirmālya* is utterly pure.

The final transfiguration of substance through Śiva's use is, in one sense, another stage in the process begun with the worshiper's careful selection, preparation, and purification of the substance before offering it. Appayadīkṣita brings this point out by comparing the transformation with that of a stone liṅga.

> A Śiva-liṅga, which is at first only a particular form of a worldly piece of stone, comes to partake of consciousness (*cinmaya*) by the consecration of establishment (*pratiṣṭhā*), which removes its impure form resulting from *māyā*, and after

> that the liṅga should not be touched by those who are not initiated. In the same way the *nirmālya* [which is initially a worldly substance] also comes to partake of consciousness by the group of four consecrations beginning with "divine glance," after which it is considered suitable for Śiva's consumption, and then becomes even more pure when consumed by Śiva. Therefore it too should not be touched by the uninitiated. (*ŚAC* p. 119)

Substances already highly refined by the ritual actions of humans become even more so when Śiva consumes them.

While human leftovers are unfit for subsequent use because they are impure, Śiva's leftovers are unsuited for human enjoyment because they are too pure. Contact with Śiva has rendered the *nirmālya* immaculate, yet human worshipers continue to inhabit bodies infested with *mala* and so are not able to bear contact with so much pureness. Says Śiva in a *purāṇa*, "A foul person of impure soul who, out of greed, consumes that which I have enjoyed and which is highly pure will be destroyed, like a *śūdra* who studies the Vedas."[13] If one does imbibe some *nirmālya* through some ill fortune, however, he may avert the ensuing destruction by performing a stiff expiation. Somaśambhu prescribes that one recite the purifying mantra AGHORA twenty-five thousand times (*SP* 2.3.58), roughly the same expiation as is required for such grave transgressions as drooling on the liṅga or touching it with one's feet. Consuming *nirmālya*, like mistreating a liṅga, is a serious infringement requiring serious restitution.

These overly purified substances pose a practical problem: how should one dispose of them? If humans cannot receive them, who can? Fortunately, there is an apt recipient for Śiva's pure, powerful leftovers right within the temple complex: the Lord Caṇḍa.

Caṇḍa is one of the Gaṇeśvaras, a member of Śiva's household entourage, where he is stationed in the northeast direction.[14] In Śaiva temples of South India, Caṇḍa most often occupies an independent shrine situated immediately to the northeast of the main sanctum. The term *caṇḍa* means "fierce," "violent," "angry," and *Kāmikāgama* describes him accordingly, claiming that Lord Caṇḍa is "an angry emanation (*aṃśa*) of Paramaśiva" (*KĀ* 4.525). If his meditation form is any indication, Caṇḍa lives up to his name.

> Arising from Rudra's fire, and fierce (*raudra*), Caṇḍa is the color of lampblack, dreadful, carries trident and hatchet, and has four faces and four arms. He spits great flames from his mouth, and has twelve red eyes. The crescent moon adorns his matted locks, a snake is his bracelet, and another snake is his sacrificial thread. He holds a rosary and an ascetic's water-pot, and sits on a white lotus throne. He removes all pain from those who bow with devotion. (*SP* 1.5.2–4)

One of the final acts of daily worship is to worship Lord Caṇḍa and to present to him the leftover *nirmālya*.[15] "Whatever remains on the liṅga, ritual platform, or sand-liṅga, and has been enjoyed and left by Śiva is for Caṇḍa's consumption" (*KĀ* 4.526–27). In contrast to humans, Caṇḍa is able to bear the intense purity of *nirmālya*, presumably by virtue of his own ardent character. Worshiping Caṇḍa has a second purpose as well. Not only does it present the *nirmālya* to an appropriate recipient, it also removes any faults (*doṣa*) the priest may have committed while worshiping the liṅga (*KKDP* p. 132). Like Śiva's own power of reabsorption, the fierce Caṇḍa removes and absorbs a host of things: the afflictions of his devotees, mistakes made in worshiping Śiva, and Śiva's too-pure leftovers.

The worship of Caṇḍa is a relatively simple rite. The priest goes to Caṇḍa's shrine northeast of the sanctum, ritually constructs an appropriate throne and embodiment for Caṇḍa using CAṆḌĀSANA and CAṆḌAMŪRTI mantras, visualizes Caṇḍa's form as described above, and invokes him with the DHVANICAṆḌEŚVARA, Caṇḍa's equivalent of Śiva's MŪLA mantra. The invocation of Caṇḍa, then, follows the paradigm of Śiva's invocation described in the previous chapter, but it is considerably less complex. The worshiper performs the proper consecrations, gives Caṇḍa *arghya*, and then presents to him the *nirmālya* that has been collected from the liṅga and pedestal. As he offers the leftovers, the priest repeats two verses that articulate the two main purposes of Caṇḍa worship.

> "By order of Śiva, I give to you what is licked, sucked, eaten, drunk, or otherwise consumed, the betel leaf, garlands, unguents, and the food that is *nirmālya*.
>
> "O Caṇḍa, whatever in the entire ritual I have done either deficiently or excessively due to delusion, may that be perfected for me through your command." (*SP* 1.5.7–8)

Even after Caṇḍa's secondary consumption of the *nirmālya*, there are still substantive remnants, and they are still not fit for humans. One final disposal remains. At this point, says one *āgama*, one should give it "to cattle and elephants, or throw it in the water, or else burn it in fire, or bury it."[16] And so ends the trajectory of substances used in worship. Perfect specimens carefully prepared, refined into nectar, presented to Śiva and consumed by him, transmuted thereby into *nirmālya*, and offered to Caṇḍa, these substances are finally disposed of among those universal recipients: cows, elephants, Water, Fire, and Earth. Human worshipers at no point enjoy these offerings themselves.

DISMISSAL

In addition to feeding Caṇḍa and disposing of the remains, other acts are necessary to complete worship. Most important among these concluding rites, the worshiper must "dismiss" (*visarjana*) Śiva from his embodiment in the liṅga. Though a much simpler rite, dismissal is in many respects the converse of invocation. Where invocation instantiates a "special presence" of Śiva in the liṅga, dismissal enables Śiva to "turn his face away" (*parāṅmukha*) from his worshipers, remaining in the liṅga as a latent presence only. Where invocation largely follows the path of emission, dismissal is an act of reabsorption.

The worshiper begins the rite of dismissal by presenting to Śiva *parāṅmukhārghya*, a special form of *arghya* that allows Śiva to avert his face, and by displaying the *mahāmudrā*. In the *mahāmudrā*, one holds the two hands together, outstretched, and moves them upward over some object, from the feet to the head, in the order of reabsorption.[17] Then the worshiper merges the members of Śiva's court back into Śiva, from where they had been drawn out, using the *mudrā* of reabsorption.[18] "He causes the divinities surrounding the liṅga to get up with ASTRA and the *mudrā* of reabsorption, and joins them so that they are united in Śiva's embodiment, using the MŪRTI mantra" (*KĀ* 4.518–19). Finally, he allows Śiva to return from his embodied state to that of undifferentiated Paramaśiva.

> Reciting MŪLA followed by the HṚD mantra, the worshiper visualizes Śiva freed from his limbs, liberated from all differentiated (*sakala*) attributes, and returned to a state of nondifferentiation (*niṣkalatā*) through the part of the *śivatattva* situated in the heart [of the embodiment]. (*KĀ* 4.519–20)

By this means, Śiva's special presence in the liṅga for the duration of worship comes to an end.

One might expect that the worshiper too would undergo some sort of "exit" rite at the completion of *pūjā*, removing himself from the high state of Śiva-ness he attained through self-purification. But there is no such rite. As far as I am aware, Śaiva authors do not consider this an omission worthy of comment, and so we are left to postulate its significance. Of course, the worshiper wishes ultimately to maintain a state of similarity to Śiva; this is the definition of *mokṣa*. If the rite of self-purification offers a quotidian taste of this climactic status, why not let its effects linger as long as possible? One will lose this unworldly purity soon enough anyway, through the impact of nonritual activities. So there is neither motivation nor necessity for the worshiper to undergo a rite counteracting the earlier effects of his self-purification.

Instead, after dismissing Śiva from the liṅga, the worshiper does clean-up duty. He washes the liṅga and pedestal and decorates them with flowers and the like. He cleans the pots used for *arghya*, bathing water, drinking water, and so on, and puts them back on their shelves. He wipes the floor with three balls of cow dung. As well as cleansing these physical objects, the worshiper must also "clear up" the ritual action he has just completed. Says *Kāmikāgama*, "he should repeat the mantra collection [consisting of MŪLA, the *brahmamantras*, and the *aṅgamantras*] in order to purify any deviations or errors" he may have committed (*KĀ* 4.536). Then, the text continues, "the priest rinses his hands and feet, sips water according to the rule, prostrates himself on the ground like a stick, and says, 'Forgive me'" (*KĀ* 4.537–38). With this final propitiation worship comes to a close.

Worship and Exchange

In *nityapūjā*, then, the worshiper gives the totality of matter, and finally himself as well, to Śiva. He supplicates Śiva, requesting (according to his aims in life) worldly pleasures or final liberation. The god Śiva is present in the liṅga to receive the offerings and may subsequently favor the worshiper by granting his wishes.

This recapitulation of the relations established in worship suggests a number of questions about the general significance of *pūjā* within the Śaiva world. Should daily worship be interpreted as a ritual of reciprocal exchange? What is the relationship between the services of worship and Śiva's bestowal of grace? Does the gift given in offering assure a return to the giver? Are the presentation of services and Śiva's boons causally linked to one another? Scholars of Indian religions have often employed terms and models drawn from human economic activity, such as "exchange," "reciprocity," and "redistribution," to explicate Hindu rituals, and so it is worth reconsidering these questions here from a Śaiva perspective.

Earlier in this chapter, I stressed the absolute hierarchy existing between Śiva and the bound soul. A parallel, and related, hierarchy subsists between a human's gift of worship and Śiva's granting of favor. For the Śaivas, these are gifts of unequal motivation, proportion, and value.

The worshiper is motivated to offer worship, as Sūryabhaṭṭa suggests, by the very nature of his relationship to Śiva. To perform *nityapūjā* is part of his "general code of conduct" (*samayācāra*), incumbent on all members of the Śaiva community; not to do so constitutes a fault, a sin. Śiva, by contrast, dispenses grace freely, without any compulsion. There cannot be any obligation to Śiva's favor, for that would contradict his autonomy. Rather, he grants his boons out of his favorable disposition to the souls (though the forms that benevolence takes may sometimes be difficult for us to comprehend), and with due regard for the propensities and capacities of those to whom he shows favor.

The *āgamas* repeatedly direct the worshiper to give his offerings *yathāśakti*, that is, in proportion to his abilities, insofar as he is able. For him, the giving over of material resources in worship represents a real and substantial "abandonment" (*tyāga*). While there is no reason for a householder to impoverish himself making offerings, the services of *pūjā* should constitute a personal sacrifice, a significant voluntary giving up of worldly possessions. And in his final supplications, the worshiper even gives up his own self to Śiva. Śiva's exercise of grace, on the other hand, is but one of his activities and does not diminish through his exercise of it. Śiva suffers no loss. There is no need for him to abandon anything else in favoring a particular soul, for he is omnipotent. Just as he is present in many temples and shrines simultaneously, Śiva can also favor many persons at the same time, without any effect on his own store of grace.

All that the worshiper gives to Śiva does not in any way add to Śiva, since he is already complete. While the offerings may represent a real sacrifice for the donor, they are without significant value for the recipient. Śiva has no need of such offerings. By contrast, the grace that Śiva may give is a thing of absolute value for the worshiper. Śiva's boon can have a complete transformative effect on the one who receives it. While bestowing grace does not subtract from Śiva at all, it may alter the human recipient totally.

The worshiper's gift and Śiva's grace, then, cannot be considered commodities of equal and exchangeable value.

Another way to consider the question of worship and exchange is to retrace the path of substantive offerings in *nityapūjā*. As we have seen, the worshiper selects the best specimens available of each article, prepares them carefully, and subjects them to a purification that renders them suitable for Śiva's consumption. Finally he presents them to Śiva, who enjoys the most subtle portion of each offering. The substantive portion left over becomes transfigured through contact with Śiva into highly pure *nirmālya*.

In many Hindu ritual schools, priests redistribute these substantive remainders of the divine meal to other participants in the ritual for secondary consumption as *prasāda*, the god's "favor." Such reuse suggests an automatic distribution of divine grace in palatable form and may lead one to think of *pūjā* as a communal exchange with the divinity: the community of worshipers gives offerings of purified food, and he gives in return transfigured food to his devotees. Śaiva siddhānta, however, denies the second phase of this apparent exchange. Food transubstantiated through Śiva's consumption is unfit for subsequent reuse by humans, because it is too pure. One cannot mechanically acquire Śiva's grace by eating his leftovers. So here too, the Śaivas stress the hierarchical distinction between Śiva and bound souls, and in so doing they confute the view that sees worship as reciprocal exchange between divinity and humanity.

If the offerings of *pūjā* are entirely incommensurate with Śiva's grace, if Śiva stands beyond any obligation or constraint, and if humans cannot even touch the food left on Śiva's plate, what does *pūjā* do? Does offering worship have any effect on Śiva at all?

While the Śaiva formulation of *nityapūjā* emphasizes the "otherness" of Śiva in many respects, it also envisions Śiva's personalization, through incarnation in a mantra body. Śiva allows himself to become embodied in a material form, and with this embodiment it is possible for the worshiper to enact a relationship analogous to certain human relations, such as that between host and guest, or between attendant and lord.

Throughout their descriptions of daily worship, the *āgamas* speak frequently of the worshiper "pleasing" Śiva. He invites Śiva to inhabit a material form as a guest in his home shrine or temple and presents to him the best he can offer in order to "satisfy" (*toṣaṇa*) and "refresh" (*tarpaṇa*) him. He entertains Śiva as the king of a divine court and sings his praises in order to "delight" (*abhinandana*) and "stimulate" (*prarocana*) him. He supplicates Śiva in order to "make Śiva favorably disposed" toward him. This notion of pleasing Śiva of course presupposes the personalization of the divinity brought about through invocation. Pleasure is not a meaningful category with respect to Paramaśiva, since Śiva in his highest state is beyond all such dualities as pleasure and pain. However, when Śiva becomes embodied as Sadāśiva and is viewed as a divine person, attempting to please this personage through one's ritual actions is eminently feasible.

In considering the efficacy of worship, it is useful to keep in mind the analogous human transactions. A host seeks to please and to satisfy the wishes of a respected guest not in any expectation of a return from the guest, but because it is *dharma*. The relationship itself compels the householder to observe certain principles of hospitality, and his own feelings of respect toward his visitor should reinforce the obligation. Similarly, one in attendance upon a king should hope to serve and gratify his lord and master precisely because the other is lord. The attendant is in no position to enforce or expect any return of favors, for he is in thrall to his king, but it is only human for him to make some petition for his lord's recognition and aid.

For the Śaivas, *pūjā* follows a similar course. The worshiper aims, through his services, to please Śiva who has become present close at hand. He does so not expecting an automatic recompense, but because service is his natural mode of relating himself to his lord, Śiva. Service to Śiva is dictated by the metaphysical relations persisting between categories of *pati* and *paśu*, by the general rules for conduct of all initiated Śaivites, and also by the worshiper's own spontaneous sentiments of devotion toward Śiva. The return on any such offering is at best uncertain, for Śiva operates according to designs beyond our comprehension in granting his favors.

The stress Śaivas place on the hierarchy of the relationship between worshiper and Śiva, and on the contingency of any profit accruing from one's donations, might lead one to regard *pūjā* as an uncertain and useless exercise. This is not a fitting conclusion. Śaiva texts obviously would not give the ritual of *nityapūjā* so much attention if it were simply uncertain, nor would they emphasize its efficacy if they considered it ultimately ineffectual. To view the full efficacy of the ritual, however, it is necessary to dissent from Sūryabhaṭṭa's definition of *pūjā*. Rather than identifying worship primarily by its core transactions between god and human worshiper, we must remember the relationship between the conscious powers of knowledge and action and view it in terms of the worshiper's own gradual mastery of a complex body of thought and practice, which does lead one ever closer both to the Lord Śiva and to attaining Śiva-ness in oneself.

CONCLUSION

IN THE FINAL SECTION of the *Śivapurāṇa*, after the wind-god Vāyu has given the eager sages of the Naimiṣa forest preliminary instruction in the *śivajñāna*, he concludes his discourse with a statement about the character of knowledge.

> Knowledge is said to be of two types, indirect (*parokṣa*, literally "beyond one's own sight") and direct. Indirect knowledge is unstable, they say, while direct knowledge is very firm. Knowledge acquired through reasoning and instruction is considered indirect knowledge; direct knowledge will arise through the most excellent practice of ritual. Deciding that you cannot obtain *mokṣa* without direct knowledge, you should exert yourselves assiduously to master this excellent practice. (*ŚPur Vāyavīya* 1.31.98–100)

Vāyu might seem here to undermine the authority of his own teachings. After all, according to this dichotomy the mediated verbal instruction he has just given the sages would be classified as indirect, unstable, and not leading to final liberation. But the sages are well-disposed to accept Vāyu's statement, since they have already been engaged in a sacrificial rite for a thousand divine years in order to gain Vāyu's presence in the first place. Immediately understanding its implication, they ask to be tutored in the superior ritual procedures so they can put them into practice themselves.

By now, we too should be able to assent to Vāyu's claim, even if we do not intend to follow his practical counsel. Śaiva daily worship, one of those most excellent ritual practices Vāyu speaks of, has provided us with a privileged entry point into the world as it was envisioned and acted upon by medieval Śaiva adepts and priests. By discursively reenacting Śaiva *pūjā* ourselves, we have seen how *śivajñāna* is embedded in every detail of its action and how this ritual engenders the direct, unmediated knowledge Vāyu declares is requisite to attaining liberation.

Śaiva *nityapūjā* employs a series of synecdochic representations to offer its practitioner a comprehensive vision of the Śaiva world within a delimited ritual terrain. Though by definition still fettered and limited in knowledge and action, the worshiper can temporarily free himself from these limitations within the sphere of *pūjā*. As he places mantras on his hands, removes impurities from his body, or mentally constructs Śiva's divine court, the worshiper regularly employs the ordering principles of cosmic dynamism, emission and reabsorption. As he reconstructs his body in self-purification, he recapitulates the central passage of the soul from its condition of bondage to liberation. When he imposes a variegated divine body onto the material liṅga and invokes Śiva into it, he enacts a condensed theophany of the Lord Śiva, a ritual metonym of Śiva's variegated being. And when he offers substantive services, he brings the three ontological categories—Śiva, bound souls, and inanimate substance—into their proper and fundamental relationship with one another.

Through regular effort, as Vāyu directs the sages, the worshiper could "exert himself assiduously to master" this ritual, to complete in himself the knowledge-in-action that would produce the highest fruits. For *pūjā* was not just a vision of an imagined world, nor even of a reconstructed historical world such as we have sought to enter, for the medieval Śaiva siddhāntins. It was rather a way of seeing into the fundamental order of things, beyond the human fetters that determine our partial viewpoint and our ignorance, and of acting thereby with greater efficacy to higher ends, beyond the bonds that normally suppress our active powers of consciousness.

Notes

INTRODUCTION
LOCATING THE TRADITION

1. The scholarly literature on *pūjā* is not large, considering its importance within Hindu traditions. For descriptions of *pūjā* in various schools, see James Burgess, "The Ritual of Ramesvaram," *Indian Antiquary* 12 (1883): 315–26; T. Goudriaan, "Vaikhanasa Daily Worship according to the handbooks of Atri, Bhrgu, Kasyapa, and Marici," *Indo-Iranian Journal* 12 (1970): 161–215; R. V. Joshi, *Le ritual de la devotion Krsnaite* (Pondichéry: Institut Français d'Indologie, 1959); K. Rangachari, *The Sri Vaisnava Brahmans* (Madras: Government Press, 1931); and Mrs. Sinclair Stevenson, *The Rites of the Twice-Born* (London: Oxford University Press, 1920), pp. 368–400. The most useful translations of *pūjā* texts are those of Hélène Brunner-Lachaux, *Somaśambhupaddhati, première partie* (Pondichéry: Institut Français d'Indologie, 1963), and T. Goudriaan, *Kasyapa's Book of Wisdom* (The Hague: Mouton, 1965). Two notable ethnographic accounts are Paul B. Courtright, "On This Holy Day in My Humble Way: Aspects of Pūjā," in J. P. Waghorne and N. Cutler (eds.), *Gods of Flesh/Gods of Stone* (Chambersburg, Pa.: Anima Publications, 1985), pp. 33–50; and Akos Ostor, *The Play of the Gods* (Chicago: University of Chicago Press, 1980).

2. The best general overview of Śaiva siddhānta literature is Jan Gonda, *Medieval Religious Literature in Sanskrit* (Wiesbaden: Otto Harrassowitz, 1977). While our knowledge of this corpus of texts has been substantially augmented since Gonda wrote, largely through the effort of scholars associated with the Institut Français d'Indologie in Pondichéry, there has not yet been any synthetic account incorporating this new information. I attempt to cite in these notes a large portion of recent scholarly work, so a diligent reader may follow up on topics of interest.

3. I use the 1975 *devanagari* edition of *Kāmikāgama* edited by C. Swaminathasiva. This edition virtually repeats the 1909 *grantha* text edited by Mayilai Alagappa Mudaliar, which in turn was based on seven separate manuscripts. I have also consulted a high-quality manuscript of *KĀ* formerly belonging to Sri Swaminatha Sivacarya of Tiruvatuturai matha, now held by the Institut Français d'Indologie at Pondichéry (T.298A). I use alternate readings based on this manuscript in a few cases where they seem clearly preferable. For *Kriyākramadyotikā*, I follow the 1927 *grantha* edition (based on four manuscript sources) published by the Jñānasambandham Press in Cidambaram, which includes Nirmalamaṇi's commentary. The 1967 edition of the South Indian Archakas Association follows the 1927 edition generally but contains numerous mistakes and adds many apocryphal passages. It is clear from a comparison of the texts that the 1927 edition of *KKD* is much truer to the text as it was available to Nirmalamaṇi in the sixteenth century. A critical edition of this central Śaiva siddhānta ritual text, based on thirty manuscripts, is currently being prepared under the direction of S. S. Janaki at the Kuppuswami Sastri Research Institute, Madras.

4. The authoritative dynastic history of the Colas remains K. A. Nilakantha Sastri, *The Colas* (Madras: University of Madras, 1935).

5. Rājarāja I adopted the practice of using a standardized *meykkirtti* to introduce his inscriptions. For one example, see E. Hultzsch, "Inscriptions at Mamallapuram," *South Indian Inscriptions* 1 (1890): 63–66.

6. An excellent account of the temple, covering diverse topics, is J. M. Somasundaram, *The Great Temple at Tanjore* (Madras: Solden & Co., 1935). For a recent architectural description, see K. R. Srinivasan's account in Michael W. Meister (ed.), *Encyclopaedia of Indian Temple Architecture: South India, Lower Dravidadesa* (Delhi: Oxford University Press, 1983), pp. 234–41.

7. These extensive inscriptions were edited and translated by E. Hultzsch, "Inscriptions of the Tanjavur Temple," *South Indian Inscriptions* 2 (1891–1913). Useful studies based primarily on this epigraphic material include: R. Nagaswamy, "South Indian Temple—As an Employer," *Indian Economic and Social History Review* 2 (1965): 367–72; K. A. Nilakantha Sastri, "The Economy of a South Indian Temple in the Cola Period," in A. B. Dhruva (ed.), *Malaviya Commemoration Volume* (Benares: Benares Hindu University, 1932), pp. 305–19; George W. Spencer, "Temple Money-Lending and Livestock Redistribution in Early Tanjore," *Indian Economic and Social History Review* 5 (1968): 277–93; and George W. Spencer, "Religious Networks and Royal Influence in Eleventh-Century South India," *Journal of the Economic and Social History of the Orient* 12 (1969): 42–56.

8. A local tradition, first reported by Burnell in 1879, claims that the liturgy of the Rājarājeśvara temple followed the *Makuṭāgama* (the "crown" *āgama*, one of the twenty-eight *mūlāgamas*). See A. C. Burnell, *A Classified Index to the Sanskrit Mss. in the Palace of Tanjore* (London: Trubner & Co., 1879). The published edition of *Makuṭāgama*, however, is highly corrupt; a critical edition would be necessary before a reasonable assessment of this claim could be made. See C. Svaminatha Sivacarya (ed.), *Makuṭāgama, pūrvabhāga* (Madras: South Indian Archakas Association, 1977).

9. Much of this brief depiction of "temple Hinduism" draws on the work of Ronald Inden, through his published and unpublished writings, classes at the University of Chicago between 1978 and 1980, and many discussions since. For a discussion of temple Hinduism as a transformation of previous ideological formations, see R. Inden, "The Ceremony of the Great Gift (*Mahādāna*): Structure and Historical Context in Indian Ritual and Society," *Asie du Sud, traditions et changements*, Colloques Internationaux du CNRS, no. 582 (Paris: Editions du Centre national de la recherche scientifique, 1979), pp. 131–36. Nicholas Dirks, "Political Authority and Structural Change in Early South Indian History," *Indian Economic and Social History Review* 13 (1976): 125–58, is also useful in specifying this transformation. Other pertinent articles by Inden include "The Ceremonial Bath of the Hindu King of Kings" and "Imperial Formations, Imperial Purānas" (both unpublished).

10. For accounts of the varied activities of medieval South Indian temples, see the well-titled essay by K. V. Soundara Rajan, "The Kaleidoscopic Activities of Medieval Temples in the Tamilnad," *Quarterly Journal of the Mythic Society* 42 (1952): 87–101; and Burton Stein, "The Economic Function of a Medieval South Indian Temple," *Journal of Asian Studies* 19 (1960): 163–76. Three important dis-

cussions of the general role of temple and temple ritual in medieval South Indian society and politics are: A. Appadurai and C. A. Breckenridge, "The South Indian Temple: Authority, Honour and Redistribution," *Contributions to Indian Sociology* 10 (1976): 187–211; Nicholas B. Dirks, *The Hollow Crown: Ethnohistory of an Indian Kingdom* (Cambridge: Cambridge University Press, 1987); and Burton Stein, *Peasant State and Society in Medieval South India* (New Delhi: Oxford University Press, 1980).

11. *ĪP* vol. 3 ch. 30. Discussed in Stella Kramrisch, *The Hindu Temple* (Delhi: Motilal Banarsidass, 1946–1976), vol. 1, pp. 261–70.

12. *Vāyusaṃhitā*, cited in *Varṇāśramacandrikā*, translated in *SP* 1 p. vi.

13. A list is given in Bhatt (ed.), *RĀ* 1, opposite p. xix.

14. For an example, see *AĀ* 1.1.35–105. But *āgamas* dispute among themselves which mouths emit which *āgamas*. See Jean Filliozat, "Introduction: Les āgamas Śivaites," *RĀ* 1 pp. v–xv.

15. E. Hultzsch, "The Pallava Inscriptions on the Kailasanatha Temple at Kanchipuram," *South Indian Inscriptions* 1 (1890): 8–24.

16. Bruno Dagens (trans.), "Introduction," *MM* 1 pp. 1–7.

17. See Hélène Brunner-Lachaux's discussion of the relation between *KĀ* and *MṛĀ* in her "Introduction," *MṛĀ (Section des rites et section du comportement)*, pp. x–xix.

18. Hara Prasad Sastri, *A Catalogue of Palm-Leaf and Selected Paper Mss. Belonging to the Durbar Library, Nepal* (Calcutta: Baptist Mission Press, 1905, 1915), vol. 2, p. xxiv.

19. Nārāyaṇakaṇṭha quotes a verse of Utpaladeva, who lived probably in the mid-ninth century; Kṣemarāja's commentary on the *SvaT*, composed in the eleventh century, in turn quotes Nārāyaṇakaṇṭha's *MṛĀV*. See Bhatt (ed.), *MPĀ* 1 p. xii, and Brunner-Lachaux (trans.), *MṛĀ (Section des rites)*, p. vii and n. 6.

20. Hélène Brunner touches briefly on these points of disagreement in "Importance de la littérature āgamique pour l'étude des religions vivantes de l'Inde," *Indologica Taurinensia* 3–4 (1975–1976): 107–24. On the various lists of *tattvas*, see Bhatt, "Introduction," *MPĀ* 1 pp. xxi–xxiv. Surendranath Dasgupta summarizes the philosophical positions of several *āgamas* and related texts (including *MPĀ*, *PĀ*, *VŚĀ*, and *ŚPur*) in *A History of Indian Philosophy, Vol. 5: The Southern Schools of Śaivism* (Delhi: Motilal Banarsidass, 1922–1975).

21. Compare Abhinavagupta's account (in *Tantrāloka*, ch. 36) of the division of *āgama*-based Śaivism into three propensities, as K. C. Pandey summarizes it:

> [Śiva] instructed the sage, Durvasas, to revive the Śaivagamic teaching. The sage accordingly divided all the saivāgamas into 3 classes according as they taught monism, dualism or monism-cum-dualism, imparted their knowledge to his 3 mind-born sons, Tryambaka, Amardaka, and Srinatha respectively, and charged each one of them separately with the mission of spreading the knowledge of their respective Āgamas. Thus there came into existence three Śaiva Tantric Schools, each known by the name of the first earthly progenitor.

K. C. Pandey, *Abhinavagupta: An Historical and Philosophical Study*, Chowkhamba Sanskrit Series, vol. 1 (Benares: Chowkhamba Sanskrit Series Office, 1935), p. 72.

22. David N. Lorenzen discusses these and many other references to the four (most often) Śaiva schools. See *The Kāpālikas and Kālāmukhas: Two Lost Śaivite Sects* (Berkeley: University of California Press, 1972), pp. 1–12. For a general summary of several individual schools of Śaivism, see also Pranabananda Jash, *History of Śaivism* (Calcutta: Roy and Chaudhury, 1974).

23. Hélène Brunner discusses the Śaiva siddhānta characterization of its main Śaiva competitor in "The Pāśupatas as seen by the Śaivas," *Schriften zur Geschichte und Kultur des alten Orients* 18 (1986): 513–20.

24. Significant secondary sources concerning Śaiva siddhānta monastic lineages include: R. D. Banerji, *The Haihayas of Tripuri and Their Monuments*, Memoirs of the Archaeological Survey of India, no. 23 (Calcutta: Government of India, 1931); V. V. Mirashi, "The Śaiva Ācāryas of the Mattamayūra Clan," *Indian Historical Quarterly* 26 (1950): 1–16; V. V. Mirashi (ed.), *Inscriptions of the Kalachuri-Chedi Era, Corpus Inscriptionum Indicarum*, vol. 4 (Ootacamund: Government Epigraphist for India, 1955); J. Van Troy, "The Social Structure of the Śaiva-siddhāntika Ascetics (700–1300 A.D.)," *Indica* 11 (1974): 77–86; B.G.L. Swamy, "The Golaki School of Śaivism in the Tamil Country," *Journal of Indian History* 53 (1975): 167–209; and Cynthia Talbot, "Golaki Matha Inscriptions from Andhra Pradesh: A Study of a Śaiva Monastic Lineage," in *Vajapeya: Essays on Evolution of Indian Art and Culture* (Delhi: Agam Kala Prakashan, 1987), pp. 133–46. For Southeast Asia, see K. Bhattacharya, *Les religions brahmaniques dans l'Ancien Cambodge* (Paris: Ecole Française d'Extrême-Orient, 1961).

25. As a tenth-century inscription from Madhya Pradesh refers to one important Śaiva siddhānta branch, the Mattamayūra. See F. Kielhorn, "A Stone Inscription from Ranod (Narod)," *Epigraphia Indica* 1 (1892): 351–61.

26. As Brunner puts it, the *paddhatis* aim at "unification of the often contradictory teachings of the *āgamas*, and have performed their function so well that they have ended up somewhat eclipsing the *āgamas* themselves" ("Importance de la littérature āgamique," p. 110).

27. On Aghoraśiva's life, see Wayne Surdam, "South Indian Śaiva Rites of Initiation: 'The Dīkṣāvidhi' of Aghoraśivācārya's 'Kriyākramadyotikā'" (Ph.D. dissertation, University of California, Berkeley, 1984), pp. xvi–xxi. Aghoraśiva's known works are listed in V. Raghavan, *New Catalogus Catalogorum* (Madras: University of Madras, 1968), vol. 1, pp. 58–59. I have attempted to summarize the intellectual background of Aghoraśiva in "Aghoraśiva's Background," in *Dr. S. S. Janaki Shashtyabdapurti Commemoration Volume* (Madras: Kuppuswami Sastri Research Institute, forthcoming).

28. For two scholarly summaries of Śaiva siddhānta doctrine based on the *paddhati* literature, see Rohan A. Dunuwila, *Śaiva Siddhānta Theology: A Context for Hindu-Christian Dialogue* (Delhi: Motilal Banarsidass, 1985) (based primarily on Bhojadeva's *TP*); and K. C. Pandey, *An Outline of History of Śaiva Philosophy* (Delhi: Motilal Banarsidass, 1986) (first printed in 1955 as *Bhaskari*, vol. 3). Jayandra Soni, *Philosophical Anthropology in Śaiva Siddhānta* (Delhi: Motilal Banarsidass, 1989), is based primarily on the works of the sixteenth-century Śaiva author Śivāgrayogin.

29. The best general account of the Tamil version of Śaiva siddhānta is M. Dha-

vamony, *Love of God according to Śaiva Siddhānta* (Oxford: Clarendon Press, 1971). Also useful are the collected lectures of V. A. Devasenapathy, with the excellent title *Of Human Bondage and Divine Grace* (Cidambaram: Annamalai University, 1963), and the study of K. Sivaraman, *Śaivism in Philosophical Perspective* (Delhi: Motilal Banarsidass, 1973). A primary agenda of most historical scholarship on Tamil Śaiva siddhānta works of the thirteenth century and later has been to develop a genealogy relating these texts directly to the works of the Tamil *nāyanmārs* of the sixth through ninth centuries. Such studies generally pay lip service to the role of the *āgamas* in the philosophical system of Meykaṇṭār and his followers, but they do not seriously investigate the connections between the Sanskrit *āgama* literature and the later Tamil works.

30. The only critical work devoted to this, as far as I know, is the brief discussion by Brunner, "Importance de la littérature āgamique," pp. 118–19. For another example of a Śaiva author working in both Sanskrit and Tamil, see Bruno Dagens's discussion of the sixteenth-century commentator Vedajñāna/Maṟaiñāṉatēcikar, in "Introduction," *ŚPM*, pp. 5–15. I am indebted to Dagens for leading me to reconsider the relation of Sanskrit and Tamil Śaiva siddhānta literature.

31. On the poetry of the *nāyanmārs*, see especially the recent study and translations by Indira Peterson, *Poems to Śiva* (Princeton: Princeton University Press, 1989).

32. On the use of texts in contemporary temple practice, see Carl Gustav Diehl, *Instrument and Purpose: Studies on Rites and Rituals of South India* (Lund: C.W.K. Gleerup, 1956). For a portrait of a Śaiva priestly community in theological disarray, see Chris Fuller's fascinating ethnography on the Madurai Mīṇākṣi-Sundareśvarar temple priests, *Servants of the Goddess: The Priests of a South Indian Temple* (Cambridge: Cambridge University Press, 1984).

33. G. U. Pope (trans.), *The Tiruvācagam, or "Sacred Utterances" of the Tamil Poet, Saint, and Sage Manikkavācagar* (Oxford: Clarendon Press, 1900), p. lxxiv. The same position turns up repeatedly in general works on Śaivism and Hinduism. For instances, see: M. Dhavamony, "Śaivism: Śaiva Siddhānta," in Mircea Eliade (ed.), *Encyclopedia of Religion* (New York: Macmillan Publishing Co., 1987), vol. 13, p. 11; and Thomas J. Hopkins, *The Hindu Religious Tradition* (Encino, Cal.: Dickenson Publishing Co., 1971), p. 118.

34. For a more skeptical discussion of the question of integration between *jñāna* and *kriyā*, see Hélène Brunner-Lachaux, "Introduction," *MṛĀ (Section des rites)*, esp. pp. xlii–xliii.

35. The texts set out an ideal program for worship that only the highly adept and devout could follow completely. Yet they also recognize and allow for individual variations and shortcuts in phrases repeated throughout, such as *yathāśakti* (in accord with one's capacity).

36. *Agnipurāṇa* (ch. 72–106), *Liṅgapurāṇa*, and *Śivapurāṇa* (*Vāyavīyasamhitā* ch. 16–20) clearly articulate siddhānta positions. (Brunner briefly discusses the purāṇic usage of āgamic material in "Importance de la littérature āgamique," pp. 117 and 121.) *Śilpaśāstras* such as *MM* also reflect Śaiva siddhānta practice, but through the eyes of the *sthāpati* rather than the *ācārya*.

37. I mention in the notes some of the disputes and differing formulations within

the Śaiva siddhānta order. In her translation of *SP*, and particularly in vol. 3, Hélène Brunner-Lachaux presents a much more variegated portrait of Śaiva siddhānta literature, focusing repeatedly on doctrinal discussion within the order.

Chapter One
Ritual and Human Powers

1. Some Śaiva texts add "volition" (*icchā*) as a third inherent power of consciousness.

2. The *āgamas* of course recognize that not everyone seeks *mokṣa* in this lifetime; the world includes *bubhukṣus* ("seekers of worldly enjoyments") as well as *mumukṣus* ("seekers of liberation"). But worldly powers and liberation do not lie along radically differing courses of action. Both result from the removal of fetters and the manifestation of inherent powers. *Sādhakas* (mantra-adepts), for instance, employ Śaiva ritual and knowledge to gain specific worldly powers. For a full discussion, see Hélène Brunner, "Le *sādhaka*, personnage oublié du Śivaisme du Sud," *Journal asiatique* 263 (1975): 411–43.

3. Contrary to what many modern advocates of Śaiva siddhānta have held, the *āgamas* do not portray themselves as derived from or in any way subordinate to the Vedas. On this matter, Hélène Brunner's "Le Śaiva-siddhānta, 'Essence' du Veda," *Indologica Taurinensia* 8 (1980–1981): 51–66, is a welcome statement. For a somewhat different formulation, see Richard Davis, "Cremation and Liberation: A Śaiva siddhānta Revision," *History of Religions* 28 (1988): 37–53. Wayne Surdam, "The Vedicization of Śaiva Ritual," in S. S. Janaki (ed.), *Śiva Temple and Temple Rituals* (Madras: Kuppuswami Sastri Research Institute, 1988), pp. 52–60, deals with the relationship as it has changed over time.

4. *MṛĀVD vidyā* 1.20, from Michel Hulin's French translation.

5. *Kāmikāgama* refers to this useful technique as an analogy to the efficacy of "interior worship":

> Visualizing with his mind, he should daily worship Parameśvara in this imagined temple, using substances that are mentally constructed. As a guru meditates that he is Garuḍa and obtains the result of removing [poison, even though done mentally], so here also one obtains the desired benefits [resulting from worship]. (*KĀ* 4.189–90)

6. This useful convention I owe to Hélène Brunner-Lachaux, who has employed it in her translations and studies of *śaivāgama*.

7. Nirmalamaṇi understands the Śaiva form of meditation, in its concern to establish a relationship between meditator and divinity, to differ from Patañjali yoga: "Yoga is the close connection (*sambandha*) during meditation with the object of meditation; not, as in Patañjali, the condition of *samādhi*" (*KKDP*, translated in Surdam, "South Indian Śaiva Rites," p. lv, n. 102).

8. *KārĀ*, cited by Nirmalamaṇi in *KKDP*, and quoted in Janaki, *ML* p. 2.

9. For detailed discussion of *mudrās* in Śaiva ritual, see the series of six articles by S. S. Janaki, "Śaiva Mudrās i–vi," *Kalakshetra Quarterly* 5–6 (1983–1984). Photographs of the *mudrās* may be found in those articles and also in *SP* 1, Plate 1, "Mudrā," and in Surdam, "South Indian Śaiva Rites," Appendix, pp. 276–313. In

S. S. Janaki (ed.), *ML*, line drawings of *mudrās* following *ML* prescriptions are provided.

10. *VŚĀ*, from Brunner-Lachaux's French translation, *SP* 1 p. xxxi.

11. On the grammar of Śaiva mantras, see Hélène Brunner-Lachaux's brief discussion in *SP* 1 pp. xxxi–xxxii. Brunner-Lachaux also includes a list of the mantras employed in *nityapūjā* in *SP* 1, Appendix 3, "Mantras utilisés pendant le culte de Śiva (d'après Somaśambhu)."

12. Vedajñāna apparently quotes *MPĀ* here. Other authors construct similar scales of forms: "Proponents of various schools describe the inherent form of the highest *mokṣa* in various ways, each in accord with its own views." With this preface, Śivāgrayogin considers, and criticizes, a whole series of alleged *mokṣas* held by other schools (*ŚPbh* pp. 335–52), including the *śivasāmya* views of Aghoraśiva that I take here as normative.

13. This includes both *pūrva* and *uttara* portions of the text. For a summary of the contents of *KĀ*, *pūrvabhāga*, see Bruno Dagens, "Analyse du *Pūrvakāmikāgama*," *Bulletin de l'Ecole Française d'Extrême-Orient* 54 (1977): 1–38. Dagens's résumé is based on N. R. Bhatt's Sanskrit *upodghāta*, in *KĀ*, *pūrvabhāga*, pp. iii–xx. Two other *āgama* résumés are available: Hélène Brunner, "Analyse du *Kiraṇāgama*," *Journal asiatique* 253 (1965): 309–28; and Brunner, "Analyse du *Suprabhedāgama*," *Journal asiatique* 255 (1967): 31–60. These two *āgamas* cover a more modest array of rituals but are noteworthy for containing all four *pādas* of a proper *āgama*.

14. *SupĀ*, quoted in *SĀSS* p. 58.

15. The *āgamas* generally present *ātmārtha* and *parārtha* as two variants of a single scheme of *pūjā*, and following their lead I will describe Śaiva daily worship in this study as a ritual unity. However, there are some practrical differences between the two. Hélène Brunner compares them in greater detail in "Ātmārthapūjā versus Parārthapūjā in the Śaiva Tradition," in T. Goudriaan (ed.), *The Sanskrit Tradition and Tantrism* (Leiden: E. J. Brill, 1990), pp. 4–23. She argues that the integral model of *pūjā* assumed by later Śaiva literature in fact results historically from the combining of two originally distinct styles of worship, one an "old public worship" of a rudimentary sort, and the other an inner-oriented "private worship" maintained by yogic adepts.

16. Frits Staal has discussed the "embedding" of ritual units within one another to constitute larger ritual wholes in the Vedic system: "Ritual Syntax," in M. Nagatomi et al. (eds.), *Sanskrit and Indian Studies: Essays in Honour of Daniel H. H. Ingalls* (Dordrecht: D. Reidel Publishing Co., 1980), pp. 119–42. As will be clear throughout this study, I depart strongly from Staal's view that such embeddings are the empty exercise of syntactic elements without discursive significance.

17. *Svatantra*, quoted by Nirmalamaṇi in *KKDP* p. 293, cited in *SP* 3 p. 9.

18. To assist those who wish to reenact Śaiva *pūjā* visually as well as mentally, the Kuppuswami Sastri Research Institute has recently made available an excellent videotape of K. A. Sabharatna Sivacarya performing an *āgama*-based worship of Śiva, with comentary in English or Tamil. Readers wishing to obtain a copy may contact Ginni Ishimatsu, Department of South and Southeast Asian Studies, University of California, Berkeley, CA 94702, or Richard Davis, Department of Religious Studies, Yale University, New Haven, CT 06520.

Chapter Two
Oscillation in the Ritual Universe

1. The classic 1918 essay by A. K. Coomaraswamy, "The Dance of Shiva," in *The Dance of Shiva* (New Delhi: Sagar Publications, 1969), pp. 66–78, remains the best published account of the significance of Naṭarāja as explicated by Tamil Śaiva siddhānta authors. On the origin of this iconic form, there is considerable scholarly debate. Starting about 970 C.E. the dowager Cola queen Sembiyan Mahādevī, grandmother of Rājarāja, began placing Naṭarāja in a prominent position on the exterior walls of the temples she sponsored, and I would date the elevation of Naṭarāja to most-favored status among Cola images of Śiva to her initiative.

2. The Śaiva scheme of *tattvas* clearly draws upon the Sāṃkhya model of emanating *prakṛti* but surpasses it by adding additional *tattvas* and an entire domain, the pure domain, not envisioned within Sāṃkhya circles. See Dasgupta, *History, Vol. 5: Southern Schools*, pp. 164–70, for some discussion of Śaiva siddhānta in relation to Sāṃkhya.

3. On the emission of language and the alphabet, see *KĀ* 2.4–7. Rāmakaṇṭha gives a more sophisticated treatment of language in the Śaiva siddhānta universe in his *Nādakārikā* (with a commentary by Aghoraśiva), included also in his *KālĀV* (1.5). See Pierre-Sylvain Filliozat, "Les Nādakārikā de Rāmakaṇṭha," *Bulletin de l'Ecole Française d'Extrême-Orient* 73 (1984): 223–55, for a translation and informed explication.

4. For a general study of *nyāsa* as a ritual technique, see Andre Padoux, "Contributions a l'étude du mantraśāstra," *Bulletin de l'Ecole Française d'Extrême-Orient* 67 (1980): 59–102.

5. Further aspects of the five mantras are set forth by Brunner-Lachaux in *SP* 1, Appendix 6, "Quelques correspondences entre les visages de Sadāśiva et le Cosmos."

6. Some texts omit NETRA from the set of *aṅgamantras*, which may account for its distinctive treatment in *karanyāsa* and elsewhere.

7. A much more detailed treatment of Śiva's *aṅgas* may be found in Hélène Brunner, "Les members de Śiva," *Asiatische Studien* 40 (1986): 89–132.

8. *MṛĀ kriyā* 3.3 offers an exception. Here the weapon mantra ASTRA should be placed on the index finger (*tarjanī*, literally the "threatening finger") because ASTRA is the mantra that "threatens intruders."

9. See Brunner-Lachaux, *SP* 1, Appendix 5, "Purification du corps grossier: les cinq maṇḍala des éléments," for a résumé of the features of each domain.

10. A shorter alternative method of bodily purification described in both *KKD* and *KĀ* involves visualizing the body as an upside-down tree and progressively destroying it (*KKD* p. 59). See Brunner-Lachaux's translation of Aghoraśiva's account in *SP* 1, Appendix 4, "Purification du corps grossier, autre methode."

11. On the thirty-eight *kalā*s and the *kalāmantras*, see N. R. Bhatt's summary in *RĀ* 1 pp. 25–28 and the table, "Les noms des Kalā dans les textes," opposite p. 28. The mantras are derived from five Vedic mantras in *Taittirīya Āraṇyaka* 10.43–47, refracted and reformulated within a Śaiva grammar of mantras.

12. See N. R. Bhatt, "Introduction," *MPĀ* 2 pp. xi–xvi; also Hélène Brunner-Lachaux, *SP* 3 p. 242 and Plate 8, "Distribution des mots du *vyomavyāpin* entre les cinq *kalā* selon l'Adhvanyāsa."

13. The classic secondary account of *vāstumaṇḍala* is Stella Kramrisch, *The Hindu Temple*, vol. 1, pp. 19–97. Kramrisch utilizes Śaiva siddhānta texts, particularly *ĪP*, as well as texts belonging to many other schools, for her synthetic description. Some of the relevant chapters of *ĪP* are translated by Kramrisch in "Īśānaśivagurudevapaddhati Kriyāpada Chs. xxvi, xxvii," *Journal of the Indian Society of Oriental Art* 9 (1941): 151–93; and "Temple, Door, Throne, Etc.," *Journal of the Indian Society of Oriental Art* 10 (1942): 210–52 (which translates *ĪP kriyā* ch. 5, 7, 12, and 13).

14. The phrase is from Mark Twain, *Following the Equator* (Hartford: American Publishing Company, 1898), p. 504, quoted in Diana L. Eck, *Banares: City of Light* (Princeton: Princeton University Press, 1982), p. 19.

15. Compare the model of a royal court presented in the *Aparājitapṛcchā* by the twelfth-century Gujarati author Bhuvanadeva and described in Ronald Inden, "Hierarchies of Kings in Early Medieval India," in T. N. Madan (ed.), *Way of Life: King, Householder, Renouncer* (Paris: Editions de la Maison des Sciences de l'Homme, 1982), pp. 99–125.

16. The architectural prescriptions of *AĀ* are lucidly summarized in Bruno Dagens, *Les enseignements architecturaux de l'Ajitāgama et du Rauravāgama* (Pondichéry: Institut Français d'Indologie, 1977), translated into English as *Architecture in the Ajitāgama and the Rauravāgama* (New Delhi: Sitaram Bhartia Institute of Scientific Research, 1984). See Table 5, "Disposition des Assesseurs selon l'*Ajita*," for a diagram of *AĀ*'s model temple topography.

17. *KĀ* 4.225–69. The *UKĀ* ch. 4 also describes these diagrams, in most but not all cases congruent with the versions in the *pūrvabhāga*. A still more detailed account is found in *RĀ* 1 ch. 20–24.

18. Compare the diagrams based on *RĀ* prescriptions, Plates 6–11, and those based on *AĀ*, Plates 2–8.

19. A fine photograph of well-dressed *śivakumbha* and *vardhanī* may be seen in Bhatt (ed.), *MṛĀ*, Plate 13, opposite p. 93.

20. The procedure summarized here is based on "Navakalaśasnāpanapaddhati," a manuscript belonging to J. Visvanatha Gurukkal of Melmangalam and quoted in extenso by N. R. Bhatt in *RĀ* 1 pp. 92–93, n. 9.

21. The *ādiśaivas* constitute a special category of "original Śaiva" brahmans, made up of five *gotras*, who alone qualify to be priests in Śaiva siddhānta temples. For a full discussion, including intriguing remarks concerning their origin, see Hélène Brunner, "Les catégories sociales védiques dans le Śivaisme du sud," *Journal asiatique* 252 (1964): 451–72.

22. *SupĀ*, quoted in N. R. Bhatt, "What Is Śaivāgama?" (pamphlet, no publication information), p. 2.

23. *ĀPV*, quoted in Bhatt, "What Is Śaivāgama?" p. 3. For similar rules from other schools concerning differentiated temple access, see Ronald Inden, "The Temple and the Hindu Chain of Being," *Purusartha* 8 (1985).

24. *KārĀ* 24.95, quoted in K. A. Sabharatna Sivacarya, "Uṟcava Vimarcaṉam," in S. S. Janaki (ed.), *Śiva Temple and Temple Rituals* (Madras: Kuppuswami Sastri Research Institute, 1988), p. 93.

25. *KārĀ* 141.1–2, quoted in Sabharatna Sivacarya, "Uṟcava Vimarcaṉam," p. 92.

Chapter Three
Becoming a Śiva

1. V. A. Devasenapathy cites the pleasing analogy of a prince raised among gypsies:

> The soul is like a prince kidnapped in his infancy by gipsies and brought up by them in ignorance of his real identity. It is natural for the prince in such a state to behave in gipsy ways mistaking these as natural to him. But when the king comes and reveals his identity, the prince will give up his gipsy ways and conduct himself as befits a prince.

V. A. Devasenapathy, *Of Human Bondage and Divine Grace* (Cidambaram: Annamalai University, 1963), p. 48. I have not been able to locate the textual source of this simile.

2. Śaiva texts refer to two other categories of fetters: *tirobhāva* (or *rodhśakti*) and *mahāmāyā*. *Tirobhāva*, Śiva's power of obscuration, is a fetter only in a secondary sense, says Aghoraśiva, while *mahāmāyā* affects only beings such as the Vidyeśvaras who dwell in the pure domain (*śuddhādhvan*) (*TPV* 17).

3. The hierarchy of souls described in Chapter 1 is based on the presence or absence of these three fetters. As bound souls, *sakalas*, we are affected by all three categories of fetters (*TP* 8–15).

4. The monist commentator Śrīkumāra, discussing Bhojadeva's *TP*, claims that the ripening of *mala* is brought about by the "fire of knowledge" (*TPD* 9), but Aghoraśiva firmly denies this (*TPV* 15).

5. Hélène Brunner-Lachaux discusses the Śaiva understanding of *karman* and its three types in *SP* 3 pp. xxii–xxvi.

6. Śaiva authors differ from one another in their discussions of *śaktinipāta*. Somaśambhu, for instance, identifies *śaktinipāta* with the act of initiation, while Aghoraśiva and most subsequent authors view it as a necessary precursor to receiving initiation. For helpful discussions of this philosophically ambiguous phenomenon, see Brunner-Lachaux, *SP* 3 p. viii, and Surdam, "South Indian Śaiva Rites," pp. cxiv–cxxi.

7. My descriptions of Śaiva *dīkṣās* are based largely on the *SP* and *KKD*. For translations of *samayadīkṣā* procedures, see *SP* 3 pp. 2–110, and Surdam, "South Indian Śaiva Rites," pp. 1–97.

8. On the several stages of initiation and corresponding ritual competencies, see Brunner, "Le sādhaka," *Journal asiatique* 263 (1975): 411–43.

9. Translations of *viśeṣadīkṣā* procedures: *SP* 3 pp. 112–56, and Surdam, "South Indian Śaiva Rites," pp. 98–112. Brunner-Lachaux argues that *samaya* and *viśeṣa* were initially two phases of a single ritual and were separated into distinct rituals at a fairly late date (*SP* 3 pp. xxx–xxxiii); these two in turn may have at an earlier date been separated from *nirvāṇadīkṣā*, the originally unitary Śaiva *dīkṣā*. To gain an idea of the variety of Śaiva treatments of *dīkṣā* generally, see N. R. Bhatt, "Introduction," *MPĀ* 2 pp. xviii–xxiii.

10. See *SP* 3 pp. 157–426, and Surdam, "South Indian Śaiva Rites," pp. 113–271. The amount of discussion Somaśambhu and Aghoraśiva devote to each of the three types of *dīkṣā* offer a good initial index of their importance in the Śaiva scheme

of things: in Surdam's translation of *KKD*, *samayadīkṣā* gets 96 pages, *viśeṣadīkṣā* 14 pages, and *nirvāṇadīkṣā* 158 pages.

11. Texts refer to this method only as *tāḍanādi*, "the set of actions beginning with striking." For a more detailed discussion of "transportation," see *SP* 3 pp. 118–25, and Plates 1 and 2, "Transport de l'*ātman* depuis le Coeur du disciple jusqu'à la matrice de Vāgīsvarī."

12. The method described here, focusing on five *kalās*, is only one of six possible "paths" (*adhvan*) along which initiation may proceed: mantras, words, phonemes, worlds, *tattvas*, and *kalās*. As the quotation from *UKĀ* below indicates, however, Śaiva siddhānta understands the *kalās* to encompass the constituents of the other paths, and hence the method of *kalā* purification offers a more comprehensive means of *dīkṣā* (at least from the time of Somaśambhu). On the sixfold path, see Brunner-Lachaux, *SP* 3 pp. xiii–xxii.

13. In *SP* 3, Brunner-Lachaux provides charts summarizing these englobements: see Plate 5, "Englobement des réalités de l'Universe par les cinq *kalā*"; Plate 6, "Répartition des *tattva* selon les cinq *kalā*"; and Plates 7 A–E, displaying the worlds encompassed within each of the five *kalās*.

14. After *nirvāṇadīkṣā*, a Śaiva initiate may undergo special additional consecrations (*abhiṣeka*) that grant him particular capacities for action. Most common is the "priestly consecration" (*ācāryābhiṣeka*), enabling the recipient to act as priest in performing rituals on behalf of others. Another consecration grants special mantra powers to the adept (*sādhakābhiṣeka*). For Somaśambhu's account of these consecrations, see *SP* 3 pp. 455–524.

15. Nirmalamaṇi distinguishes the efficacy of *ātmaśuddhi* according to the worshiper's stage of initiation. For one who has undergone *samayadīkṣā* but not *nirvāṇadīkṣā*, *ātmaśuddhi* destroys any obstructions that prevent mantras from achieving their purposes; for those who have undergone *nirvāṇadīkṣā*, by contrast, it helps complete initiation by destroying all newly arisen *karman* (*KKDP* p. 60).

16. See *SP* 1, Appendix 5, "Purification du corps grossier," for a chart of the *guṇas* located in each of the five *bhūtas*.

17. See Brunner-Lachaux's detailed discussion of this parallelism, in *SP* 3 pp. 396–405.

18. Somaśambhu's prescriptions for *antyeṣṭi* are translated in *SP* 3 pp. 567–618. For a general discussion of this ritual in the Śaiva system, see Davis, "Cremation and Liberation."

Chapter Four
Summoning the Lord

1. *MṛĀVD vidyā* 3.8–9, following Michel Hulin's French translation, *MṛĀ (Doctrine et Yoga)*, p. 121.
2. *SvāĀ vidyā* 4.3, quoted in *ŚPM* 1.2.
3. On the nonactivity of the *muktātman*, see *MṛĀV vidyā* 2.29 and *ŚSPbh* p. 37.
4. *VŚĀ* 1.22, quoted in *ŚPM* p. 56, n. 2.
5. *AcĀ*, quoted in *ŚPbh* p. 63.
6. In his "Compendium of All Schools" (*SDS*), the monist author Mādhava dis-

cusses the views of Śaiva siddhānta (*śaivadarśana*) in chapter 7. He bases his description primarily on the *MṛĀ* and Nārāyaṇakaṇṭha's commentary *MṛĀV*, on Bhojadeva's *TP* and Aghoraśiva's *TPV*; he also employs *KirĀ*, *PĀ*, *SP*, and a very few other texts. The passage here relies on *MṛĀV* 3.8. See Hélène Brunner's expert translation, "Un chapitre du *Sarvadarśanasaṃgraha*: Le *śaivadarśana*," in Michel Strickman (ed.), *Tantric and Taoist Studies in Honour of R. A. Stein* (Brussels: Institut Belge des Hautes Etudes Chinoises, 1981), pp. 96–140.

7. For general treatments of the lithic forms and iconographic representations of Sadāśiva, see Brijendra Nath Sharma, *Iconography of Sadāśiva* (Delhi: Abhinav Publications, 1976), and Thomas S. Maxwell, "The Five Aspects of Śiva (In Theory, Iconography and Architecture)," *Arts International* 25 (1982): 41–57.

8. The list of *aṅgas* is consistent, but the attributes vary somewhat from text to text. Compare for instance the discussions in *SP* 1.3.72–74 and *KKD* pp. 108–9. As noted in the previous chapter and implied in the passage quoted here, the *aṅgas* are closely related to the six divine qualities (*guṇa*) of Śiva, acquired also by the initiate in *dīkṣā*. See Brunner's two long footnotes on the subject, *SP* 3 pp. 396–405.

9. The set of weapons held by Sadāśiva varies slightly from text to text. *KĀ* specifies two possible sets (4.332–34), while Aghoraśiva gives three alternatives (*KKD* pp. 98–99). *SP* 1, Plate 7, "Āyudha de Sadāśiva," lists eight different sets of Sadāśiva's weapons attested in diverse *āgamas*. However different, these sets generally encompass all the various weapons associated with Śiva in his iconic (Maheśvara) forms.

10. Retellings of Śiva's purāṇic escapades are conveniently available in Wendy Doniger O'Flaherty, *Śiva: The Erotic Ascetic* (Oxford: Oxford University Press, 1973), and Stella Kramrisch, *The Presence of Śiva* (Princeton: Princeton University Press, 1981).

11. *RĀ* 2 ch. 35. In his "Preface," N. R. Bhatt concisely summarizes the Maheśvara forms described in various *āgama* texts (*RĀ* 2 pp. ix–xi). Also in this volume may be found drawings of these forms based on *āgama* prescription.

12. *VĀ* 63.4–5, quoted in *ŚPM* 5.151–54. As Dagens notes, the passage Vedajñāna cites does not include the expected pentad of *saṃhāramūrtis*.

13. See for instance *SP* 3.1.27–28, where the guru identifies himself with all five manifestations of Śiva.

14. For a further discussion of the relationship between "mental" and "concrete" divine images in Śaiva worship, see Hélène Brunner, "L'Image Divine dans le Culte Āgamique de Śiva: Rapport entre l'image mentale et le support concrete du culte," *L'Image Divine. Culte et Méditation dans l'Hindouisme* (Paris: Editions du Centre national de la recherche scientifique, 1990), pp. 9–29.

15. This is not to say that all liṅgas are the same. *MM* goes on to describe a great many categories of liṅgas, made of different substances and according to different dimensions, appropriate for various types of worshipers (*MM* 33.72–92).

16. Hélène Brunner, "Toujours le Niṣkala-liṅga," *Journal asiatique* 256 (1968): 445–47. For a fuller account linking this tripartite scheme to temple iconography and layout, see Doris Meth Srinivasan, "From Transcendency to Materiality: Para Śiva, Sadāśiva, and Maheśa in Indian Art," *Artibus Asiae* 50, (1990): 108–42. I thank the author for sending me proofs of her essay at the time I was revising this chapter.

17. See for instance *KKD Śivapratiṣṭhāvidhi*, p. 2. Similar sets of eighteen rites are prescribed for the establishment of an image (*pratimāpratiṣṭhā*) (*KĀ* 68.1–6).

18. For a more detailed examination of the reuse of Puruṣa imagery in an early Vaisnava establishment ritual, see Shantanu Phukan, "From the Idol to the Icon: The Transformation in the Pratimā Pratiṣṭhāna Ceremony" (unpublished).

19. The majority of *āgamas* holds that the divine throne extends from Earth up to *śuddhavidyā* (*KĀ* 4.312, *SP* 1.3.56, *AĀ* 20.157). Another school of thought, adhered to by *KirĀ* and Nārāyaṇakaṇṭha, argues that the divine throne extends all the way up to the *śaktitattva* (*MṛĀV kriyā* 3.12).

20. See Figure 9 here and the more detailed chart of throne stages in *SP* 1, Plate 5, "Āsana-pūjā."

21. The identity of this particular Śakti is not certain. She is variously assimilated to Kuṇḍalinī, Kriyāśakti, and Icchāśakti. (See Brunner's discussion, *SP* 1 p. 156.) What is never in dispute is that it must be a differentiated form of Śakti at the base of the divine throne.

22. The *nāga*-like description of Ananta in *KĀ* calls to mind another famous Ananta: the cosmic snake who serves as the couch of Viṣṇu-Nārāyaṇa. The Vidyeśvara Ananta is never identified with Viṣṇu's great servant, but the snake imagery is frequent enough to suggest that the throne of Viṣṇu has been incorporated into Śiva's more encompassing divine throne. (Brunner raises the question of Ananta's identity, in *SP* 1 pp. 158–60.)

23. See Brunner's list of the Śaktis and the Vidyeśvaras, together with her discussion of the identity of these Śaktis, *SP* 1 pp. 166–68. It is noteworthy that the names of the Śaktis "are the feminine equivalents of the divine names associated with Vāmadeva in the *Taittirīya Āraṇyaka* mantra, whose division served to form the 38 *kalā* of Sadāśiva."

24. These three categories generally include the *tattvas* of the impure domain as follows:

śiva—*māyā*
vidyā—six *tattvas* from *kāla* to *puruṣa*
ātman—twenty-four *tattvas* from *prakṛti* to Earth

These three *tattvas* also pervade the body: see *SP* 3, Plate 14, "Decoupage du corps par les trois *tattva*."

25. As an alternative method of visualizing the divine throne, *Kāmikāgama* describes it as a lotus that unfolds as the worshiper constructs it.

> The pedestal is fixed upon all paths (*adhvan*). Its great feet are the four ages of the world. Its bulb is the element Earth. The upraised stalk constitutes the *tattvas* up to Time. It is decorated with thorns which are the fifty kinds of emotions. Its main node is the *māyātattva*. The broad lotus flower is *śuddhavidyā*. The petals are the Vidyeśvaras. This lotus is ornamented with stamens which are the Śaktis, and made splendid by a pericarp and seed where the couple Śiva and Śakti are located. (*KĀ* 4.316–19)

Here again the form of the divine throne encompasses both all the constituents of the impure domain (worlds, ages, *tattvas*, states of emotion) and the powers or agents of Śiva through which he governs (Vidyeśvaras, eight Śaktis, Śiva and Śakti).

(Compare *KirĀ kriyā* 2.19–22 and *SSV* 48.) Like the divine throne of five stages, this lotus-form throne is a comprehensive ritual construction embodying Śiva's active presence in the world.

26. I follow here the account in *AĀ*, which differs somewhat from *KĀ* and *KKD*, primarily because the description in *AĀ* seems to me clearer. The main difference lies in the distinction between *sūkṣmamūrti* and *vidyādeha*.

27. According to Appayadīkṣita, still other constituents of reality are contained in the *vidyādeha*: the *kalās*, *adhvans*, *bhuvanas*, *āgamas*, and so on (*ŚAC* pp. 56–59). The *vidyādeha* is of course an inclusive body. Appaya's emphasis on this point here, however, may relate to his monistic perspective. If Śiva is considered the material as well as instrumental cause of the world, then his Sadāśiva form can and should include all manifest realities as well as his instrumentalities.

28. There are in fact several formulations of the MŪLA mantra, according to the *Siddhāntabodha*, appropriate to different categories of worshipers. See Brunner-Lachaux, "Introduction," *SP* 1 pp. xxxii–xxxiii. The name PRĀSĀDA for this mantra suggests a homology between mantra and temple (also *prāsāda*). Brunner-Lachaux points to this when describing the final dissolution of the mantra into Paramaśiva: "This is the summit of the PRĀSĀDA: the temple, which is at the same time the temple of the body, the complete domain of manifestation, and the mantra that constructs it in ascending it" (*SP* 1 p. 186, n. 1).

29. According to Anantaśambhu, each portion of the mantra is characterized by a name, a form, an illumination or color (*ābhā*), a pervasion, a location, a duration of pronunciation (*mātra*), a path, and a presiding lord (*SSV* 37). *SP* 1, Plate 6, "Recitation du Prāsāda-mantra," gives a relatively complete depiction of the mantra portions. One may also compare the three additional diagrams of mantra portions, based on three different texts, in *SP* 3, Plates 11–13.

30. This point was emphasized to me by Sabharatna Sivacarya (depicted in these photographs), who spoke of ascending pronunciation in invocation as the single most difficult ritual procedure in daily worship. The coordination of simultaneous actions requires much concentration and training.

Chapter Five
Relations of Worship

1. This episode is the frame-story of the *Mataṅgapārameśvarāgama*, the teachings given by Parameśvara to Mataṅga: see *MPĀ vidyā* 1.1–34.

2. There are two main types of *arghya*: common (*samanyārghya*) and special (*viśeṣārghya*). Common *arghya* is used generally for rites directed toward subordinate deities, while special *arghya* must be used in worshiping Śiva. As Brunner-Lachaux puts it, "The difference between these two *arghyas* resides in their composition, but particularly in the nature of the mantras that one recites over the recipient" (*SP* 1 p. 138).

3. *KĀ* 5.33–36 gives several alternative sets of substances for preparing *arghya*, though the group of eight listed here is the most common set.

4. Nirmalamaṇi quotes Bhojadeva in describing the formation of the cow *mudrā*: "When the fingers are woven together by joining little finger with ring finger, and

middle finger with index finger, the cow *mudrā* will resemble the udder of a cow" (*KKDP* p. 46).

5. The *divyamudrā* employed in this *divyadṛṣṭi* is described in *ML* pp. 19–20, quoted in *KKDP* pp. 130–31. See the photograph of *divyadṛṣṭi* employed upon entering the temple, in *ML* p. 27.

6. Attributed to *KĀ* by *SĀSS* p. 109. Cited in *SP* 1 p. 101.

7. The themes may vary in proportion according to the situation of worship. Texts like *KKD* that deal with *ātmārtha* worship in a private shrine generally stress acts of hospitality, while *KĀ* and other texts prescribing public (*parārtha*) temple worship give greater emphasis to Śiva's lordship. For a fuller account of these divergences between *ātmārtha* and *parārtha*, see Brunner, "Ātmārthapūjā versus Parārthapūjā," pp. 7–12.

8. See also the lists of twelve, sixteen, and twenty-four *upacāras* given by *KārĀ*, in *SP* 1, Appendix 7, "Upacāra du culte de Śiva."

9. J. Filliozat and P. Z. Pattabiramin, *Parures divines du Sud de l'Inde* (Pondichéry: Institut Français d'Indologie, 1966), photographically documents the crowns and ornaments used to decorate the liṅgas and images in South Indian temples.

10. *ĪP* p. 56, quoted in *SP* 1 p. 213.

11. Some texts provide suitable panegyric. In *KKD* (pp. 121–23), for instance, Aghoraśiva quotes the *stotras* from *RĀ*, *KirĀ*, *KālĀ*, and *MPĀ*.

12. Much of this discussion of *nirmālya* is based on *ŚAC* pp. 111–26. This was repeated in Nīlakaṇṭha's *Kriyāsāra* (assuming that *ŚAC* predates *Kriyāsāra*), which Hélène Brunner translates and discusses in her article "De la consommation du *nirmālya* de Śiva," *Journal asiatique* 256 (1969): 213–63.

13. Unnamed *purāṇa*, cited in *ŚAC* p. 120.

14. Readers versed in the Tamil Śaiva *bhakti* tradition will recognize Caṇḍa also as one of the sixty-three Śaiva *nāyanmārs*, whose story of devotion to Śiva is narrated by Cēkkiḻār in chapter 20 of the *Periyapurāṇam*. Eric af Edholm considers more fully the relation of the Tamil *nāyanmār* Caṇṭa and the *āgama* deity Caṇḍa in "Caṇḍa and the Sacrificial Remnants: A Contribution to Indian Gastrotheology," *Indologica Taurinensia* 12 (1984): 75–91.

15. Nirmalamaṇi points out that *caṇḍapūjā* is obligatory for the siddhānta worshiper, while it is prohibited to followers of other Śaiva schools (*KKDP* p. 132). The significant role of Caṇḍa and the notion that *nirmālya* is too pure for human consumption appear to be ritual features distinctive to Śaiva siddhānta.

16. *SupĀ*, quoted in *ŚAC* p. 113.

17. *ML* p. 13, quoted in *KKDP* p. 27.

18. *ML* pp. 9–10, quoted in *KKDP* p. 64.

Glossary

abhiṣeka — Anointment, rite by which lordly powers are affused onto a recipient.

ācamana — "Sipping-water," one of the *upacāras* offered to a guest or to a divinity.

ācārya — Śaiva priest, qualified to perform *pūjā* on behalf of others.

ācāryābhiṣeka — "Priestly anointment" conferring status of *ācārya* on Śaiva initiate.

Ādhāraśakti — The "Supporting Śakti" at the base of the *divyāsana*.

adhikāra — Appointment or assignment to perform a role or function.

adhikārin — Agent employed by a superior to carry out some assignment.

ādiśaiva — "Original Śaiva," Śaiva brāhmaṇa.

āgamas — Central texts of Śaiva siddhānta.

āgamin — "Future *karman*," one of three basic types of *karman*.

AGHORA — One of five *brahmamantras*; associated with activity of reabsorption and the south face of Sadāśiva.

aiśvarya — Lordly power.

amṛta — "Nectar," the undying food of the gods; substances ritually imbued with *śivatva*.

Ananta — First among the eight Vidyeśvaras.

aṅgamantras — Set of six "limb" mantras, considered as intrinsic extensions of Śiva's being: NETRA, HṚD, ŚIRAS, ŚIKHĀ, KAVACA, and ASTRA.

antyeṣṭi — Cremation, seen as leading to final *mokṣa*.

anuga — "Conformity," as between knowledge and ritual action in Śaiva system.

anugrāha — Grace, one of Śiva's *pañcakṛtya*, by which he grants liberation from bondage.

arghya — "Reception-water," a special ritual concoction, offered as an *upacāra* and also used to purify other substances.

ASTRA — "Weapon" mantra, one of six *aṅgamantras*, often used to burn or destroy impurities.

aśuddhādhvan — Impure domain, composed of thirty-one *tattvas* deriving from *māyā*. Antonym: *śuddhādhvan*.

ātman — The soul, the animating essence of a person, whose innate form is consciousness.

ātmārthapūjā — Worship on one's own behalf. Antonym: *parārthapūjā*.

ātmaśuddhi — Self-purification or purification of the soul, to render body suitable for subsequent parts of ritual. One of the five purifications performed at beginning of *pūjā*.

āvāhana — Invocation, rite summoning Śiva into liṅga or other support.
āvaraṇa — Entourage, a circle of divinities surrounding Śiva.
āyudha — Weapons, carried by divinities.
bandhatva — Bondage, the ordinary state of a *paśu* in fetters. Antonym: *mokṣa*.
bhakti — Devotion, the proper attitude for a person to have toward divinity.
bhāvanā — Imaginative re-creation, visualization.
bhoga — Worldly benefits; the consumption of the fruits of past actions (*bhogyakarman*).
bhogyakarman — Actions whose consequences are still to be experienced, the residue of past actions, acting as a fetter on the soul.
bhūtas — The five material elements: Earth, Water, Fire, Wind, and Ether.
bhuvanas — Worlds.
bīja — Seed, that from which other things emanate; the "seed-syllables" containing the essences of mantras.
bindu — *Mahāmāyā*.
brahmamantras — Set of five mantras, by which Śiva performs his *pañcakṛtya*: IŚĀNA, TATPURUṢA, AGHORA, VĀMA, and SADYOJĀTA. These correspond to the five "faces" of Sadāśiva.
brahmarandhra — "Divine aperture" at the top of the head, one of the *granthis*.
bubhukṣu — One who seeks worldly enjoyments. Antonym: *mumukṣu*.
Caṇḍa — One of the Gaṇeśvaras, considered a fierce emanation of Śiva; the recipient of *nirmālya*.
caryāpāda — One of four sections of a complete *āgama*, prescribing proper day-to-day conduct for members of the Śaiva community.
catussamskāra — Fourfold consecration, used as purification.
cit — Consciousness, the principal attribute of every animate being, distinguishing living beings from the inert and inanimate. Antonym: *jaḍa*.
dhāraṇā — "Cosmic supports," the five material elements seen as supports for the five *kalās*.
dhenumudrā — "Cow" *mudrā*, used when transforming substances into *amṛta*.
dhyāna — Meditation; mental activity by which the mind undistractedly centers itself on some reality, bringing about its presence.
dīkṣā — Initiation.
divyadeha — "Divine body" of mantras, imposed onto liṅga during invocation.
divyāsana — "Divine throne," imposed by worshiper onto pedestal during invocation.
dravyaśuddhi — Purification of ritual substances, one of the five purifications performed at outset of *pūjā*.

dvādaśānta — Point of reabsorption, twelve inches above worshiper's head; the location of Paramaśiva.

Gaṇeśvaras — "Lords of the Troops," group of eight deities constituting Śiva's "family": Nandin, Mahākāla, Gaṇeśa, Vṛṣa, Bhṛṅgi, Skanda, Ambikā, and Caṇḍa.

garbhagṛha — "Womb-room," innermost chamber of shrine and location of liṅga or principal object of worship.

granthis — "Subtle centers" or "joints" located at heart, throat, palate, eyebrows, and *brahmarandhra*, visualized as lotus buds binding the *nāḍis*.

guṇa — Quality, attribute; especially the divine attributes of Śiva and liberated beings.

guṇāpādana — Rite "bringing forth the qualities" of *śivatva* during initiation.

HAUM — Seed-syllable of MŪLA.

HṚD — "Heart" mantra, one of *aṅgamantras*.

iḍā — Left breath channel, one of the *nāḍis*.

ĪŚĀNA — One of five *brahmamantras*; associated with the activity of grace and the upraised face of Sadāśiva.

jaḍa — Inanimate substance. Antonym: *cit*.

japa — Mantra recitations.

jñāna — Knowledge.

jñānapāda — One of four sections of a complete *āgama*, describing the fundamental order of the universe.

jñānaśakti — The power of knowledge, one of the inherent capacities of consciousness.

jñānendriyas — Five perceptual faculties: skin, tongue, eye, ear, and nose.

kalās — "Portions" of some larger unity. Used to designate various sets:

a. Five *kalās* — Cosmological entities containing entire manifest world: *śāntyatīta*, *śānti*, *vidyā*, *pratiṣṭhā*, and *nivṛtti*.

b. Twelve *kalās* — Portions of the MŪLA mantra, reunited through *uccāraṇa* during invocation. (Often there are sixteen rather than twelve such *kalās*.)

c. Thirty-eight *kalās* — *Kalāmantras*, thirty-eight Śaktis constituting powers of Sadāśiva's body.

kalāśuddhi — Purification of the five *kalās*, a rite of *nirvāṇadīkṣā*.

kāraṇa — Instruments through which something else acts.

Kāraṇeśvaras — Five lords governing the body's breath channels, each associated with a particular *granthi*: Sadāśiva, Īśvara, Rudra, Viṣṇu, and Brahman.

karanyāsa — Imposition of mantras onto the hands, a preliminary rite of *ātmaśuddhi*.

karman — Action in general; ritual action; the residue of past actions, one of three primary fetters.

KAVACA — "Armor" mantra, one of six *aṅgamantras*, used to surround and protect.

Kevalavijñānas — Beings of the pure domain, fettered only by *mala*.

kriyā — Action in general, and ritual action par excellence.

kriyāpāda — One of four sections of a complete *āgama*, prescribing proper ritual conduct.

kriyāśakti — The power of action, one of the inherent capacities of consciousness.

liṅga — Śiva's primary icon or "mark," a smooth cylindrical shaft set in a pedestal.

Lokapālas — World Guardians, a group of eight or ten deities protecting the world in the eight directions, above and below: Indra, Agni, Yama, Nirṛti, Varuṇa, Vāyu, Kubera, Īśāna, and optionally Brahman, Viṣṇu.

mahāmāyā — Material cause of the pure domain.

Maheśvara — "Great Lord," collective name for Śiva's manifest forms, represented by Śaiva icons and related to aspects or episodes of Śiva's activities in the world.

mala — Primordial stain, one of three primary fetters.

maṇḍala — "Domain," used to refer to a variety of diagrams, ritual arrangements, that specify particularized wholes.

mantra — Powerful speech acts used to bring about presence of divine powers. In an extended sense, denotes both the speech act as signifier and the divine power as signified.

māyā — Material cause of the impure domain, the source-substance from which the thirty-one *tattvas* of material cosmos emanate; one of three primary fetters.

mokṣa — Liberation, the highest goal, by which the soul is released from its bondage and becomes a Śiva.

mudrā — Ritually prescribed hand gestures.

mukhaliṅga — Liṅga with faces.

muktātman — Liberated soul.

MŪLA — "Root" mantra, evoking Śiva in his totality; also called PRĀSĀDA and ŚIVA.

mūlādhāra — Lowermost center of the yogic subtle anatomy, situated at the base of the trunk.

mūlāgama — "Root" treatise, one of twenty-eight primary *āgamas* in Śaiva canon.

mumukṣu — One who seeks liberation. Antonym: *bubhukṣu*.

mūrti — Embodied form.

MŪRTI — Mantra of embodied form.

nāda — Undifferentiated sound, source of all audible sound and speech.
nāḍi — Subtle channels along which breath travels; the three primary ones are *iḍā*, *piṅgalā*, and *suṣumnā*.
naivedya — Food offered to a divinity.
NETRA — "Eye" mantra, one of six *aṅgamantras*.
nirmālya — Leftovers from services to Śiva, considered too pure for human consumption.
nirvāṇadīkṣā — Initiation conferring liberation, crucial ritual for attaining *mokṣa*.
niṣkala — Without parts, undifferentiated; used to describe any unity in its state of integral wholeness. Antonym: *sakala*.
nityapūjā — Daily worship.
nivṛtti — One of five *kalās*.
nyāsa — Imposition of mantras.
padārtha — Fundamental ontological categories: *pati*, *paśu*, and *pāśa*.
paddhati — Ritual manuals and other "footstep" treatises.
padmāsana — "Lotus throne," one of *divyāsana* stages.
pādya — "Foot-water," offered as an *upacāra* to guests or to divinities.
pāka — "Ripening," the process of change in *mala*.
pañcakṛtya — Śiva's five fundamental activities: *anugrāha*, *tirobhāva*, *samhāra*, *sthiti*, and *sṛṣṭi*.
pañcaśuddhi — Five purifications performed at beginning of worship: of self, place, mantras, liṅga, and substances.
parajñāna — Highest form of knowledge.
paramārthika — True "in the highest sense."
Paramaśiva — Śiva in his highest form, as limitless, formless, undifferentiated, and so on.
parāṅmukhārghya — Special form of *arghya* that allows Śiva to "turn away his face" in *visarjana*.
parārthapūjā — Worship on behalf of others, performed by Śaiva priests in temples. Antonym: *ātmārthapūjā*.
pariṇāma — Transformations, alterations in inanimate substance.
parivāradevatā — Attendant deities forming Śiva's court or entourages.
pāśa — Fetters that bind the soul: *mala*, *karman*, and *māyā*. One of the three *padārthas*.
pāśasūtra — "Cord of fetters" used as substitute body for initiate during *nirvāṇadīkṣā*.
paśu — Bound soul; *ātman* affected by *pāśa*. One of the three *padārthas*.
pati — The Lord, Śiva, and by extension others who exercise his lordship. One of the three *padārthas*.
piṅgalā — Right breath channel, one of the *nāḍis*.
pīṭhā — Pedestal for Śiva-liṅga, representing Śakti.

prakāra — Protecting walls of temple complex.

Pralayavijñāna — Beings of the pure domain, fettered by *mala* and *karman* but not by *māyā*.

prārabdhakarman — Active *karman*, whose effects have already begun, determining one's present embodiment and destined to be consumed in this lifetime. One of the three basic types of *karman*.

prasāda — Favor; leftover *pūjā* food distributed as substantive form of divine favor.

PRĀSĀDA — Mantra evoking Śiva in his totality; also called MŪLA.

pratimā — Differentiated image.

pratiṣṭhā — One of five *kalās*; ritual of "establishment" activating a temple or icon as fit support for divinity.

prāyaścitta — Expiation.

pūjā — Worship, Hindu ritual form by which devotees offer tokens of respect and adoration to embodied deity.

Puruṣa — The "Primordial Being."

putraka — "Son of Śiva," status achieved through *viśeṣadīkṣā*.

Sadāśiva — "Eternal Śiva," the body of mantras with which Śiva acts in the world; the most comprehensive manifest form of Śiva.

sādhaka — Renunciatory adept.

SADYOJĀTA — One of five *brahmamantras*; associated with activity of emission and the west face of Sadāśiva.

sakala — With parts, differentiated. Antonym: *niṣkala*.

Śakti — Śiva's instrument, arising intrinsically from Śiva's own being, with which he acts in the world.

śaktinipāta — "Fall of Śakti," a process by which one becomes ready for initiation.

samayācāra — "Common code of conduct," incumbent on all initiated Śaivites.

samayadīkṣā — "General initiation," by which one becomes a member of the Śaiva community.

samayin — "Common member" of Śaiva community, one who has undergone *samayadīkṣā*.

samhāra — Reabsorption, one of Śiva's *pañcakṛtya*, by which differentiated entities are unified. Antonym: *sṛṣṭi*.

samhāramārga — Path of reabsorption.

samhāramudrā — *Mudrā* of reabsorption.

samsāra — Worldly existence, viewed as a continuous "flux."

samskāra — Consecration, general term for preparatory rites.

sañcitakarman — Accumulated *karman*, not yet activated; a repository of *bhogyakarman* conditioning future lifetimes. One of three basic types of *karman*.

śānti — One of five *kalās*.

śāntyatīta — One of five *kalās*.

ŚIKHĀ — "Topknot" mantra, one of six *aṅgamantras*.

simhāsana — "Lion throne," one of the stages of *divyāsana*.

ŚIRAS — "Head" mantra, one of six *aṅgamantras*.

śivajñāna — Knowledge pertaining to Śiva, claimed by Śaiva siddhānta as the highest form of knowledge. Used to distinguish the Śaiva siddhānta system from all other bodies of knowledge.

śivatva — "Śiva-ness," the quality of being like Śiva.

śivīkaraṇa — To transform something into a state of *śivatva*.

sṛṣṭi — Emission, one of Śiva's *pañcakṛtya*, by which unitary entities are differentiated. Antonym: *samhāra*.

sṛṣṭimārga — Path of emission.

sthānaśuddhi — Purification of the ritual terrain, one of the five purifications at outset of *pūjā*.

sthiti — Maintenance, one of Śiva's *pañcakṛtya*.

sthūla — "Gross," relatively tangible. Antonym: *sūkṣma*.

sthūlaśarīra — "Gross body" of five *bhūtas*.

stotra — Hymn of praise.

śuddhādhvan — Pure domain, composed of five *tattvas* deriving from *mahāmāyā*. Antonym: *aśuddhādhvan*.

sūkṣma — "Subtle," relatively intangible. Antonym: *sthūla*.

sūkṣmaśarīra — "Subtle body" of the thirty-six differentiated *tattvas*, purified during *ātmaśuddhi*.

suṣumnā — Central breath channel, the most important *nāḍi*.

svabhāva — Inherent nature, essential character.

tanmātra — Five perceptible qualities: Sound, Touch, Form, Taste, and Odor.

TATPURUṢA — One of five *brahmamantras*; associated with Śiva's activity of veiling and the east face of Sadāśiva.

tattva — "Such-nesses," the thirty-six basic constituents of material being, deriving from the two source-substances *mahāmāyā* and *māyā*.

tirobhāva — "Veiling," one of Śiva's *pañcakṛtya*.

uccāraṇa — Ascending pronunciation.

udghāta — Expulsion, used to expel attributes of *sthūlaśarīra* during *ātmaśuddhi*.

upacāra — "Services," all material and performatory offerings presented to the deity during *pūjā*; partial approximation or synecdoche.

upāgama — Subsidiary treatise of Śaiva canon. Cf. *mūlāgama*.

utsava — "Festival," whether daily *nityotsava* or grand calendrical *mahotsava*.

vācaka — Signifier, that which denotes something.

vācya — Signified, that which is denoted by a signifier.

Vāgīśvara — Form of Śiva, invoked during *kalāśuddhi*.

Vāgīśvarī — Form of Śakti as "Goddess of Speech," invoked during *kalāśuddhi.*

VĀMA — One of five *brahmamantras*; associated with the activity of maintenance and with the north face of Sadāśiva.

vāstupūjā — Worship of the site.

vidyā — One of the five *kalās.*

vidyādeha — Body of mantras—literally "knowledge-body"—imposed on liṅga and worshiper's body during worship.

Vidyeśvaras — Group of eight agents assigned by Śiva to reign over impure domain.

vimalāsana — "Stainless throne," one of the stages of *divyāsana.*

visarjana — Dismissal of Śiva from embodiment at conclusion of worship.

viśeṣadīkṣā — "Special initiation," conferring status of *putraka* on recipient.

VYOMAVYĀPIN — "Space-pervading" mantra, considered the "womb" of all mantras.

yajña — Sacrifice.

yathāśakti — "Insofar as one is able."

yātrā — Procession in which Śiva leaves *garbhagṛha* and tours his temple domain.

yogapāda — One of four sections of a complete *āgama*, describing yogic disciplinary practices.

yogāsana — "Yoga throne," one of the stages of *divyāsana.*

Selected Bibliography

Sanskrit Sources by Title
(*Texts and Translations*)

Agnipurāṇa. Edited by Hari Narayana Apte. Anandasrama Sanskrit Series, no. 41.
———. Translated by Manmatha Nath Dutt. 3 vols. Calcutta: Elysium Press, 1903.
———. Translated by N. Gangadharan. 3 vols. Ancient Indian Tradition and Mythology Series, nos. 27–29. Delhi: Motilal Banarsidass, 1984.
Ajitāgama. Edited by N. R. Bhatt. 2 vols. Pondichéry: Institut Français d'Indologie, 1964, 1967.
Aṣṭaprakaraṇa. Includes *Tattvaprakāśa*, *Tattvasaṃgraha*, *Tattvatrayanirṇaya*, *Ratnatraya*, *Bhogakārikā*, *Nādakārikā*, *Mokṣakārikā*, and *Paramokṣanirāsakārikā*. Edited by N. Krishna Sastri. 2 vols. Devakottai: Saivagamasiddhantaparipalanasangha, 1923, 1925.
———. Edited by Vrajavallabha Dvivedi. Yogatantra-Granthamala, vol. 12. Varanasi: Sampurnananda Sanskrit University, 1988.
Bhogakārikā of Sadyojyoti with the commentary of Aghoraśiva. See *Aṣṭaprakaraṇa*.
———. Translated by Wayne A. Borody. "The Doctrine of Empirical Consciousness in the *Bhoga Kārikā*." Ph.D. dissertation, McMaster University, 1988.
Īśānaśivagurudevapaddhati of Īśānaśivagurudevamiśra. Edited by T. Ganapati Sastri. 4 vols. Trivandrum Sanskrit Series, nos. 69, 72, 77, 83. Trivandrum: Government Press, 1920–1925.
———. Partially translated by Stella Kramrisch. "Īśānaśivagurudevapaddhati Kriyāpāda Chs. xxvi, xxvii." *Journal of the Indian Society of Oriental Art* 9 (1941): 151–93.
———. Partially translated by Stella Kramrisch. "Temple, Door, Throne, Etc." *Journal of the Indian Society of Oriental Art* 10 (1942): 210–52.
Jātinirṇayapūrvakālayapraveśavidhi of Rāmakaṇṭha. Edited and translated by Pierre-Sylvain Filliozat. "Le droit d'entrer dans les temples de Śiva au xie siècle," *Journal asiatique* 263 (1975): 103–17.
Kālottarāgama (*Sārdhatriśatikālottarāgama*) with the commentary of Bhaṭṭa Rāmakaṇṭha. Edited by N. R. Bhatt. Pondichéry: Institut Français d'Indologie, 1979.
Kāmikāgama, pūrvabhāga and *uttarabhāga*. Edited by Mayilai Alagappa Mudaliar. 2 vols. Madras: Śivananapota yantrasalai, 1909.
Kāmikāgama, pūrvabhāga. Edited by C. Svaminatha Sivacarya. Madras: South Indian Archakas Association, 1975.
Kāmikāgama, pūrvabhāga. Institut Français d'Indologie manuscript T.298 A. (Formerly property of Sri Svaminatha Sivacarya of Tiruvavatuturai matha.)
Kāraṇāgama, pūrvabhāga, nityārcanāvidhi. Edited by R. Rajalinga Gurukkal. Madras: South Indian Archakas Association, 1969.
———. Translated by J.W.V. Curtis. *Motivations of Temple Architecture in Śaiva Siddhānta*. Madras: Hoe and Co., 1973.

Kiraṇāgama. Edited by Pancapagesa Sivacarya. Devakottai: Saivagamasiddhantaparipalanasangha, 1932.

Kiraṇāgama, vidyāpāda. Translated by Maria Pia Vivanti. Naples: Instituto Orientale di Napoli, 1975.

Kriyākramadyotikā (or *Aghoraśivapaddhati*) of Aghoraśiva with the commentary of Nirmalamaṇi. Edited by Karunkulam Krishna Sastri and Polagam Srirama Sastri. Cidambaram: Jñānasambandham Press, 1927.

Kriyākramadyotikā of Aghoraśiva with the commentary of Kacchapeśvara. Manuscript belonging to Sri Svaminatha Sivacarya of Tiruvavatuturai. Institut Français d'Indologie manuscript copy, no. 109.

Kriyākramadyotikā. Edited by V. K. Arunacalagurukkal. Madras: South Indian Archakas Association, 1967.

Kriyākramadyotikā, Dīkṣāvidhi. Translated by Wayne Edward Surdam. "South Indian Śaiva Rites of Initiation: The 'Dīkṣāvidhi' of Aghoraśivācārya's 'Kriyākramadyotikā.'" Ph.D. dissertation, University of California, Berkeley, 1984.

Kriyākramadyotikā, Mahotsavavidhi of Aghoraśiva. Edited by C. Svaminatha Sivacarya. Madras: South Indian Archakas Association, 1974.

Kriyākramadyotikā, Śivapratiṣṭhāvidhi. Edited by I. Kacchapesvara Sivacarya. Madras: South Indian Archakas Association, 1964.

Liṅgapurāṇa. Bombay: Venkatesvara Press, 1857.

———. Translated by a Board of Scholars. Ancient Indian Tradition and Mythology Series, nos. 5, 6. Delhi: Motilal Banarsidass, 1973.

Makuṭāgama, pūrvabhāga. Edited by C. Svaminatha Sivacarya. Madras: South Indian Archakas Association, 1977.

Mataṅgapārameśvarāgama with the commentary of Bhaṭṭa Rāmakaṇṭha. Edited by N. R. Bhatt. 2 vols. Pondichéry: Institut Français d'Indologie, 1977, 1982.

Mataṅgapārameśvarāgama, vidyāpāda. Edited by N. Krishna Sastri. Devakottai: Saivagamasiddhantaparipalanasangha, 1924.

Mayamata of Mayamuni. Edited by T. Ganapati Sastri. Trivandrum Sanskrit Series, no. 65. Trivandrum: Government Press, 1919.

———. Edited and translated into Tamil by K. S. Subrahmanya Sastri. 2 vols. Thanjavur: Tanjore Maharaja Serfoji's Sarasvati Mahal Library, 1966, 1968.

———. Edited and translated by Bruno Dagens. 2 vols. Pondichéry: Institut Français d'Indologie, 1970, 1976.

———. Dagens's French translation translated into English. New Delhi: Sitaram Bhartia Institute of Scientific Research, 1985.

Mṛgendrāgama, vidyāpāda and *yogapāda*, with the commentary of Bhaṭṭa Nārāyaṇakaṇṭha. Edited by Madhusudan Kaul Shastri. Kashmir Series of Texts and Studies, no. 50. Bombay: Nirnaya Sagar Press, 1930.

Mṛgendrāgama, vidyāpāda and *yogapāda*, with the commentary of Bhaṭṭa Nārāyaṇakaṇṭha and subcommentary of Aghoraśiva. Edited by K. M. Subrahmanya Sastri. Devakottai: Saivagamasiddhantaparipalanasangha, 1928.

———. Translated by Michel Hulin. Pondichéry: Institut Français d'Indologie, 1980.

Mṛgendrāgama, kriyāpāda and *caryāpāda*, with the commentary of Bhaṭṭa Nārāyaṇakaṇṭha. Edited by N. R. Bhatt. Pondichéry: Institut Français d'Indologie, 1962.

———. Translated by Hélène Brunner-Lachaux. Pondichéry: Institut Français d'Indologie, 1985.

Mudrālakṣaṇa. Edited and translated by S. S. Janaki. Mayiladuturai: International Institute of Śaiva Siddhānta Research, 1986.

Nādakārikā of Sadyojyoti with the commentary of Aghoraśiva. See *Aṣṭaprakaraṇa*.

———. Translated by Pierre-Sylvain Filliozat. *Bulletin de l'Ecole Française d'Extrême-Orient* 73 (1984): 223–55.

Nareśvaraparīkṣā of Sadyojyoti with the commentary of Rāmakaṇṭha. Edited by Madhusudan Kaul Shastri. Kashmir Series of Texts and Studies, no. 45. Srinagar: Kashmir Pratap Steam Press, 1926.

Rauravāgama. Edited by N. R. Bhatt. 3 vols. Pondichéry: Institut Français d'Indologie, 1961, 1972, 1988.

Śaivāgamaparibhāṣāmañjarī of Vedajñāna. Edited and translated by Bruno Dagens. Pondichéry: Institut Français d'Indologie, 1979.

Śaivaparibhāṣā of Śivāgrayogin. Edited by H. R. Rangaswamy Iyengar and R. Ramasastri. Oriental Research Institute Publications, Sanskrit Series, no. 90. Mysore: Government Branch Press, 1950.

———. Translated by S. S. Suryanarayana Sastri. Madras University Philosophical Series, no. 35. Madras: University of Madras, 1982.

Śaivasiddhāntaparibhāṣā of Sūryabhaṭṭa. Edited by N. Krishna Sastri. Devakottai: Saivagamasiddhanta-paripalanasangha, 1926.

Sakalāgamasārasaṃgraha. Edited by C. Swaminatha Sivacarya. Madras: South Indian Archakas Association, 1974.

Sarvadarśanasaṃgraha of Mādhava. Edited by Vasudev Shastri Abhyankar. Poona: Bhandarkar Oriental Research Institute, 1924.

———. "*Śaivadarśana*" chapter translated by Hélène Brunner. *Tantric and Taoist Studies in Honour of R. A. Stein*. Brussels: Institut Belge des Hautes Études Chinoises, 1981. Pp. 96–140.

Śataratnasaṃgraha of Umāpati. Edited and translated by P. Thirugnanasambandhan. Madras: University of Madras, 1973.

Siddhāntasārāvāli of Trilocanaśiva with the commentary of Anantaśambhu. Edited by A. A. Ramanathan et al. *Bulletin of the Government Oriental Manuscripts Library*, vols. 17–20. Madras: Bharati Vijayam Press, 1965–1972.

Śivapurāṇa. Edited by Pandeya Ramatejasastri. Kashi: Pandita Pustakalaya, 1963.

———. Translated by a Board of Scholars. 4 vols. Ancient Indian Tradition and Mythology Series, nos. 1–4. Delhi: Motilal Banarsidass, 1970.

Śivārcanācandrikā of Appayadīkṣita. Edited by Kalisvara Sivacarya. Devakottai: Saivagamasiddhantaparipalanasangha, 1922.

Somaśambhupaddhati of Somaśambhu. Edited by K. M. Subrahmanya Sastri. Devakottai: Saivagamasiddhantaparipalanasangha, 1931.

Somaśambhupaddhati (*Karmakāṇḍakramāvalī*) of Somaśambhu. Edited by Jagaddhar Zadoo. Kashmir Series of Texts and Studies, no. 73. Srinagar: Krishna Printing Press, 1947.

———. Translated by Hélène Brunner-Lachaux. 3 vols. Pondichéry: Institut Français d'Indologie, 1963, 1968, 1977.

Svacchandatantra with the commentary of Kṣemarāja. Edited by Madhusudan Kaul

Sastri. 6 vols. Kashmir Series of Texts and Studies, nos. 31, 38, 44, 48, 51, and 56. Bombay: Nirnaya Sagar Press, 1921–1935.
Tattvaprakāśa of Bhojadeva with the commentary of Śrīkumāra. Edited by T. Ganapati Sastri. Trivandrum Sanskrit Series, no. 68. Trivandrum: Government Press, 1920.
Tattvaprakāśa of Bhojadeva with the commentary of Aghoraśiva. See *Aṣṭaprakaraṇa*.
Tattvaprakāśa of Bhojadeva with the commentaries of Śrīkumāra and Aghoraśiva. Edited by Kameshwar Nath Mishra. Varanasi: Chaukhambha Orientalia, 1976.
Tattvaprakāśa of Bhojadeva. Translated by E. P. Janvier. *Indian Antiquary* 54 (1925): 151–56.
———. Translated by Pierre-Sylvain Filliozat. *Journal asiatique* 259 (1971): 247–95.
Tattvasaṃgraha of Sadyojyoti with the commentary of Aghoraśiva. See *Aṣṭaprakaraṇa*.
Tattvatrayanirṇaya of Sadyojyoti with the commentary of Aghoraśiva. See *Aṣṭaprakaraṇa*.
———. Translated by Leon E. Hannotte. "Philosophy of God in Kashmir Śaiva Dualism: Sadyojyoti and His Commentators." Ph.D. dissertation, McMaster University, 1987.

Secondary Works on Śaiva Siddhānta

Note: The Kuppuswami Sastri Research Institute has recently made available an excellent videotape of K. A. Sabharatna Sivacarya performing an *āgama*-based worship of Śiva, with commentary in English or Tamil. Readers wishing to obtain a copy may contact Ginni Ishimatsu, Department of South and Southeast Asian Studies, University of California, Berkeley, CA 94702, or Richard Davis, Department of Religious Studies, Yale University, New Haven, CT 06520.

Arunachalam, M. *The Śaivāgamas*. Tiruchitrambalam: Gandhi Vidyālayam, 1983.
Bhatt, N. R. "What Is Śivāgama?" Pamphlet, no publication information.
Brunner, Hélène. "Analyse du *Kiraṇāgama*." *Journal asiatique* 253 (1965): 309–28.
———. "Analyse du *Suprabhedāgama*." *Journal asiatique* 255 (1967): 31–60.
———. "Ātmārthapūjā versus Parārthapūjā in the Śaiva Tradition." In *The Sanskrit Tradition and Tantrism*. Edited by T. Goudriaan. Leiden: E. J. Brill, 1990. Pp. 4–23.
———. "Les catégories sociales védiques dans le Śivaisme du sud." *Journal asiatique* 252 (1964): 451–72.
———. "De la consommation du *nirmālya* de Śiva." *Journal asiatique* 256 (1969): 213–63.
———. "Importance de la littérature āgamique pour l'étude des religions vivantes de l'Inde." *Indologica Taurinensia* 3–4 (1975–1976): 107–24.
———. "L'Image divine dans le Culte Āgamique de Śiva: Rapport entre l'image mentale et le support conrete du culte." In *L'Image divine. Culte et méditation dans l'Hindouisme*. Paris: Editions du Centre national de la recherche scientifique, 1990. Pp. 9–29.
———. "Les membres de Śiva." *Asiatische Studien* 40 (1986): 89–132.

———. "The Pāśupatas as Seen by the Śaivas." *Schriften zur Geschichte und Kultur des alten Orients* 18 (1986): 513–20.

———. "Le *sādhaka*, personnage oublié du Śivaisme du sud." *Journal asiatique* 263 (1975): 411–43.

———. "Le Śaiva-siddhānta, 'Essence' du Veda." *Indologica Taurinensia* 8 (1980–1981): 51–66.

———. "Toujours le *niṣkala-liṅga*." *Journal asiatique* 256 (1968): 445–47.

Dagens, Bruno. "Analyse du *Pūrvakāmikāgama*." *Bulletin de l'Ecole Française d'Extrême-Orient* 54 (1977): 1–38.

———. *Les Enseignements architecturaux de l'Ajitāgama et du Rauravāgama*. Pondichéry: Institut Français d'Indologie, 1977.

Dasgupta, Surendranath. *A History of Indian Philosophy*. Vol. 5: *Southern Schools of Śaivism*. Cambridge: Cambridge University Press, 1955.

Davis, Richard H. "Aghoraśiva's Background." In *Dr. S. S. Janaki Shashtyabdapurti Commemoration Volume*. Edited by V. Kameshvari. Madras: Kuppuswami Sastri Research Institute, forthcoming.

———. "Cremation and Liberation: A Śaiva Siddhānta Revision." *History of Religions* 28 (1988): 37–53.

Devasenapathy, V. A. *Of Human Bondage and Divine Grace*. Cidambaram: Annamalai University, 1963.

Dhavamony, Mariasusai. *Love of God According to Śaiva Siddhānta*. Oxford: Clarendon Press, 1971.

Diehl, Carl Gustav. *Instrument and Purpose*. Lund: C.W.K. Gleerup, 1956.

Dunuwila, Rohan A. *Śaiva Siddhānta Theology: A Context for Hindu-Christian Dialogue*. Delhi: Motilal Banarsidass, 1985.

Filliozat, Jean. "Les āgama śivaites." In *Rauravāgama* vol. 1, pp. v–xv. Edited by N. R. Bhatt. Pondichéry: Institut Français d'Indologie, 1961.

Gonda, Jan. *Medieval Religious Literature in Sanskrit* (A History of Indian Literature, vol. 2). Wiesbaden: Otto Harrassowitz, 1977.

Janaki, S. S. "Śaivite Mudrās I–VI." *Kalakshetra Quarterly* 5–6 (1983–1984).

Lorenzen, David N. *The Kāpālikas and Kālāmukhas*. New Delhi: Thomson Press, 1972.

Pandey, Kanti Chandra. *Abhinavagupta: An Historical and Philosophical Study*. Varanasi: Chowkhamba Sanskrit Series Office, 1963.

———. *Bhaskarī*. 3 vols. Prince of Wales Saraswati Bhavana Texts, no. 84. Lucknow: Superintendent, Printing and Stationery, 1954.

Peterson, Indira. *Poems to Śiva*. Princeton: Princeton University Press, 1989.

Śivaraman, K. *Śaivism in Philosophical Perspective*. Delhi: Motilal Banarsidass, 1973.

Soni, Jayandra. *Philosophical Anthropology in Śaiva Siddhānta*. Delhi: Motilal Banarsidass, 1989.

Surdam, Wayne. "The Vedicization of Śaiva Ritual." In *Śiva Temple and Temple Rituals*. Madras: Kuppuswami Sastri Research Institute, 1988. Pp. 52–60.

Index

abandonment (*tyāga*), 159–60
abhiṣeka. *See* anointment
ācārya. *See* priest
action, ritual (*kriyā*), 31–32; and *karman*, 86–87; and knowledge, ix, xii, 32, 34–35, 73–74, 163–64; as power of consciousness, 23, 25, 84, 113, 133–34, 162
activities, Śiva's five fundamental (*pañcakṛtya*), 42–43, 114; and *brahamantras*, 48, 51; effects on matter of, 139; effects on soul of, 89; and Sadāśiva, 115. *See also* emission; grace; reabsorption
adept (*sādhaka*), 100n.14, 152
Ādhāraśakti, 124, 127
adhikārin. *See* agents
ādiśaiva, 41, 69–70, 70n.21
adornment, 150
Advaita Vedānta, 17, 44, 85, 135–36
āgamas: as genre of Śaiva texts, 9–14; origins of, 10–12, 29, 46, 61; and *paddhati* literature, 16–17; rituals prescribed in, 36; sections of, ix, 10; as Śiva's grace, 28–29; temple recitation of, 71; and Vedas, 29n.3
āgamin (future *karman*), 87, 93. See also *karman*
agents (*adhikārin*): of Śiva, 32, 94, 118–19; in temple, 61–62; in worship, 66, 151–52
AGHORA, 48–51, 152. See also *brahmamantras*
Aghoraśiva, 3, 13, 15–17. See also *Kriyākramadyotikā*
Agni, 7, 8; in crematory fire, 46, 110
alphabet: emission and reabsorption of, 46; imposed in ritual, 59, 124, 126
amṛta (nectar), 141, 143
Ananta (Vidyeśvara), 118–19; dominion of, 124, 140; throne of, 124–25, 127; and Viṣṇu's snake, 124n.22; visualization of, 124
aṅgamantras ("limb" mantras of Śiva), 48; and divine perfections, 108–9; imposed in ritual, 48–51, 58, 108, 126, 145; in mantra-collection, 158–59; and Sadāśiva, 116; visualization of, 67–68. *See also* mantras
anointment (*abhiṣeka*): of kings, 99, 149; of liṅga, 64–67, 149; of priests and adepts, 36, 40, 70, 100n.14, 149
antyeṣṭi (cremation), 36, 109–10
anugrāha. *See* grace
Appayadīkṣita, 20
arghya: preparation, 145; uses, 133, 146–48
Aruḷnanti, 18
ascending pronunciation (*uccāraṇa*): in invocation, 129–32, Pl. 6; in protection of soul, 105; in purification of mantras, 143; in services, 147
ASTRA, 47, 48–51, 57, 68. See also *aṅgamantras*
aśuddhādhvan. *See* impure domain
ātman. *See* soul
ātmārthapūjā, 37, 40; relation to *parārthapūjā*, 37n.15, 147n.7
ātmaśuddhi (self-purification), 40, 137, 158; and liberation of soul, 101–4; and *nirvāṇadīkṣā*, 104; procedures of, 47–60, 104–9; transformation of body in, 52–60, 134–36, Pl. 4; transformation of hands in, 47–51, Pl. 2
āvāhana. *See* invocation
āvaraṇa. *See* entourages
āyudha (weapons): of Sadāśiva, 116–17; of World Guardians, 68

bandhatva (bondage), 24, 84, 163–64
bath (*snāna*), 71, 149
bhakti, 7, 135–36
bhāvanā. *See* visualization
bhoga: as consumption of *karman*, 26; as worldly benefits, 7, 34, 46, 154
bhogyakarman, 87
Bhojadeva, 17
bhūtas, five. *See* elements
bhutas (lesser spirits), 152
body, divine (body of mantras): imposed on worshiper's body, 52, 58, 108–9; imposed on liṅga, 122–23, 125–28, 163–64

body, human: in *ātmasuddhi*, 51–61, 104–9, 163–64; in cremation, 110; distribution of mantra portions in, 129–31; and Śiva, 52; and soul, 101–4, 119; substitute, in initiation, 94–98
body, Śiva's, 52; liṅga as, 119, 133; mantras as, 48, 115; Sadāśiva as, 48, 115–17, 133. *See also* Śiva, forms of
bondage (*bandhatva*) 24, 84, 163–64
bound soul. See *paśu*
brahmamantras: and five fundamental activities, 48, 139; imposed in ritual, 48–51, 58–59, 108, 126–27, 145, Pls. 2, 4, 5; in mantra-collection, 158–59; as Sadāśiva, 48, 59, 115; as *śaktis*, 118; visualization of, 67–68
Brahman, 7, 123; as Kāraṇeśvara, 55, 119, 125, 129–30; location in temple of, 63; womb of, 96
brahmans, common and Śaiva, 41, 69–70
brahmarandhra, 55
bubhukṣu, 27n.2, 46–47; and path of emission, 50–51, 70–71; and stages of initiation, 91
Buddhism, 29

Caṇḍa, 36; as Gaṇeśvara, 68; as *nāyanmār*, 156n.14, worship of, 156–57
caryāpāda section of *āgamas*, x, 10
categories, ontological. See *padārthas*
catussamskāra (fourfold consecration), 146
causality, 86–87
cit. *See* consciousness
Cola period, 4–6, 19, 43, 63
Collingwood, R. G., ix
concealment (*tirobhāva*): as fetter, 86n.2; as form of grace, 89; as fundamental activity, 42, 89; and VĀMA, 48
consciousness (*cit*), 23; powers of, xi, 25, 28, 84; requires instruments, 32–33; Śiva as, 24, 119, 138; soul as, 25, 84; suppression of, 25–27, 84–85, 89
cord of fetters (*pāśasūtra*), 94–98, 100, 108
cosmology, Śaiva, 42–46
cremation (*antyeṣṭi*), 36, 109–11

Delhi Sultanate, 17–18
dīkṣā. *See* initiation
dismissal (*visarjana*), 157–59
dravyaśuddhi (purification of substances), 39, 52, 143–47
Durvāsas, 14n.21, 15
dvādaśānta, 55; Paramaśiva located in, 100, 122, 128, 131; soul transported to, 100, 105; as target of ascending pronunciation, 131–32

Earth, 44–45; domain visualized, 54–57. *See also* elements
elements (*bhūtas*), five: and *brahmamantras*, 50; as cosmic supports, 106–7; emission and reabsorption of, 44–45, 53, 140; purification of, 53–58, 106; as services to Śiva, 150–51
emission (*sṛṣṭi*): of *āgamas*, 10–12, 46; as cosmological principle, 42–47, 51, 72–73, 88, 140–41; path of, 43–44; as ritual order, 40, 46–47, 49–51, 58–60, 62–69, 72, 94–96, 132–35, 151–52; Śiva's activity of, 139
entourages (*āvaraṇa*) of Śiva: inside, 64, 67–69, 151–52; outside, 63–64, 152
establishment (*pratiṣṭhā*): of liṅga, 36, 122–23, 155–56; of temple, 60
expiation (*prāyaścitta*), 36, 110, 152, 156
expulsion (*udghāta*), 55–57, Pl. 3

favor, divine (*prasāda*), 7, 155, 160
fetters (*pāśa*): effect on soul, 25–27, 30–31, 84; ontological category, 22–24, 86–89; removal of, 92–94, 100, 102–3, 109–10; in ritual, 40, 94, 137–38
flowers: in invocation, 131–32, Pl 6; in *japa*, 153; purification of, 143–46, 155; offering of, 148–50
food (*naivedya*), purification of, 146
foot-water (*pādya*), 142, 148

Gaṇeśa, 63, 68
Gaṇeśvaras, 65–66, 67–68, 156–57
gift (*dāna*), 137, 159–60
grace (*anugrāha*), Śiva's, 42, 48, 72, 82; effect on humans of, 7, 27–29, 89, 142, 159–60; and initiation, 89–90, 93–94, 100
granthi (subtle centers), 54–57
gross body (*sthūlaśarīra*), 52–58, 105–8, 126–27
guṇas (perfections), 99–100, 108–9

homa (fire oblation), 36, 38, 91
householder, 46, 49–51
HṚD. See *aṅgamantras*

imposition (*nyāsa*) of mantras, 47; in *ātmaśuddhi*, 58–60, 108–9, Pl. 4; in invocation, 124–27, Pl. 5; in *karanyāsa*, 47–51, Pl. 2
impure domain (*aśuddhādhvan*), 140; in *ātmaśuddhi*, 53; in invocation, 123–25, 127
impurity, 53, 103–4, 140, 143
Indra, 7, 63, 96
initiation (*dīkṣā*), 36, 89; efficacy of, 35, 92–94
initiation, common (*samayadīkṣā*), 40, 90–91
initiation, liberating. See *nirvāṇadīkṣā*
initiation, special (*viśesadīkṣā*), 91
instruments (*kāraṇa*), 32–33, 115, 118, 139
invocation (*āvāhana*), 39–40, 112, 137, 163–64; of Caṇḍa, 157; of deities into pots, 66; of Śiva into the liṅga, 71, 112, 119–20, 122–34, 145, 163–64, Pl. 6; of soul into the body, 108
IŚĀNA. See *brahmamantras*

jaḍa. *See* substance, inanimate
japa (mantra recitations), 152–54
jñāna. *See* knowledge
jñānapāda section of *āgamas*, ix, 10
jñānaśakti: form of Śakti, 118, 125; power of consciousness, xi, 23, 25

kalās, five, 50, 123, 131; and elements, 106–7; and Kāraṇeśvaras, 119; purification of, 95–99
kalās, thirty-eight: imposed on worshiper, 58–59; imposed on liṅga, 126; as Śaktis, 118
kalās, twelve (mantra portions), 129–32
Kālāmukha school of Śaivism, 14
kalāśuddhi: and *ātmaśuddhi*, 104, 106–8; in cremation, 110; in initiation, 96–99
Kāmikāgama, 3, 19–20; origin of, 11–13; revision of, 16; rituals discussed in, 36
Kāpālika school of Śaivism, 14, 85
kāraṇa. *See* instruments
Kāraṇeśvaras: preside over mantra portions, 129–31; preside over stainless throne, 125; preside over subtle centers, 54–57; as Śiva's agents, 119, 139
karanyāsa (imposition on hands), 47–52, Pl. 2
karman: as fetter, 25–26, 86–89; removal of, 93, 97–102, 110–11, 153–54; as ritual action, 31–32; types of, 86–88

Kashmiri Śaivism, 17, 44
KAVACA. See *aṅgamantras*
Kiraṇāgama, dated manuscript of, 13
knowledge, ix; limitations of, 25–27, 113, 133–34, 139; powers of, 23, 25, 84; and ritual action, xii, 34–35, 73–74, 162, 163–64; Śaiva, 10, 19–21, 29–31; two types of, 163–64
kriyā. *See* action, ritual
Kriyākramadyotikā of Aghoraśiva, 3, 19–20
kriyāpāda section of *āgamas*, ix, 10
kriyāśakti: as form of Śakti, 118, 125; as power of consciousness, xi, 23, 25

liberation (*mokṣa*): definitions of, 7, 27, 83, 85; as human goal, 24, 27, 46, 83; levels of, 34, 34n.12; and ritual action, 102–3, 109–11, 154, 163–64; and Śiva's grace, 7, 89, 90
liṅga: and body of mantras, 125–28; dismissal of Śiva from, 157–59; establishment of, 122–23; invocation of Śiva in, 119, 128–34; location of, 62, 121; purification of, 123; types of, 120–21
lokapālas. *See* World Guardians
lordship, Śiva's: and agents, 32, 118–19; and anointment, 149; and entourages, 61–62, 151–52; and matter, 139–40; and temple, 62–64, 69; and worshiper, 142, 148, 153–54, 161

mahāmāyā: as fetter, 86n.2; as source-substance, 44–45, 53
Mahāvratin school of Śaivism, 85
Maheśvara forms of Śiva, 117–18; contradictory attributes of, 139; and images, 121–22; as Kāraṇeśvara, 119
Māheśvaras, early Śaiva school, 14
maintenance (*sthiti*), 42–43, 48
mala (primordial stain): as fetter, 25, 86; and *nirmālya*, 155. *See also* fetters
Maṇavācakam Kaṭantār, 18
maṇḍalas: of elements, 53–57; of throne, 125; of temple, 62
Manonmani, 125, 127
mantras, 33, 128–29; ascending pronunciation of, 105, 129–32, 143, 147; as beings, 26; imposition of, 47–51, 58–60, 108–9, 124–27; purification of, 143; recitation of, 152–54; as ritual instruments, 33; as Śiva's body, 48, 115; as Śiva's instruments, 32

mantra-collection (*samhitāmantra*), 158–59
Mataṅga, sage, 141–43
Mataṅgapārameśvarāgama, frame narrative of, 141–43
māyā: as fetter, 25, 86–88; purity and impurity of, 53, 105–6, 140, 144; as source-substance of world, 44–45, 53, 105–6
Mayamata, 13
meditation (*dhyāna*), 32–33, 33n.7. *See also* visualization
Meykaṇṭār, 18
Mīmāṃsakas, 16–17
mokṣa. *See* liberation
Mṛgendrāgama, 20; date of composition, 13
mudrās, 33: of cow, 145–46; *mahāmudrā*, 158; of reabsorption, 57, 68, 158
mukhaliṅga, 121–22
muktātman (liberated soul), 24; in hierarchy of beings, 26. *See also* liberation
MŪLA (or PRĀSĀDA): in *ātmaśuddhi*, 57; in ascending pronunciation, 147; in invocation, 129–32; in mantra-collection, 158–59; in *nirvāṇadīkṣā*, 99–100; in preparation of *arghya*, 145
mūlāgamas, 10
mumukṣu, 27n.2, 46–47; and path of reabsorption, 50–51, 70–71

naivedya (ritual food), 146
Nandin, 63, 68
Narasimhavarman II, Pallava king, 12
Nārāyaṇakaṇṭha, 13, 16, 17
Naṭarāja, 43, Pl. 1
nāyanmār poet-saints, 18, 71
nectar (*amṛta*), 141, 143
NETRA. See *aṅgamantras*
Nirmalamaṇi, 20
nirmālya, 155–57
nirvāṇadīkṣā (liberating initiation), 89–90; and *ātmaśuddhi*, 104; and cremation, 110; effect on soul of, 92–94; preparations for, 90–92; procedures of, 94–100; required for *parārthapūjā*, 40, 70
niṣkala: as level of Śiva, 113–14; liṅga as, 62, 121–22; and Śiva's movements, 132, 135, 158
nityapūjā (daily worship). See *pūjā*
nyāsa. *See* imposition

oscillation, 42; emission and reabsorption, 42–47; as method of study, ix–xii; in *pūjā*, 72

padārthas (ontological categories), three, 22–23; enacted in *pūjā*, 39–40, 137–38, 163–64
paddhatis, 15–17
pāka (ripening): of fetters, 26; of *mala*, 86–89
Pallavas, 12
pañcakṛtya. *See* activities, Śiva's five fundamental
Pāñcarātra school of Vaiṣṇavism, 29, 38
pañcaśuddhi. *See* purifications, five
Paramaśiva: in *dvādaśānta*, 55, 100, 122, 128, 131; as highest level of Śiva, 113–14, 140; and liṅga, 121–22; meditation on, 132; movements in ritual of, 140
parārthapūjā, 8, 37; and *ātmārthapūjā*, 37n.15, 147n.7; competence to perform, 40
Parāśakti, 118, 125, 127
pariṇāma (transformation): through emission and reabsorption, 43; of fetters, 86–89
parivāradevatās, 63, 152
pāśa. *See* fetters
pāśasūtra (cord of fetters), 94–98, 100, 108
paśu (bound soul): as ontological category, 22–24; in *pūjā*, 40, 137–38; in relation to Śiva, 112, 141–43, 161. *See also* soul
Pāśupata school of Śaivism, 14, 38, 85
pati (the Lord): as ontological category, 22–23; in *pūjā*, 39–40, 137–38, 161; in relation to substance, 138–41; in relation to souls, 141–43. *See also* Śiva
pedestal (*pīṭhā*): identification with Śakti, 62; location in temple, 62; transformation during invocation, 123–25, 127
pīṭhā. *See* pedestal
Pope, G. U., 19
Pralayakevala, 26, 140
prārabdhakarman: in *ātmaśuddhi*, 57, 105; in cremation, 109; definition, 87; in *nirvāṇadīkṣā*, 93, 96, 100
prasāda (favor), 7, 155, 160
PRĀSĀDA mantra. See MŪLA
pratiṣṭhā. *See* establishment
Pratyabhijñā school of Śaivism, 14
prāyaścitta (expiation), 36, 110, 152, 156
presence, Śiva's levels of, 119–20, 142; in liṅga, 133–34, 157–58; and Sadāśiva, 126–27
priests (*ācārya*): as audience for *āgamas*, 10; perform *parārthapūjā*, 135; requirements of, 40–41, 69–70; of Rājarājeśvara temple, 6

pūjā (worship): contrasted with sacrifice, 7–8; efficacy of, 36–37, 101–4, 159–162, 163–63; as Hindu ritual form, 3, 38–39; qualifications to perform, 37, 40–41, 69–71, 102, 159; Śaiva siddhānta formulation of, 36–38, 39–40, 163–64; scholarly study of, x, 3n.1, 158–59; and transactions with Śiva, 122, 137, 159–62
purāṇas: cosmogonic texts of temple Hinduism, 7, 20; narratives of Śiva, 117, 139
pure domain (*śuddhādhvan*), 140; in *ātmaśuddhi*, 53; in invocation, 126–27
purifications, five (*pañcaśuddhi*), 39, 52, 143; of liṅga, 123; of mantras, 143; of place of worship, 64, 143; of substances, 143–47. See also *ātmaśuddhi*
Puruṣa, 6, 123
putraka, 91, 101

Rājarāja I, 4–6, 9, 43
Rājarājeśvara temple, 4–6, 5n.8, 43
Rājendra I, 6
Rāmakaṇṭha, x, 17
reabsorption (*saṃhāra*): as cosmological principle, 42–47, 51, 72–73, 88, 140–41; path of, 43–44; as ritual order, 46–47, 49–51, 53–58, 71, 96–98, 110, 123–25, 128–32, 134–35, 147, 149; as Śiva's activity, 110, 139, 157
renouncer, 46, 49
ripening (*pāka*): of fetters, 26; of *mala*, 86–89
ritual: and exchange theories, 159–60; and microcosms, 72–73; Śaiva theory of, 22, 72–74; scholarly study of, ix–x
Rudra (Kāraṇeśvara), 55, 119, 125
Rudras, eight, 65–66

sacrifice, 7, 34, 38
Sadāśiva: and *brahmamantras*, 48; as form of Śiva, 11, 48, 115–17, 125, 132–34, 152; as Kāraṇeśvara, 55, 119; and liṅgas, 121–22, 125–28
sādhaka (adept), 10, 27n.2
SADYOJĀTA. See *brahmamantras*
Sadyojyoti, 16–17
Śaiva brāhmanas (*ādiśaivas*), 41, 69–70
Śaiva siddhānta, ix, 3–4, 3n.2; as historical order of Śaivism, 12, 14–15, 17–19; as school of thought, 3–4, 19–21, 85, 134–36, 137–38, 155, 156n.15, 160
Śaiva siddhanta, Tamil, 18–19
sakala: as level of Śiva, 114; images as, 62, 121–22; Śiva's movements, 132, 135, 158
sakalas, category of beings, 26
Śākta *tantras*, 9
Śakti: and divine throne, 127; fall of, 90–92; as pedestal, 62; as pot, 66; and Śiva, 22, 32, 118, 139
Śakti, forms of: Ādhāraśakti, 124; eight Śaktis of Vidyeśvaras, 118, 125, 127; Jñāna, Kriyā, and Icchā, 118, 125; Manonmanī, 125, 127; Parāśakti, 118, 125, 127; thirty-eight *kalās*, 59; throne coverings, 124; Vāgīśvarī, 91, 97
śaktinipāta (fall of Śakti), 90–92
samayācāra (code of conduct), 40, 102, 159
samayadīkṣā, 40, 90–91
saṃhāra. *See* reabsorption
Sāṃkhya, 44, 45n.2, 85
saṃsāra, 22, 45, 92
saṃskāras, 91, 98, 146
sañcitakarman, 87, 93. See also *karman*
Śaṅkara, 14
śānti (pacification), 36
self-purification. See *ātmaśuddhi*
services (*upacāra*), 8; lists and gradations of, 148; pattern of, 147–154; role in *pūjā* of, 39, 133, 137; transactions involved in, 137–38, 143, 147–48, 159–62
ŚIKHĀ. See *aṅgamantras*
śilpaśāstras, 20
ŚIRAS. See *aṅgamantras*
Śiva, 6; and *āgamas*, 10–12, 29; and five fundamental activities, 28–29, 42–43, 93–94, 89, 139; levels of, 113–14, 119–20, 133–34; lordship of, 9, 22–23, 26, 64, 119, 125, 147–48, 154; movements during ritual of, 40, 71–72, 122–34, 157–59, 160–61, 163–64; perfections of, 24, 116, 138; relation to bound souls of, 28–29, 112, 134–36, 141–43; relation to substance of, 138–41; supports for, 120–22; and temple, 61 64, 69, 117–18
Śiva, forms of: Maheśvara, 117–18, 121–22, 139; Naṭarāja, 43; Paramaśiva, 113–14, 121–22, 132, 140; Sadāśiva, 11, 54, 115–17, 125, 132–34; Vāgīśvara, 97
Śivāgrayogin, 17
śivajñāna: effects of, 31, 88; enactment of, 32, 41, 163–64; superiority of, 14–15, 29–31; unity of, 10–11, 16–17, 20–21
Śiva-ness (*śivatva*): of souls, 84, 99–100, 109; of substances, 141, 143

Śivārcanācandrikā, 20
śivīkaraṇa, 47
Skanda, 63, 68
Somaśambhu, 13, 17, 20
soul (*ātman*), 24–25; and body, 103–4, 119; career of, 24, 26–27, 83–85, 163–64; constraints upon, 25, 84–85, 85n.1; liberation of, 24, 27, 85, 110–11; powers of, 25, 28, 84, 109; in *pūjā*, 101, 103, 137, 153–54
space, ritual, 60–72
Śrī Vaiṣṇava school, 38
sṛṣṭi. *See* emission
sthānaśuddhi, 52, 64. *See also* purifications, five
sthiti, 42–43, 48
stotras, 141–43, 154
substance, inanimate (*jaḍa*), 23–24; body as, 24, 103–4; liṅga as, 119, 133; material world as, 23–24, 138–41; participation in *pūjā* of, 137–38, 150–51; transformations of, 143–47, 154–57
subtle anatomy, 54–55
subtle body, 52–53, 105–6, 126–27
subtle centers (*granthi*), 54–57
śuddhādhvan (pure domain), 53, 126–27, 140

TATPURUṢA. See *brahmamantras*
tattvas: and *brahmamantras*, 50; and divine throne, 123–25, 127; emission and reabsorption of, 44–45, 140; and five *kalās*, 95; and mantra portions, 129–31; purification of, 53, 105–6
temple: as Hindu religious institution, 8–9; organization of, 60–64, 121, 118, 156; and *pūjā*, 37, 69–72, 134–35; and Śiva, 61–64, 69, 71–72, 117–18
temple Hinduism: as ideological formation, 6–9, 19; schools of, 38–39
theology, Śaiva, 112–19
throne, divine (*divyāsana*), 123–25, 125n.25, 127
tirobhāva. *See* concealment
Tirumūlar, 12
transformations, ritual: of body through *ātmaśuddhi*, 52–61, 104–9; of fetters, 86–89; of hands through *karanyāsa*, 47–51; in initiation, 90–94, 100; of liṅga and pedestal, 123–28; of substances, 141, 143–47, 154–57; of worshiper and Śiva, 134–36
Trika school of Śaivism, 14
tyāga (abandonment), 159–60

uccāraṇa. *See* ascending pronunciation
udghāta (expulsion), 55–57, Pl. 3
Umāpati, 18
upacāras. *See* services
upāgamas, 10

vācaka (signifier) of mantra, 33, 128–29
vācya (signified) of mantra, 33, 128–29
Vāgīśvara, 97
Vāgīśvarī, 91, 97
Vaikhānasa school of Vaiṣṇavism, 38
Vaiṣṇava *saṃhitās*, 9
VĀMA. See *brahmamantras*
varṇas (classes), 41, 90
Vedas: and *āgamas*, 29n.3, 30; emitted by Sadāśiva, 29; restrictions of, 41; temple recitation of, 71
Vedism: gods of, 63, 123; rituals of, 34; and temple Hinduism, 6–9
Vidyeśvaras, 22, 26; as agents of Śiva, 22, 118–19, 139–40, 152; as participants in *pūjā*, 60, 65–66, 67–68, 125, 152
Vijñānakevalas, 26, 140
Vīraśaiva school of Śaivism, 14, 18
visarjana (dismissal), 157–59
viśeṣadīkṣā, 91
Viṣṇu: as image in Śaiva temple, 63; as interlocutor in *Ajitāgama*, 61; as Kāraṇeśvara, 55, 119, 125, 129–30; as primary god in temple Hinduism, 6
visualization (*bhāvanā*), ix; in ascending pronunciation, 131; in *ātmaśuddhi*, 53–54, 58n.10, 107; in imposition of mantras, 47; in invocation, 123–25, 126, 132; in *nirvāṇadīkṣā*, 96–98; of Sadāśiva, 115–16; in services, 150; in worship of the entourages, 64, 67–69
VYOMAVYĀPIN, 59–60, 126

weapons (*āyudha*): of Sadāśiva, 116–17; of World Guardians, 68
World Guardians (*lokapālas*): as Śiva's agents, 61–62, 119, 139; as Śiva's entourage, 67–68; in temple, 63–64
worship. See *pūjā*
worshiper: motivations of, 159–62; qualifications of, 40–41; relation to Śiva of, 134–36

yajña (sacrifice), 7–8
yogapāda section of *āgama*, x, 10

GPSR Authorized Representative: Easy Access System Europe - Mustamäe tee 50, 10621 Tallinn, Estonia, gpsr.requests@easproject.com

www.ingramcontent.com/pod-product-compliance
Lightning Source LLC
Chambersburg PA
CBHW050634300426
44112CB00012B/1790
* 9 7 8 0 6 9 1 6 0 3 0 8 7 *